Understanding
CHRISTA WOLF

UNDERSTANDING
MODERN EUROPEAN
AND LATIN AMERICAN LITERATURE

JAMES HARDIN, *Series Editor*

volumes on

Ingeborg Bachmann
Samuel Beckett
Thomas Bernhard
Johannes Bobrowski
Heinrich Böll
Italo Calvino
Albert Camus
Elias Canetti
Céline
José Donoso
Rainer Werner Fassbinder
Max Frisch
Federico García Lorca
Gabriel García Márquez
Juan Goytisolo

Günter Grass
Gerhart Hauptmann
Christoph Hein
Eugène Ionesco
Milan Kundera
Primo Levi
Boris Pasternak
Luigi Pirandello
Graciliano Ramos
Erich Maria Remarque
Jean-Paul Sartre
Claude Simon
Mario Vargas Llosa
Peter Weiss
Franz Werfel

Christa Wolf

UNDERSTANDING

CHRISTA
WOLF

Returning Home to a Foreign Land

MARGIT RESCH

UNIVERSITY OF SOUTH CAROLINA PRESS

Copyright © 1997 University of South Carolina

Published in Columbia, South Carolina, by the
University of South Carolina Press

Manufactured in the United States of America

01 00 99 98 97   5 4 3 2 1

Grateful acknowledgment is made to Luchterhand Verlag for permission to quote from
the following works by Christa Wolf: *Die Dimension des Autors,* books 1 and 2; *Nachdenken über Christa T.*

Library of Congress Cataloging-in-Publication Data

Resch, Margit.
    Understanding Christa Wolf : returning home to a foreign land /
Margit Resch.
        p.   cm. — (Understanding modern European and Latin American
literature)
    Includes bibliographical references and index.
    ISBN 1–57003–148–7
    1. Wolf, Christa—Criticism and interpretation. I. Title.
II. Series.
PT2685.O36Z85   1997
833'.914—dc21   96–51242

To Sibylle Lützen

und ich komme dich beschwestern

CONTENTS

CONTENTS

EDITOR'S PREFACE

Understanding Modern European and Latin American Literature has been planned as a series of guides for undergraduate and graduate students and non-academic readers. Like the volumes in its companion series *Understanding Contemporary American Literature,* these books provide introductions to the lives and writings of prominent modern authors and explicate their most important works.

Modern literature makes special demands, and this is particularly true of foreign literature, in which the reader must contend not only with unfamiliar, often arcane artistic conventions and philosophical concepts but also with the handicap of reading the literature in translation. It is a truism that the nuances of one language can be rendered in another only imperfectly (and this problem is especially acute in fiction), but the fact that the works of European and Latin American writers are situated in a historical and cultural setting quite different from our own can be as great a hindrance to the understanding of these works as the linguistic barrier. For this reason the *UMELL* series emphasizes the sociological and historical background of the writers treated. The peculiar philosophical and cultural traditions of a given culture may be particularly important for an understanding of certain authors, and these are taken up in the introductory chapter and also in the discussion of those works to which this information is relevant. Beyond this, the books treat the specifically literary aspects of the author under discussion and attempt to explain the complexities of contemporary literature lucidly. The books are conceived as introductions to the authors covered, not as comprehensive analyses. They do not provide detailed summaries of plot because they are meant to be used in conjunction with the books they treat, not as a substitute for study of the original works. The purpose of the books is to provide information and judicious literary assessment of the major works in the most compact, readable form. It is our hope that the *UMELL* series will help increase knowledge and understanding of European and Latin American cultures and will serve to make the literature of those cultures more accessible.

J. H.

PREFACE

The world changed for all Germans when the Wall fell on 9 November 1989 and the two Germanies were united on 3 October 1990. Christa Wolf calls the dissolution of the German Democratic Republic an "annexation." In the years since unification the profound cultural differences between East and West have become more acute, and more acutely felt. This book examines within the context of many great political upheavals the career of Germany's most distinguished contemporary novelist and essayist—one who *chose* to live in the East.

This study responds to several questions that have been raised by scholars and readers alike: Why did Wolf, who enjoyed unrestricted travel privileges, remain in the East, when she could have easily defected? How was she able to survive artistically in an authoritarian regime? What is her conception of the role of a writer? What are the qualities in her writing which earned the respect of major critics on both sides of the Wall? Why has she chosen not to identify with the feminist movement? What contribution has she made to German and world literature? These are the central questions explored in this chronological study of her career.

To date there is no comprehensive edition in German or English of Wolf's literary criticism and reviews, no edition of her letters or journals, and no biography. Until such materials become available, any examination of her life's work must, in many areas, be reserved. Nevertheless, a study of any major author is always to some degree a collaboration. My chief scholarly debt is to Therese Hörnigk; I have benefited from both her book and the lively seminar on Christa Wolf which she conducted in 1990 at Dickinson College under the direction of Gisela Roethke. I have also found Anna Kuhn's and Wolfram Mauser's studies on Wolf to be especially insightful.

Each major phase of Wolf's career is examined in chapters entitled with Wolf's own telling words. All translations of German text into English are mine. I use my own translations partly out of necessity, because no English text is available, and partly because the published translations often render the original text inadequately. The titles of Wolf's books will be given first in German, followed by the date of the first German publication and an English translation of the title (in italics if the English version has been published). Subsequent citations of the title will be in English, unless no translation exists, although the passages referred to come from the West German editions.

I would like to thank Günther Holst, Chair of the Department of Germanic, Slavic, and Oriental Languages, and Lester Lefton, Dean of the College of Liberal Arts of the University of South Carolina, for approving the sabbatical leave during which this book was written; James Hardin, General Editor of USC's *Understanding Modern European and Latin American Literature* series, for his support, patience, and insight; Gerda Jordan, who read the entire manuscript and made many helpful suggestions; Patricia Matson, for reading the chapter on *Cassandra;* my sister Sibylle Lützen, who did invaluable research on Wolf's publications and provided for *Wattblick;* and my husband, John MacNicholas, whose contributions to my life cannot be enumerated.

ABBREVIATIONS

Works cited in the text are abbreviated as shown. Page numbers refer to the West German editions listed in the bibliography.

CT	*Nachdenken über Christa T. (The Quest for Christa T.)*
D	*Die Dimension des Autors (The Author's Dimension)*
DI	*Die Dimension des Autors (The Author's Dimension, vol. I)*
DII	*Die Dimension des Autors (The Author's Dimension, vol. II)*
GE	*Gesammelte Erzählungen* (Collected Stories)
GH	*Der geteilte Himmel (Divided Heaven)*
ID	*Im Dialog (In Dialogue)*
K	*Kassandra (Cassandra)*
KM	*Kindheitsmuster (Patterns of Childhood)*
KO	*Kein Ort. Nirgends (No Place on Earth)*
MN	*Moskauer Novelle* (Moscow Novella)
S	*Sommerstück* (Summer Play)
ST	*Störfall (Accident)*
T	*Auf dem Weg nach Tabou* (On the Way to Taboo)
VEK	*Voraussetzungen einer Erzählung: Kassandra (Prerequisites for a Story)*
WB	*Was bleibt (What Remains)*

CHRONOLOGY

1929	Born Christa Ihlenfeld on 18 March, in Landsberg/Warthe (now Polish Gorzow-Wielkopolski).
1939–45	High school in Landsberg
1945	Flees from the Red Army to Gammelin, Mecklenburg. Assistant to mayor of Gammelin.
1946	Resumes high school in Schwerin. Tuberculosis.
1949	High school diploma *(Abitur)* in Bad Frankenhausen. Joins Socialist Unity Party (SED).
1949–53	Studies German Literature in Jena and Leipzig. Thesis under Hans Mayer on "Problems of Realism in the Works of Hans Fallada."
1951	Marries essayist and editor Gerhard Wolf (b. 1928).
1952	Birth of daughter Annette.
1953–59	Researcher for German Writers' Union.
1955–76	Member of the Executive Committee of the German Writers' Union. First of several trips to the Soviet Union.
1956	Birth of second daughter, Katrin.
1956–59	Chief editor of the publishing house for youth literature Neues Leben.
1958–59	Editor for journal *Neue Deutsche Literatur.*
1959–62	Moves to Halle. Freelance editor for the Mitteldeutsche Verlag (Halle). Trips to Soviet Union, FRG, France, England, Finland, etc. Edits (with Gerhard Wolf) several anthologies of GDR literature.
1960–61	Works and studies in boxcar factory, Ammendorf. Member of Association of Writing Workers.
1961	*Moskauer Novelle* (Moscow Novella), story. Prize for the Arts of the City of Halle.
1962	Moves to Kleinmachnow near Berlin, in 1976 to Berlin.
1963	*Der geteilte Himmel, 1965 (Divided Heaven),* novel. Heinrich Mann Prize of the Academy of the Arts, GDR.
1963–67	Candidate of the Central Committee of the SED (from the Sixth to the Eighth Party Congress).
1964	DEFA's production of *Divided Heaven* (director: Konrad Wolf, no relation). National Prize Third Class of the Academy of the Arts, GDR. Speech at the Second Bitterfeld Conference. Visits Auschwitz trials in Frankfurt, FRG.

1965   Member of the PEN Center of the GDR.

1966   *Fräulein Schmetterling* (Miss Butterfly), film script (with Gerhard Wolf).

1967   "Juninachmittag" ("An Afternoon in June" [1970], "June Afternoon" [1993]), story.

1968   *Nachdenken über Christa T. (Quest for Christa T.* [1970]), novel. *Die Toten bleiben jung* (The Dead Stay Young), film script of novel by Anna Seghers (coauthor).

1972   *Lesen und Schreiben. Aufsätze und Betrachtungen (The Reader and the Writer: Essays, Sketches, Memories* [1977]) "Till Eulenspiegel. Erzählung für den Film" (Till Eulenspiegel: Story for the Film, with Gerhard Wolf). Wilhelm-Raabe Prize of the City of Braunschweig (refused). Theodor-Fontane Prize, GDR.

1974   *Unter den Linden. Drei unwahrscheinliche Geschichten (Unter den Linden: The New Life and Opinions of a Tomcat, and Self-Experiment* [1993]). Member of the Academy of the Arts, GDR. Seventh Max-Kade German Writer-in-Residence at Oberlin College, Oberlin, Ohio.

1976   DEFA production of *Till Eulenspiegel* (director: Rainer Simon). *Kindheitsmuster (A Model Childhood* [1980], *Patterns of Childhood* [1984]), novel. Signs "Open Letter" in response to Biermann expatriation. Dismissal from executive committee of GDR writers' union.

1977   Literature Prize of the City of Bremen (awarded 1978). Member of the German Academy for Language and Literature in Darmstadt, FRG.

1978   Guest lecturer at the University of Edinburgh.

1979   *Kein Ort. Nirgends (No Place on Earth* [1982]). *Fortgesetzter Versuch: Aufsätze, Gespräche, Essays* (Continued Attempt: Treatises, Interviews, Essays).

1980   *Lesen und Schreiben. Neue Sammlung (The Reader and the Writer,* expanded ed. [1981]). *Gesammelte Erzählungen* (Collected Stories). Georg-Büchner Prize of the German Academy for Language and Literature in Darmstadt (FRG).

1981   Travels to Greece.

1982   Guest lectureship in poetics at the Johann-Wolfgang-Goethe-University, Frankfurt.

1983   *Kassandra. Vier Vorlesungen. Eine Erzählung (Cassandra: A Novel and Four Essays* [1984]). Honorary doctorate and guest professorship at Ohio State University. Schiller Memorial Prize.

1984   Franz-Nabl Prize of the City of Graz, Austria. Member of the
        European Academy of Arts and Sciences, Paris.
1985   Austrian National Prize for European Literature. Honorary
        doctorate of the University of Hamburg. Honorary fellow of the
        Modern Language Association (U.S.).
1986   *Die Dimension des Autors. Essays und Aufsätze, Reden und
        Gespräche 1959–1985 (The Author's Dimension: Selected Essays*
        [1993]). Member of the Free Academy for the Arts, Hamburg.
1987   *Störfall. Nachrichten eines Tages (Accident: A Day's News*
        [1989]), novel. National Prize First Class of the Academy of the
        Arts, GDR. Geschwister-Scholl Prize of the City of Munich,
        FRG. Guest professorship of the Technical College, Zurich.
1989   *Sommerstück* (Summer Play), novel.
1990   *Was bleibt (What Remains* [1993]), story. Prize Premio Mondello
        (Italy). Medal Officier des arts et des lettres, Paris. Honorary
        doctorate of the University of Hildesheim.
1992–93 Research fellow, Getty Center for the History of Art and the
        Humanities, Santa Monica, California. Erich-Fried Award,
        Vienna.
1994   *Auf dem Weg nach Tabou. Texte, 1990–1994* (On the Way to
        Taboo).

Understanding
CHRISTA WOLF

Introduction

The past is never dead, it is not even past.
William Faulkner, *Requiem for a Nun*

Faulkner's aphorism, distilled from experiences deeply rooted in the bitter history of the American South, captures the essence of Christa Wolf's life and work, which are both inextricably linked to Germany's traumatic past. Wolf's Germany, like Faulkner's South, was troubled by racism, violent nationalism, the shame of military defeat, catastrophic loss, and economic havoc. That Germany had engineered its own catastrophe in World War II made it no less catastrophic. Clear and vivid memory, witness to the *spiritual* as well as factual elements of epic losses, is a vital part of any true recovery. So it seems fitting that Wolf's great novel about her own past, *Kindheitsmuster*, 1976 *(Patterns of Childhood)*, begins with Faulkner's poignant words. Deeply probing her own memory's recesses, Wolf explores Germany's Nazi history and its pernicious aftermath. But her other novels also deal with the past's insidious effect on the present and future.

The past is important to all people but perhaps more so to a novelist. Wolf's life and artistic development were strongly affected by the violent and dramatic reversals in Germany's history. Wolf can only be German; she has spent her entire life on German soil. Yet she has been expatriated twice: once in 1945, when, at the age of sixteen, she and her family had to leave their home in northeastern Germany (territory that is now in Poland) to look for safety; forty-five years later, on 3 October 1990, when the Democratic Republic of Germany (GDR, also East Germany) was united with the Federal Republic of Germany (FRG, also West Germany). This unification erased the institutions and country in which Wolf had established her family, her career, and her identity. This time she was expatriated without having to leave her country. She has therefore lived in three different Germanies: one fascist, one socialist, one democratic. Any assessment of Christa Wolf must consider the historical metamorphoses of Germany and their powerful effects. Mirroring her countries' development, both her life and work have exhibited striking and often troubling transformations. Consequently, her literary and political activities have to be seen in the appropriate historical context.

1

Not surprisingly, Christa Wolf is an unusual writer. She could be called an anthropologist with a passion for exploring and representing the vexing nature and mysteries of contemporary society. Her themes stir universal interest: the pathology of societies that constitutionally represent but continually violate basic human rights; the schizophrenia of human relationships under authoritarian regimes; the compliance or resistance to authority and society's rules; the inexplicable mixtures of beauty and evil, harmony and catastrophe, indifference and conflict, in human life. All themes essentially invoke the painful and uncertain processes of self-realization.

Wolf is unusually self-conscious, even for a writer. She comments upon her writing processes with scientific precision and sharp insight, analyzing and meticulously describing her methods. Her habit of sharing with the reader detailed deliberations of a work in progress is probably unrivaled among her contemporaries. Skillfully, Wolf integrates into her fiction artistic and philosophical reflections about narrative techniques and subject matter, enlarging the dimensions of her narrative voice.

Wolf invites all readers to witness and collaborate in the revelation of complex motivations and character and in the depiction of human action within informed social reality. We are asked to share the author's own surprise at a significant turn, the disappointment of an unsuccessful search or inconclusive results, authorial doubts about her technique, and the joy of an unexpected find. Convinced that literature can be an instrument of change, Wolf endeavors to inspire her readers' imagination, unearth their true feelings, hone their intellectual sharpness, and encourage their responsible personal judgments. Her ultimate goal is to aid and further the quest for individual identity and improved social integration. Wolf always saw these as complementary.

Rarely cynical, on occasion surprisingly humorous, always fair, Wolf treats her characters with sensitivity and respect. Much of her greatness as a writer is reflected in the extraordinary verbal elegance and lucidity of her mature prose. Few if any contemporary German novelists can rival Wolf's control of language in depth, color, precision, and poetic resonance. Perhaps her own tribute honoring the famous West German novelist Heinrich Böll on the occasion of his sixty-fifth birthday identifies Wolf's greatest strengths: her work exhibits the same lessons she claims to have learned from Böll: "that abstract concepts such as kindness, conscience, hope can and should be taken and described as concretely as a house, a landscape, a family. And that kindness, conscience and hope can be political virtues; that it is, indeed, possible to combine in one person private, literary, and political virtues" (DII 231). It is easy to perceive Wolf's great purposes in writing because they are gleaned from personal experience and presented without coercion but, rather, with sincerity, modesty, and clarity. Wolf's tempestuous life, her acute sense of social and political dynamics, her sensitive reading of motivation, and her great gift for language combine to form a powerful and unignorable talent.

In her mature work Wolf does not tell a story along a contrived plot line, develop predictable characters, or weave by the logic of causality an apparently inextricable web of action and reaction which will be unraveled at the end. Wolf's stories and novels contain an idiosyncratic mixture of autobiography, fiction, and essay. Person *and* work are a perplexing web. The identity derives from Wolf's belief that reality is not an entity outside of ourselves but, instead, a fluctuating process to which we are subjected and which we create at the same time. Literature should articulate the author's experience as truthfully and precisely as possible. To this end Wolf relies upon her memory to retrieve stories, characters, historical context, physical setting, and language. During this retrieval she simultaneously submits everything to a rigorous analysis. The composition of her stories simulates the nature of her memory retrieval process, a technique scholars define as "narrative structure of remembrance." Vacillating skillfully between narration and reflection, the author invokes in one narrative stroke the past and the present. In her 1994 collection of essays, *Auf dem Weg nach Tabou* (On the Way to Taboo), Wolf describes cogently the alliance of individual experience, social context, and literary expression:

> A pen would follow as precisely as possible the spoor of life; the hand which holds it would be my hand and also not my hand; many people and things would write along; "as in life," the most subjective and the most objective would be inextricably intertwined; the person would openly show but not expose himself or herself; the point of view would be concerned, but not clouded by unresolved biases; not cold, but sympathetic, as unsentimental as possible. Thus the person would earn unprejudiced attention. (T 9)

Not only the author's life experience but also her entire being are engaged in the writing process and, as a result, are reflected in her prose.

Likewise, her work as an author has significantly enhanced her awareness of competing truths, enlarged her responsibilities to her country, and profoundly changed the way she moves about in the world. In a discussion with readers she admitted: "Just knowing that one is meant to write about it changes a lot of things" (DII 835). While Wolf the person is clearly manifested in every book, the genesis of every text has shaped Wolf the person. She has often specifically attested to these changes. This interdependence of life and work is based on a circular principle that animates both: "To feel thinking and to think feeling. Thinking and feeling are not separate from each other; every thought is permeated by the emotions in which I happen to live at the time. When I am depressed, I think differently, arrive at different conclusions than when I am in a euphoric mood" (ID 145–46). It is safe to say that to encounter Wolf's work is to encounter Christa Wolf.

Wolf's first great success on both sides of the Iron Curtain was *Der geteilte Himmel,* 1963 *(Divided Heaven).* Although the novel was imbued with the officially sanctioned principles of socialist realism, it also showed how Wolf was breaking away from the East German regime's cultural and political doctrines. The following three great novels mark her steady departure from the stranglehold of approved socialist aesthetic principles and irrefutable entry into the ranks of world literature. *Nachdenken über Christa T.,* 1968 *(The Quest for Christa T.),* a novel about individual self-realization, introduced subjectivity to GDR's list of allowable themes, significantly advancing literary boundaries in content, structure, and style. This novel widened Wolf's literary reputation in East and West, but it also signaled to the GDR regime her insurgency. From then on she was subjected to relentless surveillance by the Ministry of State Security, a vicious police bureaucracy called the Stasi. Next, her 1976 novel *Patterns of Childhood* continued to broaden and modify the socialist agenda. Exploring the capabilities of memory, the novel resurrects the officially ignored Nazi past and exposes its presence in the collective subconscious of contemporary Germany. It also contains notable stylistic innovations and authorial observations about the nature and function of writing. Then *Kassandra,* 1983 *(Cassandra),* while addressing many issues of female self-realization, describes the emancipation of a courageous individual from the abuses of authority. It also exposed the methods employed by a dictatorial regime to enhance its power, even at the cost of destroying the very people who sustain it. All of Wolf's work, including her numerous essays, contains to some extent the elements of these great novels: the search for the self, defiance of social expectations, resistance against authority, analysis of the creative process, and retrieval of the past. But these four novels are the most widely read and most important publications in her career to date.

Called the first lady of contemporary German literature, Wolf has become one of the most celebrated and controversial of German writers. Her novels, stories, and essays have been translated into more than a dozen languages and reach a large and devoted global audience. Numerous coveted literary prizes have been awarded to her. From the former Democratic Republic of Germany, where she lived and worked until the unification of the two Germanies, she received the Heinrich Mann Prize (1963) and National Prize Third and First Class from the Academy of Arts (1964 and 1987). The Federal Republic of Germany honored her with the prestigious Georg Büchner Prize (1980) and the Schiller Prize (1983). Austria, Italy, France, and the United States have also given her distinguished prizes and awards. Many critics believe Wolf deserves the Nobel Prize for Literature. She has also received honorary doctorates from the Universities of Hamburg, Hildesheim, and Ohio State and held guest professorships at the University of Frankfurt and in England and Switzerland. She served as writer-in-residence and scholar at Oberlin College, Ohio State University, and the Getty Center for the History of Art and the Humanities in Santa Monica, California. She has been elected to memberships in various academies of art and literature in several countries. More reviews and scholarly studies in many languages have been devoted to Wolf's accomplishments and her alleged failures than to any other living German writer.

It is a remarkable and unparalleled feat for an East German writer to establish a worldwide readership and to earn critical acclaim in the East as well as in the West. Some of Wolf's East German colleagues—Hermann Kant and Ulrich Plenzdorf, who remained in the GDR; Peter Hacks, who moved there in 1955; and expatriate Wolf Biermann—achieved popular success in both Germanies. But only Wolf reached a global audience and won the respect of major critics from both sides of the Iron Curtain. This occurred partly because her work, although intensely personal and firmly rooted in GDR soil, speaks to everyone. Wolf's depiction of individuals and their conflicts with society (even a now defunct socialist society) applies to all people.

Not all appraisals of Christa Wolf, the person and her work, have been positive. As a controversial public figure, she has of course found her share of harsh and persistent detractors on both sides of the Wall. It is noteworthy that reviewers have rarely disparaged her literary achievements or the quality of her mature work. Both male and female critics praise and respect her novels. But, no matter what Wolf published, it was going to be politically incorrect somewhere. In the West her political convictions and her active engagement in the socialist cause have been called into question and often severely attacked. In the East Wolf was castigated at times because she allegedly failed to adhere to the principles of socialist realism and to represent society according to the official party line. She was regarded with suspicion not so much because her books were also published in the West but because she received high praise there among readers and critics alike. The fear that the West may derive self-pronounced vindication from any criticism she might make of life under socialism was more threatening to the GDR functionaries than her disobedience to the party line.

In proportion to her growing fame, Wolf was increasingly reproached in the West for allegiance to the regime of her country, for her defense of the GDR up to its demise, for her resonant silence about the GDR's corruption, acts of harsh repression, and glaring violations of human rights. Following unification on 3 October 1990 such criticism intensified after it was revealed that Wolf herself was once briefly engaged in work for the Stasi. This revelation was ironically and sadly exacerbated by the recent publication of her story *Was bleibt,* 1993 *(What Remains)*, which depicts the espionage activities on unsuspecting innocent citizens, featuring the narrator, a woman greatly resembling Wolf, as victim of Stasi surveillance.

Unlike a number of her celebrated colleagues—Uwe Johnson, Sarah Kirsch, Christa Reinig—Wolf chose to remain in her country with her family, even when she saw clearly that its repressive political course veered away from the ideals of its original constitution. Wolf remained a GDR citizen, loyal not to the regime but to friends and readers, even though she herself was adversely affected by the blatant civil rights violations of the government, including shameless surveillance and banishment from the media. Some critics charged that she did not want to give up certain privileges she enjoyed, such as unobstructed world travel, special consideration regarding her publications, and her exalted role as "state poet." These allegations may be easily dismissed. But a more devastating accusation in the West was leveled: because she remained in the GDR, she was naturally considered a representative of that state, giving the socialist regime an aura of respectability; even worse, she helped to prolong its existence.

Wolf, deeply hurt by such accusations, repeatedly defended her position in the GDR. "I loved this country," she wrote in 1991 to Günter Grass, the most prominent of her West German contemporaries. "I knew that it had reached its end because it was unable to integrate its best people, because it demanded human sacrifices" (T 262). Proceeding from the premise that identity is only possible through bonds, she declares: "Identity becomes stronger in resistance against intolerable circumstances, which means that bonds cannot degenerate to dependence, that they can, indeed may have to, be dissolved" (T 29). In surveying Wolf's life and work, no critic can reasonably ignore the constant flux of tensions generated by loyalty, commitment, willingness to compromise, and the strict defense of one's own space.

The preposterous indictments by many in the Western media are clearly rooted in lingering animosities between East and West Germans. Many in the West resent Wolf's reluctance to embrace wholeheartedly the unification of Germany, which she prefers to call an "annexation" of the GDR by West Germany, and by the capitalist system, which Wolf regards with distrust because she believes it is incapable of solving the urgent problems facing our planet. At any rate the friendly conspiratorial attitude of the Western public and the warm critical approval that used to greet Wolf's publications vanished with the Iron Curtain, along with the West's sympathetic or condescending generosity toward the East.

In certain respects Wolf's post-Wall reputation makes a stunning, cautionary tale about political correctness. When the socialist regime's ineptness, deceit, and inhumanity were exposed, many western critics started examining her activities and work for signs of socialist proselytizing and renunciation of the West. It is supremely ironic that these western critics themselves became dupes of the Stasi machinations: they blamed Wolf for retracting her signature from a document that protested the GDR's forced expatriation of her colleague Wolfgang Biermann in 1976. But Wolf had never retracted her signature. These critics were ignorant of the fact that the Stasi had planted this lie just to discredit Wolf. The result of this and similar media persecution was devastating. Christa Wolf the person (if not the artist), long respected for her diplomatic sensitivity to most issues affecting both East and West, justly praised for resolute efforts toward cultural reconciliation, admired for courageous if circumspect criticism of a dictatorship, now suddenly found herself attacked for her apparent collaboration with that same regime. And suddenly all of her work—welcomed in the West for three decades, hailed for its humanity and its courageous advancement of literary boundaries—was now pronounced questionable or altogether deficient in either content or literary merit. Few observers have noticed a glaring irony: that hewing to the "party line" is a requirement enforced as earnestly by western critics as by those previously employed by the GDR's hated socialist regime. In a sense all of Wolf's life can be seen as a profoundly ironic navigation among the rocks of state-sanctioned taboos and mutually conflicting demands of political correctness.

The war of political correctness, especially in Wolf's case, is an unwinnable war. In time, however, after social and spiritual unification has taken place or when Wolf's role as European citizen is generally recognized, the true quality of her writing will emerge above and beyond political fashions. Then, perhaps, it will become apparent that it was not expediency that motivated Wolf's support of socialism or her decision to remain in the East but, rather, the will to realize and live out her faith in a more humane world, even though misplaced, as it were, in the doomed system of the GDR. Perhaps the basic human impulses affecting her decisions will also become apparent: that in the face of adversity or even persecution a woman may not be eager to leave her home, family, and friends and for the second time become a refugee. She may not be eager to seek political asylum in a country whose system she disdains and has lambasted for decades. She may not be eager to enter an alien and radically opposed literary arena as a "foreign" writer.

Wolf's loyalty to her readers and fidelity to her vision of how they live and have suffered remain a fact. This fact survives in her tireless efforts to unfold before them a reality that has included suicide, loneliness, adultery, pessimism, despair, political oppression, and the inability to adjust. All of these themes were nonexistent and officially forbidden in the GDR. It took exceptional courage to write about them.

Of course, any balanced assessment must also include Wolf's misguided collaboration with the regime, especially her role on the Central Committee of the Sozialistische Einheitspartei Deutschlands (SED), the German Socialist Unity Party, from 1963 to 1967; her short-lived activities as informant for the Stasi in the early stages of her career (1959–62); her membership in the SED until weeks before its demise; the mistakes she made after unification in the difficult attempt to defend herself and her career; her defense of socialism even after the fall of the Berlin Wall in November 1989. Wolf anticipated such accusations and planted throughout her work preemptive explanations to many such questions. Most sympathetic readers can understand and accept her account. But any scholarly assessment of Wolf's development must begin with three basic facts: that from early adulthood she aspired to the realization of the principles of socialism—an honorable dream; that she changed her views profoundly about her country's government from one decade to the next; and that public opposition to the SED regime normally had dire consequences for intellectuals, ranging from nonpublication of books and retaliations against family to incarceration or forced exile. Who can dismiss the dangers Wolf had to contend with?

Wolf had a keen sense of obligation to her society. Believing that books help to shape who we are, she assumed the role of the writer as moral conscience. This responsibility presents certain liabilities under any circumstance but especially if one criticizes an authoritarian regime. Wolf's record of negotiating a desire for the truth and her state's rigid guidelines and of accommodating official mandates while at the same time questioning their source is no small feat. She deserves great credit for being absolutely sincere in these endeavors and for advancing artistic freedoms to serve humanity. This had always been her most ardent, enduring, and credible aspiration; speaking in 1972, she declared: "I am interested in today's development of mankind while trying to secure its survival, and possibly more than survival; interested in the tensions between social groups and individuals that result from this process; in ways of harnessing these, finally, for the production of humanity and not for destruction" (DII 766).

Wolf's personal story, the development of her career as a critic, essayist, and fiction writer, and the evolution of her work are closely related to the history of her three countries: the Third Reich, during which she grew up; the Democratic Republic of Germany, in which she completed her schooling, raised a family, and established her career and international fame; and, finally, the Federal Republic of Germany, most likely her final national identification. The extraordinary flux and strife of these three political entities provide the historical matrix that is essential to understand Wolf's life and art.

CHAPTER ONE

Understanding Christa Wolf
Some Prerequisites

History of Germany since 1945

When the Third Reich capitulated to the Allied forces in 1945 and World War II ended, Germany was physically, politically, and spiritually in ruins. After twelve years of oppression by the dictatorial regime of Adolf Hitler and the National Socialists, including five years of the most destructive war in history, every aspect of national and individual life had to be reconstructed. Most important, a new political structure had to be devised. After centuries of monarchic rule the Weimar Republic, lasting a little more than a decade from the end of World War I in 1919 until Hitler's ascent to power in 1933, offered the German people their first experience in democracy. Therefore, when Germany was divided into two distinct political entities four years after the end of World War II, each depended on the powers administering its affairs for establishing a new political order. These powers could not have been more divisive: the Soviet Union on the East, the United States on the West.

The German people share a turbulent history spanning more than a millennium. Even though the various German states were politically not reintegrated until 1871, centuries of collective experiences and traditions shaped a national identity, forged a common language, and yielded a rich culture. The division of Germany in 1949 marked the beginning of a social and cultural separation that can be observed in every area of life, including the language. Within a few years incompatible ideologies, disparate political and social orders, different economic systems, alliances with opposing powers, and antagonistic propaganda on both sides precipitated a profound alienation that, to this day—years after unification on 3 October 1990—affects political, social, and personal discourse and impedes true understanding and consolidation. At the same time, the two German countries, each backed and prodded by one of the two world powers, were the battlefield of the Cold War between the Soviet Union and the Western powers, the residue of which will linger well beyond this century.

The Federal Republic of Germany, under the guidance and control of the three Western allies that had occupied its territory—the United States, the United Kingdom, and France—quickly adopted democratic constitutional principles and the free market system, emulating the political, economic, and cultural creeds of its new sponsors. With the generous financial support of the United States the FRG vigorously launched its physical and spiritual restoration. Within a decade the so-called economic miracle enabled the West German people to heal the most glaring physical wounds of the war, rebuild their cities to provide universal housing, restore to full capacity the nation's industrial complex and its agricultural production, engage in lively trade with other countries, and establish strategic alliances with West Germany's former conquerors. By 1960 most citizens enjoyed financial and social security. The standard of living and the quality of life were compatible with and expected to supersede that of most industrial nations. Insofar as possible, moral rehabilitation from a shameful past appeared well under way, and full integration into the community of free nations had taken place.

The West Germans basked in the unaccustomed climate of freedom and progress. The artists, musicians, and writers, who had suffered severe control and censorship under Hitler's dictatorship or who had gone into inner exile during the Third Reich, revived their zest for experimentation and courage of expression. To bridge the cultural hiatus they looked to their new friends in the West for inspiration and training in modern aesthetics. They absorbed with special fascination anything American, ranging from theater to jazz to modern dance. They looked back into their own national past, to the fertile and colorful two decades before Hitler ascended to power and at once silenced all voices not speaking the National Socialist idiom. The artistic community of West Germany rediscovered what were in the 1920s avant-garde movements such as expressionism and surrealism in literature and the visual arts, modernism in architecture, and atonality in music. The writers also caught up with the diverse literary and artistic styles developed by colleagues whose books had been banned by the Nazis and who had sought safety from persecution in exile. They eagerly employed these modern aesthetics and structures in new creative endeavors until they found their own artistic vocabulary.

There was much to be concerned about after the war and much to be expressed. As the voice of a collective national conscience, the artists and writers endeavored the daunting task of helping the German people come to terms with their immediate past. The phrase *Vergangenheitsbewältigung* was coined for this painful and ongoing process—literally, "conquering the past." But they also scrutinized the postwar years, the emerging political constellations, the impact of guilt and shame about the monstrosities of the war and the Holocaust upon Germans old and young, the ensuing generation gap, the problems of the individual in an increasingly fragmented society, the reverberations of the division of Germany, the future of the country and the world. The themes were as diverse as life itself. Under the patronage of a liberal society and with the government's unparalleled financial support, both eager to see the country's rich cultural heritage continued after the Third Reich hiatus, the arts in West Germany flourished and began to traverse the international arena. Soon other nations looked to the FRG for artistic stimulus.

The history of the German Democratic Republic evolved in a markedly different manner and direction. The Soviet Union, holding the eastern part of Germany occupied, served as a model for the ideological foundation and political structure of the GDR. The constitution proclaimed the republic to be a socialist state of workers and farmers. The SED, a combination of the Socialist and the Communist Parties, became the most powerful political force, with the party's general secretary eventually holding the post of head of state. The SED derived its legitimacy from the Marxist axiom that its constituents, the class of workers and farmers, are the "creators of socialism" and are destined to lead mankind to the ultimate form of socialism: communism, the classless society. For the first time in German history the majority theoretically held power and represented the interests of society at large. In effect, the government controlled by the SED held power. According to the GDR's last long-term head of state, General Secretary Erich Honecker, it is the mission of the party to serve the people, the architects of a new society, to ensure their happiness and to lead them toward a socialist order. The party members, in turn, assume the prescribed responsibility to protect the unity and purity of the party, to fight for the enforcement of its resolutions, and to follow faithfully the party canon. Like the participants in the Bolshevist October Revolution of 1917, the socialists in East Germany celebrated the arrival of a new, more humane, peaceful order. The ideals of a gentler era with a classless society, with true equality and justice for the historically disenfranchised, with a fair redistribution of land and wealth, held great appeal for many, energizing them to work toward these lofty goals and make the necessary sacrifices to reach them. When the GDR was established in 1949, few Germans could have foreseen how badly these ideals would be betrayed by a totalitarian regime.

A state that believes that politics, the economy, and culture form an interdependent entity will monitor the internal dynamics carefully, if not relentlessly. A state that follows Lenin's maxim that a person's mind does not simply reflect the objective world but also creates it will attempt to mold and control its citizens' consciousness to achieve its goals. To this end the GDR established an elaborate network of organizations. The centralized political apparatus, culminating in the Central Committee of the SED and its general secretary, reached down into every corner of the society. Additionally, organizations such as sports leagues and youth groups, schools and universities, the unions and the army, were vested with the task of educating or controlling the population. They were to ensure the early recruitment of the youth into the system, to provide continued instruction in socialism according to the party line, and to safeguard against ideological intrusion from the outside. To guarantee continued concord the state instituted a personal file for every citizen, the *Kaderakte,* which was to be kept by schools or workplaces. Only the Ministry of State Security, the infamous Stasi, had access to the file. The Stasi's pervasive arms conducted covert surveillance of persons whose loyalty seemed in question—rightfully or not—recruiting ordinary citizens to spy on their neighbors and friends. Millions of people were inducted into their service, more often than not against their will. A system of reprisals for failure to conform served to preserve the apparent unity and discipline, including dismissal from universities, demotion or loss of job, jail terms and expulsions from the country. The East Germans learned soon that they were free to express only what was sanctioned by the party and free to move west only as far as the border. Only the privileged, the ideologically steadfast, and some renegades with loud voices were allowed to cross and leave the country; the latter were given a one-way ticket like the prominent songwriter Wolf Biermann, who was exiled in 1976.

Severe restriction of personal freedom, especially pertaining to travel and communication, affected relations among all citizens within the GDR and among all Germans. Visiting the West was considered fraternizing with the enemy. This astonishing leap of political argument was based on the historical fact that the founders of the republic, the socialists and communists, had constituted an important segment of the opposition to Hitler. As members of the resistance against fascism, they and by extension the entire GDR, were not responsible for the past—only the West Germans were. Consequently, the state's claim to be qualified to lead the new republic to a better future, its alliance with the ideologically exemplary Soviet Union, and their Cold War declaration to the West seemed wholly justified. The antifascist doctrine became a major ingredient of the GDR's propaganda repertoire. It meant on the one hand a sincere abdication of the fascism of the Third Reich, precipitating a rigorous cleansing of all institutions of former Nazi collaborators. It meant on the other hand the renunciation of fascism's alleged revival in the West in the form of capitalism, which, it

13

was said, created a powerful military and industrial complex to sabotage the progress of socialism.

Furthermore, the elimination of any effective opposition in the political structure prevented the formation of an internal enemy; therefore, an external foe, the capitalists on the other side of the Iron Curtain, was appointed to serve. The result of these political constructs was increasing "security" along the border to the West—minefields, watchtowers, guard dogs, barbed wire fences—and more and more restrictions affecting communication in either direction. Casting the other Germany in the role of adversary only served to further divide the two German countries, to estrange families and friends and destroy a national identity. Eventually, these propaganda stratagems were used to defend the building of the Berlin Wall: it was hailed as protection against fascist aggression. But the real reason for drawing the Iron Curtain completely closed was an economic one.

Even though the GDR developed into one of the most productive industrial nations in the world, with the highest living standard in the Eastern Bloc, its population suffered from an erratic and insufficient supply of basic food and consumer products. Moreover, what was actually produced was generally mediocre. Even in the late 1950s it was still an experience of daily life to stand in long lines at the store only to find the desired item sold out. Ordinary consumer goods were scarce—an especially inconvenient political fact next door to the West German economic miracle, where provisions exceeded need. The restoration of the country's infrastructure was slow, health and social services were lacking, and home construction did not keep pace with population growth.

There were several reasons for the persistent economic malaise. The Soviet Union, unlike the Western allies, insisted on the full payment of war reparations and appropriated what was left of the industrial machinery. This stymied economic growth for many years. West Germany took full advantage of the Marshall Plan, which provided generous financial subsidy from the United States to restore economic vigor. No such plan was available to the GDR, whose natural resources were scarce and whose trading partners were mainly limited to economically depressed Eastern countries. The swift redistribution of real estate and the collectivization of farms in the GDR, at first welcomed as an essential step toward communism, generally did not have the desired effect on production. Farmers expected to have decision-making powers, but government bureaucrats with no farming experience appropriated the right to devise long- and short-term agricultural production plans, determine distribution of harvests, prices, length of work hours, and vacation. Bureaucratic decisions often collided with the natural course and schedule of farming activities. Consequently, farmers lost their ties to the soil, which they no longer controlled, and production declined. But the major culprit for the chronic economic infirmity was the socialist system itself: ostensibly, the workers, not capitalists, owned the industrial facilities and shared in management as well as in profits. Workers, not the consumers or the market, determined the nature and volume of products. But workers, of course, were controlled by the SED, and the party functionaries actually devised production plans, which, according to a facetious saying, were always surpassed but never fulfilled.

The results of the endemic economic woes ranged from resigned discontent to escape to the West. In the summer of 1961 an average of thirty thousand people a month arrived in the refugee camps of West Berlin, in August almost two thousand every single day. The economic and social consequences of such massive flight were devastating. A country of some seventeen million people was bleeding to death. The intelligentsia and the professionals led the exodus: for lack of qualified employees, factories and stores had to close; crops could not be harvested on time; school classes had no teachers; hospitals lacked enough doctors and nurses. Worst of all, many young people, for whom this new society was supposedly constructed, defected to the West. On 13 August 1961 the GDR found itself completely surrounded by an ugly impenetrable border made of concrete and barbed wire, collectively called the Berlin Wall. The population of the GDR was physically isolated from the Western world. The tragedy of this total separation of the two Germanies is immeasurable. Its impact can still be felt, years after the unification on 3 October 1990.

In the West the Wall was denounced as a symbol of totalitarian oppression and national incarceration. Yet the Wall also created the illusion of protection against aggression, and a feeling of security emerged on both sides. The Cold War, which had heated up to boiling point by 1961, began to simmer down. For the East Germans the Wall was ostensibly erected to protect the GDR against antifascist aggression and celebrated as a "Friedenstat," an act to preserve peace. In effect, the hermetic seal created an enclave in which the socialist society could finally consolidate and develop without a constant drain of the workforce. The spatial boundaries compelled the population to adjust its existence to the political boundaries. No longer able to leave their country, except for the privileged and retired, East Germans began to adjust to their circumstance and to make the best of it. A period of economic growth and stability followed. The standard of living, materially and culturally, rose; cultural policies relaxed; relations to the FRG improved; in the 1970s visitation rights began to loosen.

Nevertheless, the failure of the regime to realize the socialist dream became increasingly evident. The population grew disillusioned. East Germans were dissatisfied with the constant scarcity of consumer goods and their lack of quality, with terribly inadequate housing, with the poor condition of the infrastructure, and with the careless destruction of the environment through pollution. They resented the state's unrelenting control and intrusion into their private lives. They wanted to express their opinion without reprisals; they wanted to travel freely. Their discontent was fueled by images of the West's standard of living, brought straight into every citizen's living room via West German television: images of prosperity, cultural diversity, freedom to travel; unfettered exchange of ideas and opinions, personal international relations. Yet calls for reform and democratization of socialism, demands for more participation in the political process and freedom of expression—which were actually written into the constitution but never practiced—were answered only with increased repression.

In 1986 Mikhail Gorbachev announced fundamental political, economic, and social reforms in the Soviet Union. He further proclaimed that the independence of all Eastern Bloc countries was inviolate. The consequences were immediate and historic. Poland and Hungary were the first to follow with sweeping political reforms and to open their borders to the West. The SED, however, declared that the GDR was highly developed and there was no need for refurbishing the house just to keep up with the neighbors. Honecker and the GDR's government rejected Gorbachev's reform policies. But the population articulated its desire for change more and more dramatically. East Germans began leaving the country by the thousands through Hungary's open borders to the West, assembling in churches for passionate debates, holding mass demonstrations for peace and human rights, declaring defiantly, "Wir sind das Volk" (We are the people)—all in spite of massive arrests. Finally, on 9 November 1989 the new government of the GDR announced the right to free travel. That was the signal for liberation. The same night, the Wall crumbled; thousands of people streamed to the West, now carrying slightly revised signs: "Wir sind *ein* Volk" (We are *one* people). The process of unification had begun.

When the actual process of merging the two countries with their different economic, social, and cultural standards of living began, the jubilations on both sides gave way to sober reflection, if not outright resentment. Generally speaking, the West considers the former GDR "an accident of history." Consequently, it proceeded to eradicate its legacy and permeate its territory and its population with western values. The citizens of the western part have trouble accepting eastern customs and persistent habits such as system-induced lax work ethics. They resent the GDR's initial refusal to accept responsibility for Nazi atrocities and the financial sacrifices required to make GDR industry and infrastructure equal to western standards. The eastern citizens feel more and more "annexed" or "colonized" rather than united with the West, a view affirmed by the appropriation of eastern real estate by western developers or former owners. But the act of eradicating the eastern heritage is also perceived in the gradual absorption of their cultural and social characteristics by western precepts, which are themselves defective and whose flaws—disintegration of the family structure, isolation of the individual, profit motives, ruthless competition—ironically have become more glaring in the wake of unification. Politically an entity, Germany has yet to unite as a people.

Literature in the German Democratic Republic

East Germany was a nation of avid readers. Book sales relative to the size of the population—around seventeen million—were the highest in the world. A book's first printing of a half-million copies was not unusual, and it would be quickly sold out. Even a volume of poetry would have an average first edition of twenty thousand copies, compared to the West, where a quantity of two thousand is considered large. Public readings were always filled to capacity. Conveying a sense of solidarity rarely found in public life, they frequently became lively communal confessionals, in which the audience would exchange experiences and thoughts not normally discussed in public. The East German readers turned to their writers not so much for entertainment and diversion but for assistance in the challenges of living under authoritarian rule. Ironically, the GDR regime granted prominent writers extraordinary privileges, such as travel to Western countries, large apartments in the city and second homes in the country, Western cars and bank accounts.

Yet the significant and privileged role authors played in their society came at a high price. All writers were subject to the exceedingly restrictive cultural policies of the GDR, which were based on two premises: that all forms of culture have a notable impact on the character and course of a nation; that politics, economy, and culture are interdependent ancillary tools of the national government. One can hardly expect an authoritarian state to leave the nature and the direction of its people's culture to chance or to the creative discretion of the artists. It will as a matter of course conscript the arts into the service of the government and focus all artistic endeavors toward the goal articulated by the party. In 1967 Walter Ulbricht reiterated this view: "The planning and control of culture, which is especially necessary in the transition from capitalism to socialism and in which the masses themselves participate more and more, endeavors the very best development of mankind and of human relations, as Marx said." To this end the Ministry of Culture was founded in 1954 with the express purpose of orchestrating all cultural activities from the genesis of a work of art to its public presentation. The intrusiveness of national authority into the life and work of the artist in the GDR can scarcely be imagined by anyone born and raised in the United States and other Western democracies.

As an ally in the struggle to build the socialist society, the arts were compelled to communicate in one idiom: "socialist realism," a set of artistic guidelines adopted from the Soviet Union and incorporated into the political program of the SED. Thus, socialist realism did not evolve naturally from a historical and social context, from a waning established style, as is often the case with other artistic movements; rather, it was the result of political fiat.

Like the Soviets, the SED believed that the artist is the engineer of the human soul and his work the servant to the state. Literature was ordained to play an especially important function in the engineering of the human soul and the promotion of social change. Since most East Germans were passionate readers, the party chose books as a favorite medium to propagate socialist ideology, hail its virtues, convey the party's resolutions, and inspire the reader to enroll in the common cause. Therefore, every phase of the literary process was controlled, from conception to publication to distribution to critical review and scholarly debate.

The entire literary establishment had to abide by a powerful ideological oath. Writers were expected to follow official guidelines concerning style, structure, and content. Publishers had instructions to select manuscripts that conformed to socialist principles. Distribution and publications in other countries were carefully monitored. Critical review (in the GDR a contradiction in terms) consisted chiefly of measuring the worth of the book against the cultural and political party line. Controversial debate arose only when critics disagreed whether doctrine was observed properly. A system of awards and prizes served to highlight exemplary books and, thus, affirm the successful passing of the institutionalized process.

In 1950 the community of writers was organized as the German Writers' Union. Its first president was Anna Seghers, who was revered not only for her prose work but also for her courageous struggle against fascism as a member of the Communist Party and who had just returned from exile in Mexico. A series of widely read literary journals appeared. The writers' union published a monthly journal called *Neue Deutsche Literatur.* This publication, along with the other literary journal of national significance, *Sinn und Form,* represented a self-portrait of contemporary East German literature and served as a mouthpiece of official cultural policy. Contents typically included previews of works in progress, analyses, reviews, and debate about literary theories, aesthetics, and themes in East and West. *Sinn und Form* was founded in 1949 by Johannes R. Becher, a well-known poet and head of the Ministry of Culture until his death in 1958. Becher was president of the Cultural Alliance for the Democratic Restoration of Germany and had returned from exile in the Soviet Union.

Party arbiters of culture decided that writers through the ages had generally catered to the educated classes but ignored the masses. Consequently, authors living in the GDR had to express the concerns of all citizens, and their work had to be plain enough to be understood and enjoyed by all, especially the workers. The task of the artist was to depict the people in the context of a new social order and to help propel the development of a new man: an individual of strength, optimism, and willingness to work not for his own gain but toward the formation of a new society.

To serve this agenda GDR culture bureaucrats devised a set of mandates to which every writer was expected to conform. These mandates specified the following criteria: objective reflection of reality, partiality, national orientation, portrayal of the typical and of a positive hero. A brief examination of these somewhat self-contradictory criteria will help us grasp how difficult it was for Wolf (or any serious writer) to work in East Germany.

"Objective reflection of reality" means roughly the artistic portrayal of life in harmony with the socialist interpretation of history, the evolution from a capitalist to a socialist society. By way of historical and dialectical materialism the GDR author is able to discern the objective historical progression of history and can, therefore, understand and describe reality more accurately and profoundly than a bourgeois writer. The author should depict life in the GDR, especially that of the workers and farmers, not as if reflected in a mirror but, rather, filtered through the lens of the socialist ideology. He is to bathe the current social fabric in a promising light that precludes the presentation of antagonistic conflicts—that is, conflicts that cannot be resolved harmoniously. Literature has to generate impulses that work toward the transformation of society.

The concept of "partiality" alludes to the honest desire of the author to employ his talent in the service of socialism and to interpret the historical development in light of received communist principles. In contrast to the bourgeois writer, who chronicles the human condition independent of political affiliations, the GDR author is committed to the party and thus depicts reality in accordance with party doctrine and the national interest. He or she expresses the will of the people, not his or her own individuality, and exposes impediments to the fulfillment of the socialist dream. The interests of the whole must always supersede the interest of the individual. Obviously, partiality precludes any informal dissent of the author.

"National orientation" is an inadequate translation of the word *Volkstümlichkeit,* which describes something that derives from and appeals to the common folk. National orientation is properly fulfilled when the writer addresses the masses and tries to bridge the historical gap between the lower classes and the elite. A work must be comprehensible to the population at large and must articulate themes of concern to the majority of citizens. It observes the customs of the people and is firmly rooted in the national soil and soul.

The "typical" refers to character and occurrences that convey universal truth. To be authentic, individuals in a novel must represent human nature in general. They must typify some of the characteristics of the ideal socialist, characteristics that will be typical of the aspirant socialist society. Since this society will be void of conflicts that cannot be solved and people are expected to be generally happy, optimism is an ancillary ingredient of the typical. This principle precludes depicting individuality but presents "people in quotation marks," a phrase coined by the poet Gottfried Benn. The criterion of the typical, then, abolished anything sui generis. How suppressing individuality while pursuing universal truths can be accomplished is not at all clear.

The "positive hero" is the most distinct characteristic of socialist realism. The protagonists are exemplary prototypes of the new human being and, therefore, sketched in bright and appealing colors. They are people in the throes of contemporary life who work for the good of their country because their individual well-being derives from the well-being of society. They know how to overcome conflict, how to change, and how to live or learn to live in harmony with the new social order. They are effective and tireless proponents of truth, justice, equality, and universal peace, and they promote the interest of their fellow man, community, and nation. They serve as role models in which readers can recognize themselves.

After a decade of more or less enthusiastic adherence to these principles, writers began to perceive them as serious obstacles to creative expression. Even the party recognized the stifling impact of the restrictions, and at the Second Bitterfeld Conference in 1964 the chief of state, Walter Ulbricht, declared, tongue in cheek, that socialist realism was not a dogma, a collection of rules into which life had to be pressed, but that the realistic method had evolved historically and would continue to develop. This did not mark the end of state mandates, but small allowances were made, and the writers felt encouraged to seek new paths.

Several developments in the political and social arena helped loosen the iron grip. The Wall, perceived as a shield against the intrusion of western thought, contributed to a more relaxed climate and a less stringent application of the rules. The regime had organized the literary professionals into a close community in which communication about the literary scene was easy and became increasingly lively, much more so than in the West, where authors had to make special personal efforts to establish contact with their colleagues. In the GDR there was constant exchange about artistic and aesthetic concerns, a fact that contributed substantially to the incremental changes made in cultural policies. The criteria of socialist realism were passionately debated in the annual SED conventions, writers' union conferences, and literary gatherings. As a consequence, in the course of the GDR's history they were frequently revised and refined, although their basic tenor remained restrictive: the elementary antagonism between a political mandate and artistic autonomy just cannot be resolved.

The definitive separation of East Germany, while fostering a climate of security and growth, also prohibited the formation of a corral of critical thinkers fundamental to any effective change. Many intellectuals who had misgivings with the power structure and the inability to articulate their criticism found ways to escape to the West, or they were isolated through incarceration or expatriation before they could rally an effective following. Thus, the seeds of productive resistance and protest perpetually shriveled to ineffectual innuendo and powerless encoded pleas. Nevertheless, some of the remaining writers were able to forge a small space for the expression of their artistic dreams through shrewdly veiled language and concerted efforts in the various cultural organizations.

An emerging suspicion that the party's self-proclaimed infallibility, moral authority, and ability to realize the concepts of socialism were possibly fraudulent fueled these writers' clandestine rejection of dogma, particularly the notion that the individual's interests must be subsumed by society's interests and that social postulates are always more important than individual needs. Since the late 1960s some writers such as Stephan Hermlin and Hermann Kant began to follow their own artistic instincts and visions, finding ways to circumvent the mandates of socialist realism, even when they saw themselves as advocates of socialism. In spite of, perhaps partly because of, these criteria, the individual, often in conflict with society, became a major theme in GDR literature. The limiting precepts of structure and style were concomitantly expanded. Christa Wolf, more than any other writer of her generation who remained in the East, was a pioneer of such reforms. Aware of the author's vital function in GDR society, she felt keenly and embraced sincerely her role as mother confessor and her responsibility as guidance counselor and reformer. In fact, her commitment to change and to the realization of socialism as she envisioned it were the major reasons for her decision to stay in the East.

After the unification of Germany many eastern writers felt exiled without leaving their home. Alien western customs and habits quickly dominated the cultural life of the eastern states. Many authors had difficulties adjusting to western standards, to the more competitive, less nurturing cultural atmosphere. In many cases their works suddenly lost appeal, if not relevance. Formerly prominent authors found they had no audience. Bookstores and publishers discarded thousands of books because they were considered obsolete. It is a tragedy that unification has relegated many of these courageous writers, including authors who used to be respected in the East and West, such as Hermann Kant and Heiner Müller, to mediocre positions in the artistic arena of Germany. Even Wolf struggles to maintain her ranking among the celebrities.

CHAPTER TWO

"Identity through Bonds"

Growing Up

When studying photographs of Christa Wolf, we look into dark, probing eyes; they look "startled and aloof," to use her own words. From her round face—framed by dark brown, slightly wavy hair—emanate sincerity and curiosity, qualities that animate alike her friendly smile and contemplative gaze. Her work, too, reveals sympathetic and fervent inquisitiveness into all aspects of human reality, yet she has resisted revealing much about her own life. What we do know is filtered through her novels and stories, which are unabashedly autobiographical; in her own words they include the "dimension of the author." Prose, she once said, is where subject and object meet. It requires, she went on, fantastic precision, strict order, endless freedom, creative and magical transformation of facts into new reality. All this she applies to her own prose, in which the facts lifted straight from her life are imaginatively transformed. To a large extent the protagonists embody Wolf's temperament, feelings, and musings. They move in a space and time she has divined in accordance with her own; they populate episodes from her personal history; they experience many of her experiences; they relate to people resembling her own family and friends. Although most scholars warn against identifying any of the novels' characters with the author and Wolf states in most books that all of her characters are inventions, she herself noted in her diary on 27 September 1993: "When will I, or when will I ever again be able to write a book about a distant invented character; I myself am the protagonist, I can't help it, I am exposed, I exposed myself" (T 298). To read Wolf's work is necessarily to meet Wolf the person.

Christa Ihlenfeld was born on 18 March 1929 in the small, mostly Protestant town of Landsberg on the Warthe River. In Polish territory now, it is called Gorzow-Wielkopolski, located approximately twenty-five miles from Germany's eastern border. The characteristics of Landsberg, with its modest but sturdy red brick houses lining the river, and of the surrounding countryside, with its dark pine forests and sandy hills, feature prominently in several novels. The leisurely sagacious tone of the area's dialect resounds unmistakably in the dialogue. Most of Wolf's ancestors—middle-class people, civil servants, farmers, and tradesmen—flourished here. Her parents successfully operated a grocery store in Landsberg, providing Christa and her younger brother a comfortable home and a carefree childhood.

When she started public school in 1935, the National Socialists, though in power for only two years, had already infiltrated the curriculum with their racial, political, and cultural theories and set up a system of organizations to educate the youth in national socialism. Wolf has often addressed the difficult task of her generation to cleanse their outlook and instincts from the fascist indoctrination they received throughout their childhood. Already in March 1933 the Nazis held a much heralded auto-da-fé of undesirable books and quickly expunged them from the libraries and the market. Christa, the avid consumer of books, read authors like Grimm, Jost, Binding, Carossa—popular but inconsequential "stuff," as she herself said. The first forbidden book, Erich Maria Remarque's *All Quiet on the Western Front,* touched her deeply because it helped her understand that a German soldier, too, could die miserably of his wounds. For the first time she understood the agony and horror of death. She remembers little of the discrimination against the Jews and other minorities that climaxed in the Holocaust—after all, she was only a child in the Third Reich—but she cannot forget the "false sadness, the false love, the false hate" with which her generation was infused and how much sincere effort it took to pluck those perversions from the soul.

Wolf was only ten years old when the Nazis invaded Poland. The ensuing war remained distant from the perspective of a child in a small town. But in January 1945 the battlefront drew near Landsberg. Like millions of other refugees, her family left their home in a small truck with only a few possessions and supplies to flee westward from the invading Soviet army. Wolf has rarely spoken about this ordeal. She has expressed shock about the big difference between seeing brutally killed enemy soldiers in the movies and witnessing the monstrosities of war firsthand. She lived through weeks on the road with thousands of other refugees and found herself holding a baby frozen to death and having to hand it to its mother.

Wolf also remembers a cold night by the roadside sitting around a fire with a German communist just liberated from a Nazi concentration camp. She was accustomed to seeing communists as criminals. His exclamation "Where did you live all these years, for crying out loud?" rang meaningful to the teenager, although she didn't quite understand it then: Was everyone deaf to the lies and blind to the horrors perpetrated by the Nazi regime? Wolf used this scene several times in her works to signal a change of consciousness in the protagonist.

Eventually, the question made her realize that every belief she had held and defended needed to be examined for its validity. Wolf felt shame for having been a part of such an inhumane system, although she was only a child during the Third Reich. In a symbolic gesture of restitution (or was it because her mother feared the content could implicate the family?) she burned her diary. Thirty years later, in an attempt to come to terms with man's willingness and ability to live under a dictatorship, she recounts these experiences in meticulous detail in her book *Patterns of Childhood*.

When the war finally ended, the trauma over the loss of home, in the all-embracing sense of that word, was more acute than the joy over liberation from an inhumane regime. In the little village of Gammelin, in Mecklenburg, her family took temporary refuge, the first of eleven different moves until Wolf finally settled in Berlin in 1976. This mobility was a new phenomenon in Germany, set in motion by the war, and it became typical in the postwar period. Millions were searching for a new place, new values, new relations, but they were also responding to the genesis and the challenges of rebuilding a new society. In 1945 Wolf found work in the Gammelin mayor's office. The following year, in the nearby town of Schwerin, she continued her high school education. During a protracted stay at a sanatorium to cure tuberculosis, she read incessantly—books that had been banned by the Nazis. They had the effect of revelations, she admitted, which gave her life a new direction. Especially Anna Seghers's novel *Das siebte Kreuz,* 1942 *(The Seventh Cross),* deeply influenced her worldview. When she attended the university in 1949 she was obliged to study dialectical and historical materialism, to read Marx and Engels. That provided an intellectual basis to understand recent history, and it led her to embrace socialism. "The old dying reality was replaced by a new feasible reality," she said.

On the Way to Socialism

Wolf recalls the feeling of exhilaration as she began to perceive her own destiny and that of her country being forged at the same time. Both her generation and her society were in search of a new identity and new forms of existence. There were so many conflicts to be resolved, changes to be made, old convictions to be reexamined. She found that it was much easier to feel shame about one's country after the truth was revealed than to learn to love it again, that it was easier to say no than yes—either to past or present—because any yes had to be based on knowledge, honesty, and fairness, not on misconceptions and illusions. She was ready to embrace her country and to say yes to socialism, with its enticing promise to remove the political, physical, and moral ruins left by the Third Reich and to move toward a new reality, a new social order. She believed then that a fundamental economic change, particularly a change in the allocation of property, would lead to the next phase in social development, the socialist phase. It was not until thirty years later that Wolf wondered how, as Marxists, they could have presumed a swift, smooth passage to socialism within a society that had been unable to free itself from the shackles of fascism and which was, moreover, under the whip of a world power that was experiencing a dreadful perversion of that very system under the Stalinist regime. But in the 1950s she had high hopes that her generation was going to witness and enjoy the advantages of the realized socialist society. And there was no time to lose.

At twenty years of age, mobilizing her new convictions, Wolf became an active member of the recently founded SED, the German Socialist Unity Party. In 1949 she began studying German literature and history at the Friedrich Schiller University in Jena to become a teacher. In 1951 she married Gerhard Wolf, a fellow student. She followed him to Leipzig, where he had been offered a job at the radio station, with a modest income for the young family. Their daughter Annette was born in 1952. Wolf and her husband have since collaborated on many different projects, including anthologies, film scripts, literary essays, and reviews.

Christa finished her studies at the University of Leipzig. She studied under some well-known teachers, such as philosophy professor Ernst Bloch. His principle of hope, which defines Marxism as the practice of concrete utopia projecting life onto the horizon where it will be realized, can be readily perceived in Wolf's thinking. And literature professor Hans Mayer, who resurrected in his lectures the literary history and texts forbidden during the Third Reich, directed Wolf's thesis about "Problems of Realism in the Works of Hans Fallada." Fallada wrote the first published German postwar novel in 1949, *Jeder stirbt für sich allein,* (Everyone Dies All Alone), continuing in his forte of entertaining common people with tales about common people.

In 1987, in her address honoring Hans Mayer on his eightieth birthday, Wolf recalled her student days and confessed that the class debates about purity of faith, about the correct point of view or departure from the norm, which was not desirable but often unavoidable, had left her feeling alienated and doubtful. She decided that Leipzig at that time was not the place for her. And teaching, she realized, was not the profession for her, either. Even before her graduation in 1953, at the age of twenty-three, she published her first book review for the daily paper *Neues Deutschland,* the voice of the SED. Praises of her frank and insightful opinion about a contemporary novel must have been encouragement to pursue a career as critic and editor.

Christa Wolf as Literary Critic

Wolf started her career as research assistant at the German Writers' Union, which had just been founded in 1950. Here she received her introduction to the cultural policies of her country, the aesthetics and content of socialist realism, as well as the politics of criticism. She also met many writers, celebrated authors such as Bertolt Brecht from the older generation who were returning from exile in various countries. There was a lot to learn from them because they had personal knowledge of the literary traditions and activities before 1933—a blur to Wolf's generation. Wolf was especially eager to learn from Anna Seghers, the first president of the writers' union, whose work and thought became a model for her and inspired her to explicate the function and effect of prose.

Wolf's career advanced rapidly—too rapidly, she thought in retrospect. Early on she was placed into positions of authority in a professional and political process that she was still trying to understand. She was entrusted with overseeing the development of contemporary literature in the writers' union. At twenty-six she was already a member of the union's executive committee, at twenty-seven chief editor of the publishing house Neues Leben, and at twenty-nine editor for the writers' union's publication *Neue Deutsche Literatur*. In all these positions she had to make crucial decisions on many manuscripts and literary projects by seasoned as well as aspiring authors—challenging responsibilities for a young woman. The disparity between power and her self-perceived competence was hard for Wolf to overcome. In 1956 she escaped by having another child—in her own estimation a typically female refuge.

Her brilliant career would not have been possible without a vigorous representation of the ideological program of the party. It is not surprising, then, that her early reviews and essays rest more on the official canon of literary standards than on individual opinion. In her first reviews she still favored the representation of the typical rather than the individual, objective description rather than a narrator's subjective intrusion, partiality with the party line rather than individual conviction, a real plot rather than a chain of loosely related events, conflicts that could be resolved harmoniously. Characters were examined for their ideologically correct orientation and positive outlook. Protagonists had to be appropriate socialist models for the readers' opinions and lives. In short, she followed prescribed guidelines.

Following Stalin's death in 1953, socialist ideology began to be cleansed from Stalin's authoritarian dogma, and cultural policies were reviewed. In the wake of the "new political course" Wolf and others began to criticize the absence of sharp conflict in the new fiction and, by extension, the absence of the tragic element. It may not have a place in socialist literary theory, she wrote, but conflict and tragedy happen in real life, and because they are not typical—only the positive is considered typical—they are ignored in GDR literature. Readers want to know why it is that people in our new society can still cause someone else's death, she pointed out, or that party functionaries can commit harmful errors. At this time she still blamed the authors for paucity of conflict and want of variety of characters. Perhaps writers misunderstood the parameters of socialist realism, she speculated apologetically; perhaps they feared that the editors could misunderstand. She praised books such as Erwin Strittmatter's novel *Tinko* (1954), which uses original language and describes the tragic element. *Tinko* depicts the main characters' physical and moral demise because they are unable to accept or comprehend their current historical situation, which is, "objectively" speaking, beneficial for them.

In her essays, too, Wolf began to scrutinize doctrinal inconsistencies, define the responsibility of the publisher as disseminator of ethical guidelines, wonder how contemporary literature could appeal to a diverse public, and query the function and possibilities of literature beyond the prescribed notions. She expressed her belief that the written word is able to expand the horizon of the "new man," the socialist whom society was aspiring to develop, that a book could strengthen his moral judgment and sense of beauty and that it could enrich his emotional life. To that effect she pleaded in an essay "Achtung! Rauschgifthandel," 1955 (Beware! Drug Trade), that the level of reading matter be raised by removing comics, cheap romances, and similar publications from the market. They are poisoning our youth, she claimed. Instead, we should offer entertaining but decent, humane books dealing with themes that meet the readers' interests and reflect their lives. The books should make clear that, with the advent of socialism, contemporary social needs were finally corresponding to man's deep longing for perfection and for a holistic development of the individual. The socialist world could be empowered by honorably satisfying this longing.

After the birth of her second daughter in 1956, Wolf contributed many reviews and essays to a variety of publications, among them *Neue Deutsche Literatur,* a literary journal, *Forum,* a widely read student paper, and daily newspapers such as *Neues Deutschland,* voice of the SED, the *Berliner Zeitung,* and many others. She reviewed important authors and became known as a critic with principles—not necessarily the sanctioned kind. Especially in view of the evolving technology and increased emphasis on science, Wolf warned that one could not forget the ultimate goal of all our economic, scientific, cultural, and political efforts: the whole human being. Moreover, she argued that literature above all had to investigate the emotions, thoughts, and psychic structures of the individual. Clearly, she was moving further and further away from the party line. In 1962, in one of her last reviews, she contributed to the debate about war books. She echoed the official proclamation when she wrote in veiled terms that, on the one hand, "the recent past" (fascist ideology), though appearing in new clothes, was again state doctrine in West Germany and that, in East Germany, it had been politically overcome—ludicrous claims in either case. On the other hand, she observed that the past still affected people in many ways, and its residue needed to be purged. Being well aware that the party version placed the blame for the Nazi reign squarely on the West Germans, she nevertheless demanded that GDR literature admit and come to terms with the unfortunate role all Germans played in the war.

Therese Hörnigk, who knows Christa Wolf and her work well and whose study of Wolf's career is most insightful, observed that the aesthetic, thematic, and political idiosyncracies characterizing her later work emerged even in the early reviews and essays. This fact, Hörnigk rightly argues, distinguished her clearly from other critics. Wolf's passionate engagement in the political process, her moral foundation, her honest and deeply probing exploration of reality, her search for the right direction, her attempts to facilitate society's dialogue about its concerns, her efforts to interest her readers in moral issues and in individual change—all are orchestrated to improve radically both individual and corporate life in the GDR.

Wolf's critics also charged, however, that her critical work is characterized by advocacy of SED policies and persistent admonition of GDR writers to illustrate the promises and virtues of socialism. In 1965 Wolf still expressed gratitude to have been in a position in those years to help administer the birth and growth of a new society. In 1972 her retrospective opinion was at once more critical and apologetic. She would write those reviews differently today based on different experiences, she said. They were based on sterile ideological concepts of literature that were common then. They were honest errors and not products of opportunism, but she acknowledged that honesty does not justify errors (DII 766). In a discussion with professors from Ohio State University in 1983 Wolf expressed "horror" at having written critical reviews "in the wrong sense" and of having been a critic "who measured books by a certain standard" (DII 897).

Moskauer Novelle

Since early childhood Wolf had tinkered with fiction: fairy tales, stories of revenge and other fantasies, daring little lies for practical use, occasional poems, portions of novels and plays—all these were mentioned in her list of writing attempts in younger years. But her manuscripts fell victim to her own censorship, as she phrased it, until *Moskauer Novelle* (Moscow Novella), which was published in 1961. She had been encouraged by her colleague Louis Fürnberg, who insisted that she was eminently qualified to write prose: "Who if not you? Come on, write! Just try it!" He added that she could continue writing critical reviews on the side, the way the English playwright George Bernard Shaw did all his life.

By Wolf's admission *Moskauer Novelle* was the first tangible result of her attempts to give literary shape to her own experiences. The story contains a great deal of autobiographical material, including most prominently her ideological position at the time. It reflects her experiences as a guest of the Soviet Union on several occasions, the personal story of a Russian soldier and acquaintance, and her desire to describe the complex transition from national socialism to communism which her generation was undergoing. The central theme of the relationship between the Soviet Union and the GDR, the victor and the culprit of the war, coupled with the political regeneration of the protagonists as a result of solidarity between the two countries, was popular with both the GDR public and writers. It was frequently couched in the microcosm of two lovers and their double encounters who recognize past failures and guilt and, through restitution and socialist brotherhood, overcome conflict.

Wolf takes the reader on a trip to Moscow with the pediatrician Vera Brauer, member of a delegation of medical experts. Vera recognizes their interpreter Pawel Koschkin as the Russian lieutenant whom she first met at the end of the war, when the Red Army's occupational forces established outposts in the eastern zone. Vera and Pawel's growing mutual affection is both kindled and burdened by their past encounter. Fourteen years ago Pawel had inspired Vera, a clerk in the mayor's office (like Wolf at that age), to pursue a healing profession and study medicine. He had also been instrumental in her conversion from fascism to socialism. He himself had wanted to be a surgeon, but he was wounded in an act of German sabotage, a fire at an ammunition depot of the Soviet army, and had suffered impaired vision. As a result, he was forced to relinquish his dream and settle for the profession of interpreter. Nonetheless, Pawel was a facilitator of communication between nations, so he, too, was serving society, helping to heal the maimed relations to East Germany. We discover that Vera had known of the planned arson and could have warned Pawel. She could have saved him from injury and averted his professional misfortune. But at the time he was, of course, her enemy sworn to an alien political persuasion and a Russian to boot, so she let him walk into calamity. Her guilt of yesterday can only be atoned through ethical behavior today. Since both Pawel and Vera are married to others, she decides to do the decent thing: sacrifice her love for Pawel and return home.

This novella is an exercise in socialist realism. It is constructed in compliance with its prerequisite ingredients: objective reflection of reality, partiality, national orientation, the typical, a positive hero. An objective, all-knowing narrator chronicles the events in a simple and mostly straightforward manner, retrospectively bringing to life the past to prepare and motivate the actions of the present. The narrative camera focuses on external action, scanning the scenery and actors in sharp detail. Only occasionally the story is marred by symbolic ballast. The action is set in the Soviet Union, which is lovingly laid out. The panorama of the city of Moscow emerges in great splendor as we are led through the colorful streets buzzing with the daily activities of cheerful, relaxed, but energetic citizens—pictures reminiscent of any capitalist metropolis. To offset the sinister image of the eastern neighbor, whom Germans have always feared, Wolf draws visions of a compassionate and benign Russian. Through the protagonists we meet a cast of helpful, courteous, and kind individuals, each one representing a specific desirable characteristic. The mosaic of characters depicts the ideal society, communism, which is also delineated and exalted in lengthy dialogues.

The love story unfolding on this backdrop of self-righteous partiality and correct national orientation is symbolic of the historical relationship between Germany and the Soviet Union. It is ironic that Wolf chooses a woman to represent Germany's collective burden of guilt and restitution for crimes devised by an exclusively male political apparatus, while a male functions as the virtuous victim and savior. At any rate the story depicts the change from bellicose animosity to growing friendship between the two nations. The behavior of the German who recognizes and assumes her responsibility for the fate of the other and atones for her shame with a sacrificial act mirrors the national situation—enormous war reparations, the penance for Germany's culpability. The recent solidarity between the two countries is driven by a common utopian goal: "One day we'll all wake up . . . and the world is a socialist one. The atom bombs were dropped in the ocean and the last capitalist gave up his stock portfolio voluntarily" (MN 68).

The protagonists Vera and Pawel are positive heroes, both acting in accord with the overall principle of socialist brotherhood: "To live with an open visor. Not having to mistrust one another. Not envy the other's success, help others cope with failure. Not having to hide one's weaknesses. To be able to tell the truth. Credulity, naiveté, softness are no longer curses. The ability to survive no longer means: ability to delude" (MN 55). Pawel is the socialist par excellence from the start. His star lights Vera's path to socialism, and by its position in the socialist heaven Vera navigates the waves of her feelings for Pawel. Empowered by socialist verve, rationality triumphs over emotion. Conflict is resolved by engaging instruments of morality: loyalty, altruism, family responsibilities.

The reception of Wolf's debut as a writer was generally positive, and public interest in her country for both novella and author was quite lively. Years later Wolf herself was one of the severest critics of her first published work of prose. She lamented its lack of stylistic versatility: ill-conceived images, wooden dialogue, unraveling of the plot like a wound-up clock, prefabricated construction of the conflict. But most of all she frowned on the lack of reality in her story. After all, she observed, the social morals of an author require that he share with his society what he knows about it and not use thoughtlessly the official stamp called "partiality." She wished "a cloak of mercy" would cover her first work of prose.

It appears that in the early 1960s Wolf the creative writer began to unlearn everything that Wolf the student, critic, editor, and official guardian of contemporary literary endeavors had learned about literature. And she gradually removed the instruments of socialist realism from her literary arsenal so thoroughly that only her admirers and detractors would recognize socialist vestiges in her later work. In the course of the purge, her writing underwent dramatic changes. The nature of her latest publications has but the faintest resemblance to that of her earlier ones. Hans Mayer, on the occasion of his famous student's sixtieth birthday, opined that Wolf was a writer who "had to write her way to her self."

Her retrospective criticism of *Moskauer Novelle* also reflects a dramatic change in self-perception: what appeared to be slightly smug self-confidence about her work as an official agent of literary culture gave way to thoughtful questioning and constant reassessment of content, purpose, and techniques of her creative writing. This rigorous self-examination is reflected in the numerous essays, lectures, and interviews accompanying her creative work, which document the genesis of a text or describe its nature and significance. Often Wolf previewed her own unorthodox work in the context of current cultural politics to smooth the path to official acceptance and publication. The most important result of this continual process of textual introspection is its inclusion in the text itself. Analysis and revision of the fiction became an integral and essential part of that same fiction, frequently determining even the structure of a novel. For instance, if, during the process of writing, Wolf has doubt about the desired impact of a chosen word, she may rephrase her statement. If the accurate portrayal of a character is in question, she may offer an alternate rendition. If an event appears to be depicted inadequately, she may present a second version of the episode or introduce another character's view to yield a more complete picture—all in the name of a precise rendition of reality. The continual review of her progress included in the text makes the reader a collaborator in this technique: the reader is constantly invited to join in Wolf's search for the most accurate presentation and to arbitrate her decisions. This process of reassessment and revision of the text as part of the content and structure of fiction became one of Wolf's unique characteristics. In her next novel, *Der geteilte Himmel,* 1963 *(Divided Heaven),* though still adhering largely to the recently refined principles of socialist realism, she experiments with some of these techniques. The story, as Wolf preferred to label this book, was a major step toward artistic individuality characteristic of Wolf's mature work.

CHAPTER THREE

"So Much Light in So Much Darkness"

Divided Heaven

In the fall of 1959 the Wolfs moved to Halle, where the publishing house Mitteldeutscher Verlag had offered both Christa and Gerhard editorial positions. Halle is located in the southwest of the GDR in an industrial area with a spirited cultural life. Under the motto "Chemistry provides bread, wealth and beauty," local industries, the arts, and, of course, the SED had initiated a series of conferences in 1958 in an attempt to interest writers in current social concerns and to help them present contemporary life more realistically. A year later the Bitterfeld Conference convened one hundred and fifty professional authors and three hundred workers with an active interest in creative writing. With the slogan "Take to the pen, comrade! The socialist culture of your country needs you!" they debated national cultural goals and revised the latest official literary doctrine, which had been formulated at the fifth SED party convention in 1958. Concern about the lack of books dealing with present-day problems and misgivings about the perceived separation between art and life spawned the idea of motivating the workers to write and the writers to work. Who, they argued, could better give literary expression to the life of the working class and to the country's struggle toward a true socialist society than someone who had experienced both firsthand?

The call to the pen was sounded in every industrial plant, and professional writers were encouraged to take to the factories to learn about the world of labor. It was, not surprisingly, a world teeming with disappointments, pain, frustration, discontent, full of conflict—all of which literature was of course not allowed to discuss. One writer posed this problem to Secretary-General Walter Ulbricht. "You must be joking," Ulbricht answered. "The Party, which is based on dialectic materialism, which leads in the struggle for the new life and for progress, for a solution to the existing conflicts—this very Party should object to the artistic depiction of the conflicts as they exist in real life. . . . This is unthinkable! That would be a contradiction in terms!" Thus, a far-reaching change in the definition and practice of literature and a new phase in the evolution of socialist realism were inaugurated, generally referred to as the "Bitterfelder Weg" (Bitterfeld Movement). The efforts to engage the working class in the creation of a new socialist literature ultimately failed. But quite a few professional writers followed the call to the factories and acquainted themselves with the work and life of the working class. Some had the courage to take Ulbricht at his word and give voice to the problematic conditions they had observed. The most dedicated of those writers was Christa Wolf.

Following the Bitterfelder Weg, Wolf joined the labor force of a local plant manufacturing railway cars to study the production process and to gain more insight into the life of her fellow workers. She soon questioned the value of an experience that was perhaps socially desirable but otherwise meaningless to the person not suited for such work. One can learn many things, she said, but can we really assimilate all of them? Nevertheless, her exposure to labor prompted her to write a story about a team of workers—a so-called brigade. In a diary entry of September 1960 she noted:

> I am looking over the first pages of my manuscript piled up on my desk. The tediousness of the process which is called writing depresses me. A few faces have emerged from the simple brigade story, people whom I know better and have brought together in a story which is much too simplistic as it is, I can see that clearly now. A young woman from the country who, for the first time in her life, comes to the city to study. But first she does an internship in a factory, in a difficult brigade. Her boyfriend is a chemist, he does not get her at the end. The third person is a young master craftsman who had made a mistake and was sent to the brigade to prove himself. . . . It is strange that the banality of these commonplace occurrences, 'true to life,' is unbearably magnified on the pages of a manuscript. I know that the real work does not begin until the overall idea is found which allows the material to be told and which makes it worth telling. (GE 321)

Transforming the reality of her work experience into a literary reality challenged Wolf's writing skills. She needed a theme to animate the central characters. Some critics believe that the building of the Berlin Wall, the final Iron Curtain call on Sunday, 13 August 1961, provided the overall idea. Wolf seemed to have approved of what was euphemistically called "securing the border to the West." Like many others, she expected that, as a result, internal politics would take a turn toward true democratization: "August 13 makes it possible to expand the borders within our own country, within us—in discussions with our people, in working together," she said publicly a year later. It is not surprising, then, that this historic event should have had an impact on Wolf's new project. After all, according to the new Bitterfeld dogma, the treatment of current affairs was encouraged.

The prologue of *Divided Heaven* makes veiled reference to 13 August: it describes a day in the fall when people interrupt their work to listen to the voice of a radio announcer and even more closely to those "inaudible voices of very close dangers all of which are deadly these days. But this time they were averted. A shadow had fallen over the city, but now it was hot again and alive . . . it gave life and it took life, every day" (GH 7). Life goes on as usual after the Wall. The seemingly final division of Germany may have inspired Wolf to center the novel around the theme of separation rather than labor in a factory, mirroring the national situation in the constellation of the protagonists Manfred and Rita. The differences between East and West resound in their unhappy love affair, which ends when Manfred departs to the West and his lover, Rita, decides to stay in the East. Their personal conflict and separation, finalized by the subsequent construction of the Wall, has been read as a metaphor for the conflict between the two Germanies and the tragedy of their separation. Wolf did not seem to perceive either rift as tragic, however, which is strongly implied in the title *Divided Heaven.* Heaven's offerings are presumably divided equally between the estranged halves. For Rita and her country the Wall marks a new phase in their development. They both recuperate from a period of pain, anxiety, and doubt, and they can expect a life in which personal and national dreams can be fulfilled—a happy end reflected in the book's final words, which express the hope and even the certainty that "we will get used to sleeping peacefully. That we live with abandon as if there was plenty of that mysterious stuff we call life. As if it would never end."

Yet the "overall idea" Wolf sought in order to make the story worth telling is not its historical relevance. In spite of the importance accorded by critics and scholars to the theme of Germany's division, both the literary inclusion of the Wall and Manfred's defection to the West are not the thematic center around which the plot revolves but simply historically meaningful and elegant devices to effect the lovers' separation. If the few allusions to the political situation were removed and the separation of the lovers caused by, say, Manfred's move to another city, the tenor of the story would not change substantially. Wolf herself said in a radio interview that she had considered a version in which the couple would separate but would both remain in the GDR, and she went on to explain that the basic theme was not the division of Germany but, rather, the question: Why do people have to part?

Why must the protagonists, Rita Seidel and Manfred Herrfurth, part? Even before they meet the reader suspects that their love is doomed and that the forces that will separate them come from within. When Rita returns home from work one evening, she notices Manfred for the first time, standing under a wind-torn willow tree by the road. "The same kind of longing drove her to her village and him to this road leading to the highway and, for that matter, to all streets of the world" (GH 11), the narrator observes. Rita is obviously content with her peaceful and quiet little village. Manfred is restless and seeks contentment elsewhere. Of course, other forces will interfere with their relationship—social pressures, professional obligations and disappointments, friends and family, ideological differences, personal preferences. But these are simply designed to affirm the internal disposition of the protagonists, which is shaping their destiny and forcing them apart. Not surprisingly, then, the more Manfred and Rita get to know each other, the more deeply they love each other, the more apparent their differences and discord become which eventually drive them apart.

Rita is the quintessential positive hero. She grew up in a secure little village in which her mother had found refuge in the home of an aunt after the war. Rita was content in her village, where everyone liked her, but her teacher noticed that she was often lonely. He gave her books to read and encouraged her ambitions, her expectations for "extraordinary joys and sorrows, extraordinary events and realizations" (GH 14). After graduation she felt obliged to help with household expenses, and she started to work in an office. Soon she registered "signs of getting used to the monotony of her days" (GH 15), and she felt a little lost. When Manfred came to town on his summer vacation to relax before completing his dissertation in chemistry, he awakened Rita to the promises of life.

They met at a village dance. Rita, sensitive and observant, detected a shade of arrogance, indifference, cynicism, in his eyes, the very characteristics that perpetuate his eventual fall from socialist grace. She asked him a question that launched their relationship: "Is it difficult to become the way you are?" Not until they reach her front door did Manfred respond: "Could you fall in love with someone like me?" "Yes," she said simply (GH 12). By Christmas "their love reached a perfect balance," and, while taking a walk through the snow-covered village, Rita felt like the "two halves of the earth fitted precisely, and on the seam they strolled as if it were nothing" (GH 16). She thought that "everything was possible, only that they would lose each other again, that was not possible." Her optimism clashed with Manfred's apprehensions: "He was annoyed that she awakened hopes in him he had buried" (GH 19). But for a while she was able to lay the intellectual cynic and emotional skeptic in Manfred to rest and to give him the feeling of being needed—the perceived absence of which ultimately drives him away.

The rift began later that spring, "one of the strangest days in her life," when Rita suddenly decided to become a teacher. It was her habit to make important decisions intuitively and quickly, but they always turned out to be beneficial. Erwin Schwarzenbach, devout communist and educator, who had come to town to recruit potential teachers, had encouraged her to go to school—if she couldn't do it, who could? "That was possible that someone would come and simply say: Quit all of this. Start all over again. If that was possible, everything was possible . . . . This sleepy little town could wake up, from the edge of the world she could be hurled into its very center" (GH 21).

The location of this "center" was the big city where Rita had to move in order to study education. Moreover, as part of her studies, she was obliged to work in a factory. The trying nature of all these changes—city life, her studies, her work—hastened the demise of Rita's love affair but, ironically, also steeled Rita for the difficult decision to part from Manfred and prepared her for a future without him, a productive life in the service of her community.

In the city, counterpoint to the security and harmony of her village, Rita discovers all the ills of the industrialized age: pollution—smog hanging over the roofs, the river water too polluted for swimming and fishing; crowded living conditions and inadequate housing; relentless pressures, stress, isolation. "I am not one for premonitions," she said to herself while looking down on the city from an observation tower, "but I knew that I would be down at times . . . . Hundreds and thousands of faces . . . . Among the hundreds of faces in my village I was never as lonely" (GH 27).

But Rita made friends soon, as can be expected from an exemplary positive heroine. As part of her training, she worked in a railway car factory with a "brigade," a team of twelve carpenters installing windows. Through her involvement in the production and planning processes and her easy adjustment to this small circle of men, she quickly became a fully integrated member. She enjoyed her work; she felt proud that she was contributing her share to the new society and said so to the foreman: "You know . . . railroad cars—that was exactly what I needed. Of course, I could have felt comfortable somewhere else. But I can't imagine that I would have liked something else as much as the whistling of our engine when it takes off at night with the two new cars" (GH 37)—cars that would almost kill her at the end of the story. Working alongside the men, Rita observed their strengths and weaknesses, their professional ambitions and personal worries, and she learned to observe the same in herself. As she felt the dynamics within the group, the internal conflicts, she began to understand the social and economic forces at work in the production process and life at large. She especially liked the foreman, Rolf Meternagel. He had introduced her to her tasks, and, living in her neighborhood, he walked home with her every evening. She admired him, like the "heroes in old books," for his boundless energy, his dedication to his work, his perseverance in the face of back-stabbing and deceit. It was through his example that she learned about the role of the individual in a socialist society, "that she crossed the threshold to adulthood, that she entered the realm in which results are the arbitrators of a human being, not his good will, not even his efforts if they happen to be inadequate" (GH 60). When at the end of the novel Meternagel fell seriously ill, Rita consoled his wife: "Without him, we wouldn't be able to manage." She had learned the most important principle of the socialist community: each individual as a part of the whole is essential.

Although Rita progressed in exemplary fashion, she was not immune to doubt, even serious ideological crises—necessary obstacles in the development of a strong character. Those are largely staged in the university environment. She was suspected of complicity in a defection. When the parents of Sigrid, a fellow student, had gone to the West, Sigrid had not denounced them, as was expected, and Rita respected her confidentiality. Their teacher, Mangold, threatened punitive action by the party. When Rita's attempts to find counsel and encouragement from people she had learned to trust (Meternagel, Schwarzenbach) failed, Rita was devastated. Her fragile belief in the new man and the socialist fraternity began to crack, and it seemed she had fallen for a scam: "Man is good, he just needs to be given the opportunity. What nonsense! How stupid the hope that the greed in most faces can one day change to understanding and kindness" (GH 125).

She returned home to her village to recuperate and gather the strength to master the crisis alone. Finally, Schwarzenbach, her inspiration, friend, and political mentor, and now savior, advised Mangold that the party was there to help people, not to punish, and the danger was averted. From Schwarzenbach she learned that rigid adherence to ideology without sensitivity was detrimental to socialism, that forgiveness and patience are revolutionary virtues, and that "in the long run nothing but pure, unadorned truth is the key to humanity" (GH 186).

While Rita was turning into an emancipated and mature woman who identified sincerely with socialism, her relationship with Manfred deteriorated. Her spontaneous decision to study education cast the first shadow. He was angry that she did not consult him and that her decision forced him to make allowances. He was jealous because she would not live solely for him. And he doubted that she would be tough enough to survive the challenges of city life. Nevertheless, he invited her to live with him in the attic of his parents' house so that they could be together. Daily family dinners in the evening were hard on Rita. The silence across the table was as threatening as the verbal battles between Manfred and his parents.

But there were many happy moments also. When Rita and Manfred retired to their little room under the roof, they experienced an immediate regeneration and were able to restore harmony to their relationship, at least temporarily. Rita felt that she was coping quite well in spite of the many demands on her—the feeling of loneliness in the big city, Manfred's needs, the excitement and troubles at work and in school, new acquaintances, the tiresome evenings with the family, her mother's woeful letters. Manfred began to understand that she pursued her professional goals with the same fervor and determination with which she had approached him and that she would succeed.

Manfred was not insensitive to Rita's growth. He liked it yet feared it. He liked her new cheerful self-confidence, but he feared her growing independence. It made him feel more excluded and less needed. He began to deflect Rita from her destined course, disputing what he perceived to be the greatest threat to their relationship: her budding faith in socialism. Did she really believe, he challenged, that long meetings of her brigade could change things? That suddenly enough materials would be available for production? That the incompetent party functionaries would suddenly be competent? That the workers would suddenly consider the large social context rather than their own purse? Rita did not argue but wondered how Manfred could fear that something important to her could drive her away from him. "Listen," she said after a while, "let's not be jealous of a meeting anymore, o.k.?" When she returned home from work one day totally exhausted, Manfred, at once sympathetic and angry, told her to quit. But she shook her head: "You cannot just simply quit." "One can if one wanted to," he gave her to consider. "Well, then I don't want to." She had achieved independence from Manfred, too.

More than any other character in the book, including Rita, Manfred is complex and developed in careful detail. We learn more about his background and his motivations than about Rita's. Ten years her senior, Manfred grew up during the Nazi years. With revulsion he regularly participated in the activities of the Hitler Youth, "jumping off every wall with closed eyes when it was so ordered" (GH 44). He learned both obedience and rejection of authority at the same time. The latter ultimately prevailed. At the end of the war he saw his father exchange casually his Nazi uniform for an SED party emblem, a swift and easy modification of allegiance. But Manfred observed this change of guard with skepticism: "Everything will be different now. Different? With whom, may I ask? With those very same people?" (GH 45). He doubted whether young Rita could understand that he was part of a generation that had "early on been infected with this fatal indifference which is so hard to shed" (GH 44). She was often offended by what she perceived to be his antagonistic view of society. She regretted that he could not believe in the progress and the benefits of socialism because of his misguided conviction that history was always based on indifference. But how about reason? "Forget it! Reason has never been a factor in the creation of history. Since when has reason made man happy?" (GH 86). Manfred's dark cynicism and Rita's cheerful optimism clashed more and more frequently, affecting the most fundamental aspects of their lives and the most intimate facets of their love.

Manfred despised his parents, and he resented having to live with them under one roof—a necessity due to the GDR's persistent housing shortage. He perceived their house to be "the coffin of his life"—divided into coffins for sitting, dining, sleeping, cooking—"where nothing alive had ever taken place" (GH 24). He despised his father's opportunism and placid subservience to his wife's ambitions. He hated his father for having beaten him in the presence of his superior just to demonstrate his authority. He hated his mother for her pretensions, for her pathetic attempts to gain his love, for having subjugated her husband to her will. Just to anger his mother, Manfred did not become an actor. But he found he couldn't enjoy her disappointment either, and since then he had not enjoyed anything much except for his profession: "Only my job, that is good. Just enough exactness, just enough imagination. And you. You are also good" (GH 47), he said to Rita. But Rita saw "that every day when he set down to work, he had to overcome a strong resistance, a feeling of inadequacy, a fear that in the long run he would be unable to measure up to the task" (GH 112). Unlike Rita, the reader is beginning to suspect that Manfred may leave the GDR. Ironically, it was his mother who arranged for a refuge in the West even before he decided to leave.

Rita's fears that Manfred would encounter his greatest obstacle to contentment in his professional life soon proved to come true. Manfred had collaborated on the development of a textile machine with Martin Jung, an engineer and his only friend. At a party with other scientists he heard that this project had been rejected. Manfred was devastated. Not only had he invested much hope, time, and energy but, secretly, he had attached portentous value to the project: if it succeeded, everything else would succeed; if it failed, nothing would go well. Now he knew: "They didn't need him. There were some people who could destroy the hopes of a person with the stroke of a pen. All this talk about justice was nothing but talk" (GH 110). This rejection confirmed his deep suspicion

41

about the regime that he had so often criticized in his discussions with Rita. His personal fate seemed symptomatic of the course society was taking, which, he once argued, is wasting hopes and energy to accomplish the impossible: "To bring morality into this world!" (GH 147). Once he, too, had thought that pulling up the roots of evil would remove evil from this world. But evil has thousands of roots. It cannot be eradicated. "The facts are: the human being is not made to be a socialist. If you force him, he performs grotesque contortions until he has arrived where he belongs: at the horn of plenty" (GH 180). One day the socialists would also have to admit that. "To our lost illusions" was a toast he chose to conclude a party with his superiors shortly before his defection.

Gradually, Rita realized that because of her emancipation and Manfred's disillusionment their love had become vulnerable. "We are exposed to all dangers just like everyone else. Anything that happens to others can happen to us" (GH 156). And sometimes she was aware that she was waiting for a disaster. One evening, while Manfred was in West Berlin, presumably for a conference, Mrs. Herrfurth handed her a letter: "He finally got smart. He stayed over there." Rita was stunned. "He left. Like some incidental acquaintance he left the house and closed the door behind himself. He left to never return" (GH 157). But Manfred had written: he had found a job; he would notify her when to join him; he was only living for the day when they would be together again. Yet Rita sensed something deeply wrong with Manfred's move: "This is how one drifts along when one has lost control and everything is irrelevant" (GH 162). And she wondered whether he wasn't right when he insisted that love and friendship were not possible these days, that it was ludicrous to fight the great forces between us and our dreams (GH 88).

Rita bought a return ticket for her trip to West Berlin. She knew before she left that she would return to her village, her city, her family and friends, her society. For her West Berlin was "worse than a foreign country because one heard one's mother tongue." She would stay where she loved to be: home. And as soon as she was in Manfred's arms they both knew it: "It bothered her that they had to go through the motions, that the words had to be said, the day had to be spent. He knew it, too, and that made it easier" (GH 170). Rita found her suspicions about Manfred's defection confirmed: "He had given up. Those who don't love or hate anything, can live anywhere and nowhere" (GH 179). But she also detected his self-loathing for "not withstanding the pressure of the harder, stricter life" (GH 181). Rita never quite understood what Wolf articulated twenty-five years later when she was questioned about the frequent theme of failed love in her work: it is often the case that men and women "cannot use their relationship to make each other productive, that the inevitable damages they suffer in our civilization in early childhood seem to compel them to destroy each other" (ID 62–63). Rita did not, could not, see that internalized societal forces had destroyed their relationship.

A week later, on 13 August, Rita and Manfred were separated. Had Manfred stayed a little longer, so his friend Martin speculated in a letter to Rita, he would not have been able to escape, he would have had to cope with the system, and he would have learned that his project, his machine, had been accepted, after all. Had the Wall not been built, we could speculate further, Christa Wolf would have had to find another escape for Manfred to complete the internal and irreversible separation between the two protagonists. In her novel defection is more a personal than a political act: Manfred's decision is the result of an inability to believe; Rita's decision is an act of faith.

In Rita's transformation to personal independence and political affiliation the secondary characters play an important role. The negative individuals, mainly devout party member Mangold and Manfred's parents, appear to be wooden stereotypes personifying reprehensible attitudes. The positive supporting characters, on the other hand, are more rounded, embodying the complex and wide range of features that affirm life. Although exemplary, they are not without blemishes. Equipped with strengths and frailties, they have a history of successes and failures. The failures, of course, occur mostly in the private arena, within the family and their personal relationships. Thus, the conflicts that move the protagonists Rita and Manfred cut through the lives of the secondary characters as well.

The modern structure of *Divided Heaven,* unusual in the context of the place and time of its origin, was generally praised as suiting the theme. The unhappy tale of love, told in the past tense, is embedded in a story of victory over the crisis precipitated by the separation, told in the present tense. The novel begins shortly after Rita's return from West Berlin. We meet her lying in a hospital bed regaining consciousness after an accident: two railroad cars in her factory almost crushed her. The accident is described as a subconscious attempt to escape—a suicide attempt, not out of desperate love but, rather, out of desperation that love, like everything else, is transitory. She is not physically hurt, but she is suffering from a deep psychological crisis. While she is recovering from her failed love, from "this nagging feeling: they are aiming exactly at me," Rita recalls her life since she met Manfred. The process of recollection is an essential part of her therapy.

Wolf weaves Rita's memories of the past two years into the present, into her hospital stay, highlighting important vignettes in conversations with friends who come to visit. Through the narrative technique of questions and speculations Wolf invites the reader to participate in the therapeutic process. Having survived, Rita can be given her own narrative voice, and Wolf often lets her tell—in the first person—her experiences and her catharsis. A trivial story, Rita thinks, in part even embarrassing, but she has lived through it: her life in the village, a symbol of harmony and security; her move to the city signaling isolation, alienation, and discord; her love of Manfred, the conduit to her maturation; her studies and work, both forging independence and social responsibility, which ultimately motivated her decision to stay in the East. The end of her story coincides with the end of her psychological crisis, and she can return to her room in the attic of Manfred's parents' house. With her usual good cheer she resumes her life in the city, studying and working in the rail car factory.

The structure of retrospectively unfolding and analyzing the past would be better justified if Rita were, indeed, suffering a mental crisis and if the therapy of recall and reflection of the past were necessary for her recuperation. It is true that she had just gone through a period of dramatic growth and suffered the end of an intense love affair. It is true that, at first, she cannot or will not speak and that she cries often. But neither her distress nor recovery is reflected in the manner in which she tries to come to terms with these experiences. She ponders and narrates them as coherently and judiciously in the beginning, when she has just returned from a long period of unconsciousness and her memory and judgment should be expected to be bleary, as toward the end, when she is declared healthy and her improved faculties should produce improved insight. The language in which her recent ordeals are presented speaks neither of trauma nor of improvement.

Somewhere in the middle of the novel, unexpectedly, a curious change occurs in Rita which is intended to indicate her cure. It is the moment of catharsis induced not by lucid discovery of the internal and external forces that shaped her trials and tribulations but, instead, by a dream. She is amazed that her dream featured Ernst Wendland, the production manager of Rita's company, an admirer of hers and Manfred's ideological counterpart. While Ernst and Rita were in the room of her childhood, he said to her, "You need to forgive me, but not him!" The dream is clearly admonishing Rita to properly align herself with people of her roots and not with Manfred. Yet one fails to see how this dream can improve Rita's health. We are to believe that this is the point when Rita discovers that she is an adult with a "new feeling of self." We share her bewilderment, which is compared "with the amazement of a child who thinks for the first time: I." Had she not become an adult with a new sense of self and place in society while she was still living with Manfred? Was it not that sense of self and place which prompted her circumspect decision to stay where her roots are?

Upon her return to the city Rita herself says that she now knew what lay behind her and what awaited her and that this was the only change she had experienced, invaluable though it may be (GH 188).

If we cannot experience Rita's anguish or follow the change supposedly inducing the healing process, the story of her mental breakdown and recovery has little credibility, and we see no need for Rita's therapeutic recall, and, ultimately, no inherent need for the novel's elaborate structure. Yet we know that an unhappy love affair causes great pain and that dreams are often harbingers of change. Therefore, we are willing to suspend disbelief and follow with interest and suspense the author's sensitive, intelligent explorations of her characters' lives to their happy or unhappy end. The technique of retroactively unfolding and analyzing a biography and the subject of self-discovery—in this first novel matters of literary exercise rather than inherent elements of the story—shall become the major structural and thematic devices of Wolf's next novel.

The publication of *Divided Heaven* in 1963 was a milestone in the history of the cultural bond between East and West, in the literary life of the GDR, and in Christa Wolf's career. Within the first year 160,000 copies in ten editions were sold, several magazines carried the novel in installments, translations appeared in many languages, including Russian, Polish, Finnish, English, Spanish, and Japanese, and a film scripted by Christa and Gerhard Wolf was made from it. The book was a stunning success not only in the East but also in the West—altogether a remarkable occurrence on the international book market. Few if any books published at that time enjoyed as much attention and popularity on both sides of the Iron Curtain.

Critics in both Germanies immediately recognized *Divided Heaven* as an important literary event. Even in the West the novel was welcomed as a fairly objective contribution to the literary debate about a divided Germany, but Wolf was also reproached as an apologist of the Wall. The book's critical but constructive analysis of GDR society and its modern structure and narrative style were seen as signs of a thaw in the frigid climate of politics and social realism. It seemed to speak of resistance to cultural autocracy and was considered a first step toward literary emancipation of GDR writers and the programmatic beginning of a national literature. Today it is valued mainly as a historical document marking a turning point in the development of literary history in the GDR and launching Wolf's career as a creative writer.

In the East *Divided Heaven* was seen as a contribution to the fundamental question of nationhood under socialism, which was rarely brought to an open forum. The book unleashed an immediate and passionate debate among people from all walks of life, unique on the contemporary literary scene. Few books have been welcomed so universally, inspired such diverse opinions, and, at the same time, been judged so strictly, wrote Martin Reso in 1965 in the introduction to his collection of the book's reviews called *"Der geteilte Himmel" und seine Kritiker. Dokumentation* ("Divided Heaven" and Its Critics: Documentation).

The polemics focused primarily on the political and social implications of the novel. Some thought that Christa Wolf's treatment of the so-called national question, the division of Germany, was based on a grave misunderstanding of the actual historical situation. Others relished her exemplary renunciation of any hope that there could or should be an undivided heaven in Germany's future. Some alleged that her view of history as a process influenced by individual action was decadent, but most appreciated the book's affirmation of life and society as they themselves envisioned it. Awards such as the Heinrich-Mann Prize by the Academy of the Arts and the National Prize concluded the debate. The overwhelming response to her first novel motivated Wolf to write full-time and to use writing as a means "to become one with her time."

In an interview with the Dutch writer and journalist Aafke Steenhuis in 1989, Wolf confessed that it took her a long time and great effort to escape the net of theories and ideological concepts in which she had been trapped in the 1950s by her studies of literature and her professional activities in the GDR's literary arena. *Divided Heaven* represents the first self-confident steps toward emancipation from prescribed literary doctrine. In her next great novel, *Nachdenken über Christa T.*, 1968 *(The Quest for Christa T.)*, she also frees herself from many of the ideological entanglements.

CHAPTER FOUR

"To Be Honest, To Be Lonely"

The international success of *Divided Heaven* opened the world for Christa Wolf. She accepted invitations to many European countries east and west of the Iron Curtain to read her work and to lecture about literature and the writing process. Traveling widely, she developed acquaintances with West German authors such as Heinrich Böll and a close friendship with Peter Weiss, and she familiarized herself with international artistic trends and literary theory. Her popularity in the GDR caused a frenzy of public service activities. In recognition of her contributions to society and her prominent cultural role, she was confirmed as a candidate of the Central Committee of the SED. In her speeches at the party congresses from 1963 until 1967, she expressed her profound agreement with the concepts of socialism, as she did in a speech in 1964 celebrating the fifteenth anniversary of the GDR: "This part of Germany, which, twenty years ago, was still controlled by fascists and populated by bitter, confused, hateful people, has laid the foundation for rational cohabitation of its citizens. Rationality—we call it socialism—has permeated daily life. It is the yardstick by which we measure here the ideal, in whose name we praise or reprimand" (DI 398).

In spite of such expressions of surprisingly blind loyalty to the system, or perhaps because of them, she used her public stature to effect more liberal cultural policies. As a new member of the prestigious PEN Center of the GDR (a branch of the International Association of Poets, Playwrights, Editors, Essayists and Novelists), at national conferences and meetings of the literary community she joined in the voices for reform of the confining guidelines of socialist realism. At the second Bitterfeld Conference in 1964 she spoke to the literary establishment about the relationship between society and the artists. She argued that any artist had the duty to understand and depict the complex structure of society and its conflicts and, more important, that disseminating the truth about society did not harm but benefit it (DI 390). What is remarkable here is her courageous public proclamation that problems actually existed in the socialist community and her call to write honestly about them. She acknowledged the "antagonistic" conflicts that could not necessarily be resolved and had become "officially" nonexistent. Clearly, Wolf believed that the artist should not be merely a voice for the state.

In the student paper *Forum* in 1963 she enumerated some of these conflicts: the contrast between ideal and reality, between expectation and fulfillment, the desirable economic, social, and political possibilities versus the actual imperfect reality for which everyone was responsible. These conflicts are mostly rooted in the individual rather than in society—an indication that Wolf was ready to reveal publicly her interest in the mysteries of the individual. Wolf appealed to the GDR youth to consider such conflicts not as obstacles but, rather, as challenges to be resolved. And she rallied the literary community behind her cause: it was irresponsible and dishonest to present a picture of harmony and optimism in view of the many obvious problems in everyday life. In structuring a genuine socialist society, she urged, candid depiction of the actual conditions in the GDR, including the problematic aspects, and illumination of the whole human being would be more productive.

Wolf also attacked literary criticism in the GDR, joining in the polemics of writers such as Franz Fühmann, who had gained notoriety with his provocative accusation that critics tended to blame "a green bench" for not being "a blue table." She observed that the reading public had far more discerning taste, judgment, and ability to be moved by literature (*Erschütterungsfähigkeit*) than the literary critics, who seemed to write not for the benefit of the readers or the author but, rather, to please some imaginary authority. She demanded that critics cast aside caution and fear, "vestiges of a time when independent thinking and responsibility were not as self-evident as today," and take responsible risks (DI 394). Wolf knew very well that independent thinking was not self-evident yet. Perhaps she hoped to shame the cultural bureaucrats to acknowledge it as part of a new phase in social development.

The style of her continual crusade to expand the perimeters of literary activities shows intelligent circumspection. She prefers to coax rather than demand, to suggest rather than insist, to appeal to the public rather than to the bureaucracy—always conscious that her voice could be silenced if she were to raise it too high. Based on the official understanding that the regime represents the interests of the people, she strongly implied that the government needed to adjust its policies to the demands of the public, whose notions of literature's responsibilities were far ahead of party guidelines. She even urged that the state allow, indeed *mandate,* the depiction of all aspects of reality in order to harness its constructive powers.

The years after the Wall was built reverberated with possibilities for change. Society was becoming more complex, and so were its members' lives. The arts were developing self-confidence and the willingness to articulate current concerns. Wolf rallied these forces to debate the issue of self-realization in a socialist environment—not a topic favored by the bureaucracy. She reiterated her conviction that art should not serve an ideology but society and that the development of individual responsibility and creativity, based on political and moral integrity, was the key to social welfare. The artist's main task was to uncover reality and to raise new questions, even if answers were not readily available.

Wolf must have delighted in the heated ideological debates about the function of literature which followed her (and other colleagues') call for reforms but probably was not prepared for severe reprisals, most notably the rejection of two major film projects in which she and her husband, Gerhard Wolf, had collaborated. Shortly afterward, in 1965, she suffered a heart attack. While recuperating, she began preparations for two new prose works: the short story "Juninachmittag" ("June Afternoon") and the novel *The Quest for Christa T.* It is typical for her resiliency to use a major setback as the basis for starting a new creative phase.

An important influence on her upcoming work were the essays, fiction, and poetry of Ingeborg Bachmann, an Austrian contemporary poet. She had deeply moved Wolf and would continue to be a source of inspiration. Wolf's 1966 essay entitled "Die zumutbare Wahrheit" (The Truth to Which We Can Be Subjected) presents her analysis of Bachmann's prose, emphasizing the Austrian's intrepid attitude against unreasonable authority and her passionate defense of the truth. Not surprisingly, Wolf finds in Bachmann's work the narrative, structural, and philosophical elements that most closely resemble her own vision of writing. Thus, many of her observations read like a portrait of her own creative and political voice. Moreover, while presenting Bachmann as a model of contemporary writing, Wolf wielded, once again, her pen against the oppressive policies in her own country.

When reading Bachmann's prose, her essay begins, "one should not anticipate stories or the depiction of plots. Information about events is no more to be expected than characters in the usual sense or bullheaded pronouncements. A voice will be heard: bold and lamenting. A voice speaking about things known and uncertain—truthfully, that is: in accord with its own experiences. And truthfully keeping silent when the voice fails." Bachmann's voice—and in turn Wolf's voice—would never fall silent without defiance and struggle. Bachmann boldly defends the supreme mission of prose, which is to "see honestly what is, to realize what shall be." She laments the terrible temptation to conspire in the perpetuation of the world's evils "through conformity, blindness, consent, resignation, deception, and betrayal" (DI 87). Wolf identifies with Bachmann's creative raison d'être: "to continually revive the courage to her own experience, and assert it against the overwhelming number and discouraging power

49

of empty, meaningless, and useless phrases. . . . Also: to stand up, show one's own self, even weaknesses. . . . Affirmation of self as a process" (DI 88). In sharing the "heartlands" of her self, Bachmann opens up another dimension in the nature of writing: the reader who works on her book while reading. She is one of those authors, Wolf believes, "who depend on the collaboration of their readers" (DI 100). Bachmann's reliance on her own experience, her affirmation of individuality and of the right to unfold the self, her narrative style, and her intimate collaboration with the reader all inform Wolf's new projects. It appears that in Bachmann Wolf found an apologia or artistic credo for her own work.

"June Afternoon"

The short story "June Afternoon," written in 1965 but not published until 1967, is a small, well-wrought piece. It has been marked a turning point not only in Wolf's writing but in modern prose in the GDR. All of Wolf's observations at the beginning of her essay on Bachmann, quoted earlier, are pertinent to this story and are captured in the provocative opening metaphor: "A story? Something solid that can be touched like a pot with two handles, to hold and to drink from? A vision perhaps, if you know what I mean. Even though the garden was never more real than this year. Since we have known it, for only three years" (GE 34). At the onset Wolf indicates time and place, her narrative devices, and the nature of the story—a technique found more or less explicitly in all future texts. This more or less plotless story is not constructed in the usual manner. It does not depict "typical" reality but, rather, a vision, indicating a subjective view of reality. There is an "I," who is both a character in the vision and the narrator. The I is a member of a familiar group, a "we." The reader has already been included in the proceedings, "if you know what I mean." The time is an afternoon in June, as we know from the title, probably in 1965, the year Wolf wrote the story, and the place is a garden located in the vicinity of the border to West Berlin, probably in Kleinmachnow, where Wolf and her family had been living for three years.

The narrator turns out to be the mother of two children, the same age as Wolf's children. Her husband, like Gerhard Wolf, is versed in literature: he suggested the book the narrator is reading in the garden—from all indications probably one of Ingeborg Bachmann's texts. The family is engaged in various summer activities: the pruning of grape vines, discussions with the children, playing games, carving an owl, conversations with neighbors, daydreaming. But the physical and spiritual space of this family idyll is occasionally punctured by the threat of external dangers: a deafening sonic boom overhead—a chilling sound of the volatile Cold War. The clouds in the summer sky, which had just inspired the family to lofty flights of the imagination, were suddenly dotted with helicopters patrolling the border or with planes ferrying people from east to west or, politically speaking, from West to West, since they were flying from West Berlin to West Germany—a reminder of Germany's division. The tabloid story of a husband's corpse in a trunk which the eight-year-old child relished reading and a neighbor's report of a train derailment in which a friend of the family died present inexplicable evidence of evil lurking at paradise's gate.

Within the skillful framework of the garden idyll and the sinister provocations from the outside, the narrator contemplates this mundane little world and her own role in it. The process of the story is a deliberate unfolding of complements; an episode from the microcosm of the garden is accompanied by an insight alluding to the macrocosm of history or capturing an epiphany of human interaction: the older daughter's teacher had staged a dance for the school, and father questions the choice of lighting, which launches a serious argument with the daughter. Mother observes that it was not a question of proper lighting "because coping with all sorts of lighting we should have learned by now." The mother's witty reply refers to the ideological illumination provided by the regimes of Hitler and Stalin. Then she elaborates the causes of the father-daughter conflict: "No: he just cannot bear his daughter's pained dedication to everything she considers perfect; he cannot bear seeing her vulnerability; he continues to stand, foolishly, in the middle of the field in a thunderstorm to deflect the lightning bolts intended for her. Which earns him either ecstatic affection or raging ungratefulness" (GE 43).

The narrator may also use an incident to project into the future and express her ineffable fears: the tabloid report of the corpse in the trunk, she thinks, will still frighten her girl when the garden is no more, just as she, the mother, is still frightened by her grandfather's story of a murderer who was sentenced to suffer water torture until he was driven insane—a drop of water falling on his shaven head day in and day out. Using this image as a metaphor of today's threats, the narrator says: "I admitted that I am afraid these days of the next drop that will fall on our exposed heads" (GE 41).

This technique of describing a day's events interspersed with revelations of very private feelings and retrospective reflection, which gives universal meaning to personal experiences, resembles the form of a diary. Strict chronological order need not be observed; the text is often inconclusive and fragmentary; a wide array of unrelated subject matters is strung together casually; excursions into the past delay the advance into the present; the writer is always the protagonist; and she is uncertain about experiences not her own. Yet a diary normally addresses only the writer; it excludes others. But the narrator of "June Afternoon" explicitly addresses the reader and makes him a participant. This marks a stylistic change from Wolf's earlier work.

Wolf's narrator implores the reader to believe her when she says "that it is disquieting when her quiet neighborhood gets really quiet. One just never knows for what reason everything is holding its breath" (GE 36). She uses many conversational techniques to engage the reader, recurring phrases like "I am not saying that," "You may consider it strange but," "Did I already mention," "Forgive me." She may ask a rhetorical question, such as the one concluding her reflection of boredom in children and adults: "What should we fear more than the deadly boredom of entire nations?" (GE 39); or a touching personal one, prompted by her daughter's question whether she (the mother) would rather be pretty or smart: "Do you know the feeling, when a question hits you like lightning? I knew immediately, this was the question of all questions" (GE 45). Enforcing a dialogue with the readers is not just a means of keeping their attention, but it is an invitation to critical thought and to wide-ranging scrutiny of commonly held beliefs.

In all vignettes of "June Afternoon" individuality of character continually unfolds. There is nothing "typical" about each member of the family; they are not approved models of socialist virtues. Even the readers are challenged to set aside commonly held notions and to articulate their own opinion. The technique of telling a story in the first person sets strict limits on the narrator's range of knowledge. Therefore, the development of authentic rounded characters is restricted by the narrator's perspective. Only when predictable characters are depicted, as in orthodox socialist realism, can the narrator seem all-knowing. Consequently, the narrator in "June Afternoon" often expresses uncertainty about her family's thoughts and motivations: "What he really looked at, I do not know" (GE 40). The impressionistic sketch of real people with distinct personalities, individual needs, and different goals, a garden island in socialist society, could be entitled: "Dem eenen sin Ul is deem annern sin Nachtigall," an aphorism in low German, which is placed prominently between two paragraphs at the beginning of the story: "An owl to one person may be a nightingale to another." The child inquires: "What is an owl?" and proceeds to carve one out of wood, an activity that would "reveal what this darned thing of an owl really is" (GE 34).

Every narrative technique practiced in "June Afternoon" shall become a stroke in Wolf's literary signature: placing the narrator and other characters of the story in close autobiographical vicinity, a technique that emphasizes the subjectivity of the narrative perspective; making the narrator both object acting in the story and subject telling it, which imparts the illusion of authenticity; bearing witness to contemporary daily life punctuated by flashes of external threats, "this uncomfortable situation between catastrophe and idyll" (DI 457), as Wolf said twenty years later; and, most crucially, involving the reader as arbitrator and commentator. Almost every text from "June Afternoon" to *Sommerstück,* 1989 (Summer Play) employs these literary devices in various degrees. But, most important, Wolf sets out to explore the mysteries of the individual: she carves owls to find out what these darned things really are.

In preparation for her book *The Quest for Christa T.* Wolf wrote several essays in which she articulated her ardent interest in the process of self-actualization and the significance of individuality in a socialist system. The most important of these, "Interview with Myself," invents an interviewer who questions Wolf on the theme of the book. It was presented in 1966 at a reading of excerpts from *Christa T.* No doubt the essay was intended as an introduction to the novel in order to facilitate a welcoming reception by the censoring bureaucracy and preempt misunderstandings. In the interview she liberates the concept of the individual from the prison of socialist precepts, "the typical," cleverly enlisting socialism in this endeavor, when she proclaims: "It is a great thought that we cannot find peace unless we find ourselves. I believe the deep root which both genuine literature and the socialist society have in common is this: both have the goal of helping us realize ourselves" (DI 33). As a supplementary thought, she reversed the socialist notion that the individual was a cog in the wheel of history: "The individual lives more confidently in a society which he knows to be his handiwork." To help develop the self, on behalf of society's continued growth, the author "must try at any cost to break through and go beyond the limits of what we know or believe to know about ourselves" (DI 35). This became Christa Wolf's goal in what has been called her greatest prose work, *The Quest for Christa T.*

CHAPTER FIVE

"Reality Broken in Two"

The Quest for Christa T.

Christa Wolf did not think that *The Quest for Christa T.* fit the literary genre of the novel. Therefore, she asked that the label "novel" not be printed on the book cover. This is the first sign of an act of courageous defiance—creating a book that challenged the most sacred tenets of socialism and violated the essential principles of socialist realism. To smooth the arduous path to publication and to placate the cultural functionaries who would determine the book's fate, Wolf introduced her work carefully. She held public readings, explicated excerpts, described her narrative techniques, and boldly bent the official literary and political position to her concepts. In "Interview with Myself" she expounded the need for change: "The absurd opinion that socialist literature cannot treat the fine nuances of emotions, the individual differences of characters; that it is reduced to create types moving in prescribed sociological tracks: this absurd opinion is not held by anyone any longer. The years when we laid the practical foundations for the self-realization of the individual, created a socialist economy, are gone" (DI 32).

Even in the novel itself Christa Wolf planted various statements to preempt criticism and advance her concepts. Early in the text the narrator issues a plea for more artistic freedom: "Just once, only this one time, I would like to be permitted to experience and to say how it really was, nothing exemplary, nothing useful" (CT 49). Particularly clever was Wolf's selection of the book's epigraph, which articulates the nature of Christa T.'s quest: "Was ist das: Dieses Zu-sich-selber-Kommen des Menschen?" (What is that: this coming-to-oneself?) In other words: this finding oneself, this discovering the self, this process of self-realization. The extended quotation from poet Johannes R. Becher's diary entry of 1950 reads: "Because this deep unrest of the human soul is nothing else but the sense and the suspicion that the human being has not come to himself" (DI 32–33). Having served as minister of culture until his death in 1958, Becher was one of the most prominent proponents of socialist realism. Wolf realized her book's message violated the most sacred tenet of socialism: self-realization through conformity, through identification with socialist society. So enlisting the authority of Becher's own words to defend her book was a stroke of genius—and a great irony. It also epitomizes the political schizophrenia from which writers straying from bureaucratic criteria suffered.

Christa Wolf's steps to shield her new book from ideological objections were skillfully taken. Even though the manuscript was finished in 1967, it took one year before the authorities reluctantly allowed the publication of a small number of copies. That estimates of the press run of the first edition range from a mere five hundred to fifteen thousand indicates how controversial the book was then viewed. The SED functionaries decried the lack of evidence that the book conformed to the guidelines of socialist realism. They accorded Wolf "honest intentions" in observing "partiality," but the way the story was told was deemed harmful to the socialist view of life. This official assessment did not change until after the Eighth SED Party Convention in 1971, when the secretary-general of the SED, Erich Honecker, proclaimed that in socialism "there could not be any taboos in the area of art and literature" and that writers should address the "entire spectrum and variety of life" with the "entire wealth of their signatures." While this official position clashed flagrantly with established literary practice, it did relax the codes of socialist realism, and Wolf's book finally conquered all hurdles—a great tribute to its author's persistence and rhetorical skills.

As if to spite its difficult birth, *The Quest for Christa T.* was a remarkable literary event in both East and West Germany; it soon became recognized as a prominent entry in the world's literary canon. Not surprisingly: its theme—the attempt to realize one's individuality in a vast sea of enforced conformity—is of critical importance in any society.

As in "June Afternoon," Wolf immediately articulates the essential elements of the novel (which the book is still called in the absence of an appropriate term). Translation does not represent properly the title, which in German is *Nachdenken über Christa T.* (Thinking about Christa T.). The novel begins: "Nachdenken, ihr nach-denken. *Dem Versuch, man selbst zu sein*" (to paraphrase: Thinking about Christa T. and the attempt to be oneself). Unfortunately, *think* does not convey the significance of the verb *nachdenken,* which means "going after, pursuing something or someone through thinking." The narrator, a major character in the novel, will follow Christa T. through reflection. *Nachdenken* appropriates additionally the exercising of powers of judgment and conception. The process strives for becoming conscious of or reaching a conclusion about its object. It is a nonlinear activity that tends to meander and leap about. Thus, *Nachdenken* in Wolf's title leads us to expect an intimate, subjective narrative account that will reflect the complex and surprising patterns of contemplation. Furthermore, Wolf chose the infinitive form of the verb *think,* which is identical to the imperative: a strong signal for the reader to participate in the thinking process. Finally, Wolf's opening sentence uses the neutral pronoun *oneself*—which could refer to anyone—implying that the quest for Christa T. entails a search for her own self or that of the narrator and the reader. Probably no title in Wolf's oeuvre has richer connotations.

Christa T. is obviously the protagonist. The name indicates a real person whose anonymity is to be protected; otherwise, the author would have given her surname. Because the *T.* could stand for many names, the protagonist might be representative of a whole group of individuals who have something in common. Because the author has the same first name, we are led to expect autobiographical references, as is typical for Wolf's work. In less than ten words the basic elements of structure and content are laid out for a novel tremendously complex and rich in narrative devices, language, and subject matter.

Scholars have debated the crucial issue of whether the two characters, Christa T. and the narrator, are authentic or fictional. Did Christa T. actually exist? Could she possibly be Christa W., Wolf herself? Is the first-person narrator Christa Wolf? Or are they both inventions? The answer to these questions is both yes and no.

Christa T.'s life, as gleaned from the text, is hardly intriguing, except that it is conspicuously similar to Christa Wolf's. The bare biographical data scarcely make a story. She was born in 1927 in a small town east of the Oder River, the daughter of a teacher. She commutes to high school, where she meets the narrator. As a refugee, she settles in a village in Mecklenburg after the war, enrolls at the University of Leipzig in 1951, majoring in literature, and after graduation teaches school in Berlin. She has a couple of love affairs, marries a veterinarian named Justus in 1955, moves to the country and builds a house, has three children, tries to write prose and poetry, and dies of leukemia at age thirty-five.

Although Christa T. is outwardly an ordinary woman, the narrator is fascinated by her, from the very first day they meet in high school. They become friends, are separated by the war, and renew their friendship when they run into each other in a literature seminar at the university. They see each other regularly in Berlin, where Christa teaches school and the narrator lives with her family. The narrator visits Christa in her country house, and they spend holidays together at the beach. After Christa T.'s death the narrator is entrusted with her writings, which consist of diaries, letters, prose fragments, a few poems, plans for stories. This legacy and grief about her death motivate the narrator to

write an account of Christa T. Significantly, each woman's life story has conspicuous parallels to Wolf's biography.

Wolf herself contributed gleefully to the controversy about the characters'
authenticity and identity. She did have an old friend, Christa Tabbert, who died
in 1963. Her untimely death moved Wolf deeply and motivated the writing of
this book: "A person close to me died, too early. I defy this death. I look for an
effective mode of defiance. I write, I search. I find myself having to record this
search, as honestly as possible, as precisely as possible" (DI 31). Before the
prologue to the novel, however, "C. W." assures us that "Christa T. is a literary
figure. Authentic are some quotations from diaries, sketches, and letters. I did
not feel responsible for adhering faithfully to external detail. Secondary characters and situations were invented. Real living persons and real events are
similar only by chance." The narrator, who functions as biographer and analyst
of Christa T.'s life, as character in her story, and as reviewer of the writing
process, also seems to be a literary figure. But in the "Interview with Myself"
Wolf admits that, in the course of telling the story, manipulating the documents
and adding her inventions "to do justice" to her image of Christa T., a curious
thing happened: both Christa T. and the "I," the narrator, changed. They changed
identity from fictional character to the author herself. The implication that this
text is nonfiction explains Wolf's refusal to call it a novel. This metamorphosis
from protagonist to author is affirmed by another of Wolf's experiences associated with the writing process: "Later I noticed that the object of my story was
not—or was no longer—unequivocally she, Christa T. Suddenly, I stood in front
of myself, I had not expected that. The relationship between 'us'—Christa T.
and the first-person narrator—suddenly became the focal point" (DI 32). When
the invented interviewer wants to elicit a definite answer to the question of
whether Christa T. and the narrator are authentic characters, Wolf recoils: "Did
I admit that? You would be right if both characters were invented, after all."

Authentic or not, it appears that Christa Wolf externalized herself in both
characters: their lives are her life. The issue of identity transfer is frequently
built into the text, as we will see. It is demonstrated by the imprecise delinea-
tion of narrator and Christa T. They cannot always be clearly distinguished
because the narrator tends to switch abruptly from the third-person *she* to the
first-person *I,* as if the two were identical; often she uses *we* in the sense of the
pluralis majestatis, the royal we, or the inclusive pronoun *one,* which could
refer to either character. Christa T. in her writing often alludes to herself in the
third person: "SHE with whom she consorted, whom she refused to name, because what kind of name should she have given HER? SHE who knows that she

has to be new again and again . . . and will not let anyone infringe upon her right to live by her own laws." The narrator understands the "secret of the third person, who is present without being tangible, and who, when circumstances are in her favor, can draw more reality than the first person: I. About the difficulty to say I" (CT 168). Christa T. uses "SHE" as a matter of caution, to distance herself: this SHE could be either Christa T. herself or someone else, someone she "can inspect thoroughly as is her habit with others" (CT 116). Likewise, Christa Wolf frames her self in both Christa T. and the narrator to create distance, to be able to inspect them thoroughly—that is, to inspect herself thoroughly. The death of Christa T. precipitates the birth of the narrator, and *The Quest for Christa T.* must ultimately be a quest for Christa Wolf.

Thinking about Christa T. is the author's and, by extension, the narrator's way of dealing with grief. But there is a more critical reason: "Let us not pretend we are doing this for her. Once and for all: she doesn't need us. Let us make certain, then: it is for us, because it seems we need her" (CT 10). Why do we need her? Christa T.'s life is not exemplary. There are no extraordinary achievements; in fact, she is a failed writer who is unable to finish a text; she is not heroic in the socialist sense of successful immersion in socialist society. Then why does the narrator present her to us? In preparation for this question she discovered to her surprise that she needed to tell the story of Christa T.'s success. Success can be many things—"fame, for instance, or the belated conviction that one must do this and nothing else" (CT 90)—which is another way of saying that one must be oneself. The story of Christa T., then, is the story of her attempt to find and be herself. We need her example, made vivid, palpable, and real, so that we can discover "the unending possibilities lying within us."

Before examining aspects of Christa T.'s story, we should identify the other quest in the novel, no less important and described with equal passion and meticulousness. The narrator constantly searches for new means to tell the story in order to do justice to Christa T., and, while she practices various techniques, she considers their inherent problems and their effectiveness. "I find myself having to capture this search, as honestly as possible, as precisely as possible," Wolf said in "Interview with Myself" (DI 31). The narrator's role of explicator of her craft warrants her role as a protagonist in the book; her role as Christa T.'s friend and, thus, as a player in the story is secondary.

The narrator uses many different methods of narrative structure and language to delineate character. She uses a host of authentic sources to inform herself about Christa T. and to enrich her picture through different perspectives. Although the most important is her own memory, "the color of memory is deceptive," she warns in the prologue. Several times she admonishes herself and us to forget our memories, forget what we know, "in order not to cloud our view" (CT 139). The narrator's distrust of her own memory introduces powerful tensions in the novel. If one person's recollections cannot be trusted, other sources of information are needed to unearth the true Christa T. Thus, the narrator solicits the memories and opinions of her family, friends, and teachers. She peruses Christa's written legacy—her poetry, incomplete stories, notes, diaries, letters. In her narrative she uses Christa's work freely, indicating direct quotations in italics. Thus, the narrator lends an air of authenticity to the story, but Wolf herself leaves no doubt about the fictional dimension: "I treated the material efficaciously. I supplemented memory with invention. Faithful adherence to documents was not important to me" (DI 32). Unfortunately, says the narrator, corroborating Wolf's view, one cannot rely on facts or the accounts of witnesses or even on Christa's own legacy. They are tainted by too much uncertainty and hide more than they reveal. Therefore, invention is necessary, "on behalf of the truth" (CT 29). And so she builds upon what seems to be an assemblage of authentic material and factual accounts with materials made from her own imagination.

The narrator invents characters she does not know or who did not exist in order to bring to life an important event or feature of Christa T. The principal of Christa's school is such an invention. Christa called upon him to arbitrate a conflict between her and her students: what she considered unacceptable lies they believed to be justified by the rules of ordinal life—the classical friction between an idealist and realists. She gets little comfort from the principal. They have different views of the world. His generation is not her generation. He has discarded ideas she still holds dear: no compromises, the truth and nothing but the truth, act according to the way you think. But he understands her generation's desire for power and kindness, all at the same time, and she treasures his admonition: "What is brought into this world through us can never be pushed out again." The narrator concludes: "Perhaps the man, her principal, was not like that, but he could have been." In this episode the narrator even tampers with Christa T.'s identity: the person sitting in front of the principal could have been another person her age, one of many. In this way the narrator not only places the portrait of one person into the context of the time, specifically the 1950s, but she renders it a prototype of an entire generation of Germans—Wolf's own generation.

Christa T. herself liked to invent people to scrutinize her experiences and herself. One of these was a "general," whose psychic gifts were well-known and whom she went to consult: "Invented him with the sincere intention to be precise, to be objective." The narrator devotes an entire chapter to this séance, which, most likely, took place only in Christa T.'s mind. She concedes that Christa's account of the general and his predictions is fair, but it only contains Christa's perception, and, therefore, she takes the liberty of correcting Christa's version and reinventing the general, "being fair like everyone else" (CT 83). This episode—Christa T.'s self-analysis refurbished by the narrator—is designed to reveal in a nutshell the past, present, and future of the protagonist, but the life story extracted from Christa T.'s palm is suspiciously like Christa Wolf's: a job in a publishing house, insecurities at first, then assertiveness and success, fame in the field of literature, her character a rare mixture of "romantic-poetic" and "pedagogical-practical" qualities. Only the premonition of impending death seems to apply particularly to Christa T. No wonder, then, that Christa, or the narrator, ends the scene with the low-German expression "Ick glöw doar nich an" (I don't believe it) then adding in high German, "But it is strange." It is doubly strange, because there is an interesting role reversal taking place here: the literary character, in her attempt to find herself, describes the author. A subtitle for Wolf's novel might take after Pirandello: "A literary character in search of an author in search of a literary character."

The narrator continually frets that the net she casts is not sufficiently fine to capture Christa T. "Sentences she wrote—yes. Also paths she walked, a room in which she lived, a landscape that was dear to her, a house, a feeling even—but not her" (CT 117). Therefore, the narrator often presents two versions of one event, one seemingly factual, the other creative conjecture—one of Wolf's unique techniques to better capture reality. Both could have taken place; both are intended to expose as many components of the central experience as possible. Christa's encounter of the veterinarian Justus and her decision to marry him represents a great change in her life. Moreover, love is a complex feeling, "ein zusammengesetztes Gefühl," as Wolf describes it: "a feeling put together from many separate pieces." Two approaches to undo the puzzle of love are presented. One episode depicts a costume ball that ends in the couple's engagement. Christa attends as a literary character, Fräulein von Sternheim, created by the nineteenth-century writer Sophie la Roche. Like many other allusions to literature contained in the novel, this fictional character mediates a message. Von Sternheim's virtuous, sad life in the country suggests Christa's life with Justus. Through this choice of costume the narrator shows the reader what Christa was trying to show Justus, namely "what she was giving up, if she went with him"—sacrificing her freedom and her pursuit of a vision. But other issues are involved in the decision to marry. So the narrator provides another version in a new chapter. Not a costume ball—"which was an invention, anyway"—but a trip to the country, where Christa visits Justus, marries him, and gives birth to her first child. In this version Christa is quite changed. Rather than seeing marriage as a threat, she finds a state of security, motherhood, happiness. "She recreated herself all over again, from the bottom up, for Justus, that was by no means an effort but the greatest earthly joy she had ever encountered" (CT 123).

The narrator appropriates this technique of rewriting reality from models she finds in Christa T.'s own diaries and prose. For example, one of her students, Hammurabi, accepted his classmates' challenge and, for a few pennies, bit off a live toad's head. Christa's colleagues consider this a mere prank and find her tears puzzling: Was she not a country girl? To Christa this act of violence is a painful reminder of the everlasting evil in this world. She encounters the "dark side" of life for the first time as a ten-year-old child, when a drunk in inexplicable anger killed her cat with a brick. She also finds it reaffirmed even in contemporary times when she shares a hospital room with a woman who has been repeatedly raped and abused by her husband—yet she returns to him. Tampering with fact, Christa molds the toad story to her desire for a decent mankind, drafting a morally pleasing conclusion of repentance: Hammurabi rushes in, brushes his teeth, and then cries like a small child—a conclusion that bears witness to Christa's unwillingness "to accept the naked, true reality" (CT 110). Both writers, Christa and the narrator, either illuminate reality from various angles by creating several versions of it or reshape it in order to create an ideal. The unspoken premise here could well be—it is in future works—that civilized life cannot continue without the conception and pursuit of ideals as they occur in the individual person as opposed to the perpetuation of ideals through a government bureaucracy or a sterile society.

In all these narrative journeys the reader is a constant companion; we are always included in the genesis of the fiction. But Wolf worries that her efforts may not have the desired effect: "Even if I could manage to recreate faithfully everything that I still know or found out about her, even then it could be possible that the one to whom I am telling all of this, the one I need and am now begging for support, that at the end this person knows nothing about her" (CT 117). Wolf uses the pronoun *we* frequently to include the reader: "Once and for all: she does not need us. . . . we need her." Through frequent questions she forces us to interact with the text: "Forcing, whom? You? And what for? To stay?" Even secondary characters address the reader, like Christa T.'s landlady, who worried about Christa "Until the girl started to cry, that was a relief, wasn't it?" This constant interaction, the presence of "another person with no name," fashions an intimate relationship between author and reader, kindling the author's responsibility for honesty and fortifying the reader's willingness to participate in the fiction.

The assemblage of episodes, analyses, descriptions, quotations, and explications is divided into twenty chapters. They are loosely held together by a thread of chronology—a countdown to the day Christa T. dies—and by a web of repeated previews or reviews of certain events. These emphasize a different aspect of Christa T.'s character or of her attempt to assert and, at the same time, preserve herself in society. The narrator need not have worried about the picture of Christa T. that emerges at the end. It is a sharply focussed full portrait, surrounded by vaguely sketched secondary figures, on a broad but looming background of the early history of the GDR. Moreover, the narrator gives voice to the woman to say finally what she was unable to say in her lifetime. The concluding words of the novel are the often repeated refrain of Christa T.: "When if not now?" They launch not only the writing of Christa T.'s life but also the success story of the narrator as writer: the ending feeds into the beginning, the genesis of the novel.

We meet Christa T. playing the trumpet. She is actually blowing into a rolled-up newspaper, "hooohaahooo, something like that," marching ahead of her class. We wonder: Is this an expression of spontaneity? An act of liberation? A call of defiance? To rally people behind her like Pete the Piper? Christa had the potential to raise her voice to all these effects, but she was unable to articulate—for everyone to hear and understand—the meaning of this "hooohaahooo." The narrator, who would have liked to have made this call herself, saw it as an expression of Christa's vision, a vision of herself, "her secret." In her thesis about Theodor Storm, a nineteenth-century writer, Christa T., who wanted to be a writer herself, pursues the question "how—and if at all and under which circumstances—one can realize oneself in art" (CT 97). She observes that Storm's artistic being is one with his human being. This is her vision for herself. But, in spite of valiant attempts—"When if not now?"— Christa is not able to realize her art, so she is unable to merge her humanity with her creativity. The tragedy she observed in Storm is her tragedy: "The conflict between wanting and being unable has pushed him into a fatal corner" (CT 98). That is why she had to die.

"I would like to write poetry," the ten-year-old Christa wrote on the cover of her first diary, "and I also love stories." In the course of her life Christa discovers why she needs to write: "she has an intense aversion to anything that has no form" (CT 22); she derives consolation from the written lines in her diary, for instance, when her cat is murdered (CT 26); "she can only get beyond things through writing" (CT 39); she was afraid she would disappear without a trace and wanted to leave verbal tracks (CT 38); she wanted to work with and for others, but indirectly, through writing (CT 74); and, of course, she wanted "to find herself inside and outside of herself," to realize her self through writing. Achieving an authentic identity is the novel's central theme, expressed in many different contexts.

Unfortunately, Christa's periodic refrain "When if not now?" is sounded in vain. An occasional hesitant poem, disorderly notes, lists of titles, sketches, fragments—that is the extent of her literary legacy. She worries early that she will not be able to write, to put into words what is important to her. It didn't have to be perfect, but she wanted everything new and fresh, not pale and mundane like in reality. She wanted to pronounce something new, not what everyone else already knew. But her "originality," she noted, was wasted, "given away, out of cowardice" (CT 142). In other words: she did not think herself courageous enough to write. Why does writing require courage? The narrator supplies an explanation:

> She must have had knowledge early on of our inability to say things as they are. I am even wondering whether one can learn about it too soon and be discouraged forever, whether one can be enlightened too early, be robbed of one's self-deception too early. So that one gives up and lets things take their course. Then they have no way out: not into ambivalence, not into lies. . . . Then they make the best of themselves, or the worst. Or the mediocre, which is often the worst. And which when it feels threatening cannot be ignored any longer in silence. (CT 38–39)

The narrator expresses herself with great circumspection here. She cannot say explicitly that the political environment prohibited Christa T. from portraying things as they are, from letting her originality, her individuality, emerge. It took great courage to write against the political grain. It is for this lack of courage in the face of political adversity that Christa T. did not finish "Malina, the Raspberry," a story about the Nazi period told from her perspective as a child. The Third Reich was not a topic that the GDR regime, in the 1950s, wanted to see analyzed honestly. In Christa T.'s lifetime one spoke "only half sentences" about the subject. But in 1975 Christa Wolf would write just such a story: *Kindheitsmuster (Patterns of Childhood)*.

Christa T. lacked self-confidence, a form of courage directed inward. She was plagued by doubt about her work, as the narrator says: "She could never have written: 'My stories.' She did not believe that her "currency" was worth anything. In a letter to her sister—never mailed—she describes herself as "not equipped for life. Intelligent, all right. Too sensitive, brooding unproductively, full of scruples" (CT 74). Indeed, how could Christa have believed in her social worth when she did not fit the social norm, let alone the icons? Not that she did not believe in her country. She speaks about her deep "agreement with her time." She may not have agreed with the narrator's opinion (often erroneously attributed to Christa T.) that their new world would always be their cause and that, among all the alternatives, there was not one worth turning around for (CT 55). Yet she ardently wished for such a world. But, if she could not doubt the society in which she lived, then only self-doubt remained, corroding her creative worth, too. The major reasons for Christa's inability to become a writer, however, are rooted in her unmitigated restlessness. She lives at continual odds with the world.

The image of Christa's peculiar walk, leaning forward as if against a slight but constant obstacle, captures her persistent struggle to move deterrents to her self-realization out of her way. She was always an outsider, deliberately excluding herself, asserting her right to live by her own laws. She recoiled from any "branding iron whose mark would determine with which herd she had to go to which barn." She could not conform to the "new man," who believes that the key to health is adaptation and who has, consequently, relinquished any moral responsibility, like her former student Hammurabi, who became a physician. She could not identify with these "Hopp-Hopp-Menschen," people who forge thoughtlessly ahead, revere facts, and lack imagination. She could not easily follow rules or work with regularity. She was able to oversleep a final exam, wake up happy, and invent a plausible explanation without scruples. And, rather than study for a team project, endangering everyone's grade, she would read Fyodor Dostoevsky and think about this Russian writer's idea that only the softest could conquer the hardest. Her inability to adapt to the norm may render her "unzeitgemäß," not in harmony with the time; it may disqualify her as a model, but not as a friend. She was not a loner. Even Hopp-Hopp-Menschen, like the successful writer Blasing, who "worked on his career" and "brought his vocabulary to the level of the capital" (Berlin), were part of her social circle. Her unwillingness to conform was not motivated by rebellion; she just wanted to be herself—an innocence more threatening than open rebellion, more vulnerable, and more powerful at the same time—the very reason why the narrator is presenting Christa T. to us.

Wolf thought that "literature, just like our society, attends especially to the restless. Depicting people to whom restlessness is alien—the self-satisfied, flat, all too compliant ones—that seems rather boring and unproductive" (DI 33). Christa T. is the epitome of restlessness that extended to body and mind. The narrator pegged Christa T. as someone who would just come and go already in high school; one who did not need others and, therefore, did not seek acceptance by her classmates—a fragile self-sufficiency, however, and a defensive pose that she tried to overcome by marriage and motherhood. In Berlin Christa walked for hours after school, wondering whether behind the lighted windows there were others infected by this restlessness. Into her diary she then entered the line: "Longing, you bird with the lightest of sleep" (CT 41). She left her family, even though it would have been sensible to stay. But she needed to leave behind what was too familiar, what did not pose a challenge any longer. She loved motion more than reaching the goal. Christa hated the word *complete* or *completely* because it signaled an end, a dead end. She deplored the concept "facts"—too definitive. "How could everything that happens become a fact for everyone?" She, Christa T., chose the facts that suited her, like everyone else (CT 171). She was apprehensive about any kind of commitment. Even her relationship with Justus was conditional upon not making any promises. The need for order, a form of commitment, did not affect her way of keeping house or paperwork.

In Christa's penchant for change, in her aversion to completion, lies the key to her inability to write. She felt great reluctance to commit her thoughts to the definitive word, because "everything, once 'placed' on the page—this very word!—is so hard to set in motion again, which is why one must, from the start, keep it alive, even while it is forming, within. It must constantly be created, that is the key. One must never, never allow it to be finished. Only, how can that be done?" (CT 166). Christa is always striving—a female twentieth-century Faust.

Christa's dilemma manifests itself in deep despair, which is magnified by an unhappy love affair. "Kostja or the beauty," as Christa called him, was a fellow student. They spent poetic moments together, and when he left her for the blonde Inge—alluding to a character in Thomas Mann's "Tonio Kröger" who resembles a Hopp-Hopp-Mensch—Christa had a breakdown. In a literature seminar treating Friedrich Schiller's drama *Kabale und Liebe* ("Intrigue and Love"), she had just discussed that unhappy love, in this new society, was no longer reason for suicide. Yet Christa wanted to die. This is the veiled but resonant message in the unmailed letter to her sister. She recalls that as kids they used to encourage each other with the slogan: "When—if not now? When should one live if not in the time one is given?" But this time given to her, she wrote, felt alien, like a wall in which there is no opening for her. "I do not know why I exist. . . . I know what is wrong about me, but it is still mine. I can't pull it out of me, can I? And yet: I know a way to get rid of all this misery once and for all . . . I can't quit thinking about that" (CT 74). Living in the company of other people who failed in life was out of the question. Compared to that option, the "other way," suicide, is "more honorable, more honest. . . . Also stronger." Her doctor's diagnosis was death wish due to lack of adjustment. He prescribed therapy: "You are intelligent. . . . You can learn to adjust" (CT 76).

It did not occur to Christa that it was not she who needed to change. So she tried to adjust, to become a useful member of society through her marriage to Justus ("the just one"), compensating her inability to be a creative writer by the act of procreation. Of course, one could also say that she fled into married life from despair. Initially, she engaged with enthusiasm in the daily activities of housekeeping, child rearing, and husband care. She accompanied Justus on his house calls in order to get acquainted with her community. She even wrote a little, usually on the back of his discarded correspondence and receipts—tentatively, nothing complete. She even built a house to "connect more intimately with life," a place that was familiar and secure because she had created it. But slowly she felt like her "work was pushing the day forward" and that her two hands were not enough for so much weight. She grew increasingly tired: "Never can one tire as much from what one does than from what one doesn't do or can't do" (CT 138). She began to feel that she was losing "the secret that enabled her to live: the consciousness of who she really was" (CT 156). Her restlessness set in, and she responded to the dreaded banality of her daily life with a brief affair—to find out whether there was still sense in her senses—and by having a child. But she ran out of time to find new options of spiritual survival. This poem is her witness:

> Why torture oneself so devilishly?
> May never happen again what happened here:
> The closeness of two strange souls,
> The strangeness of those who are close . . .

The fatal cancer, arrested during her years of contentment, returned. "Piece by piece she takes herself, something takes her back." She died shortly after the birth of her third child.

The narrator had wanted to present Christa T.'s life as a success. How could a story of failure to realize one's ardent desire, the inability to adjust to the demands of society, a story of despair and death, be a story of success? In spite of her personal failings, her lack of tangible achievements, Christa T. did not give up. Within the sliver of time allotted to her, thirty-five years, she explored earnestly the wide range of her strengths and weaknesses—especially the latter. She created opportunities to experience the emotional spectrum of joy and pain: disappointment, pride, jealousy, loneliness, pleasure, fear. "She did not try to run away, which many people began to do, especially in those years" (CT 59). Whether that meant escaping to the West or evading personal responsibility, she stood her ground, defending her place in life and filling her space with her individuality. She represents what her generation should have been. Her legacy inspired a tale of courage to live and to be oneself at a time of adversity.

The reactions to *The Quest for Christa T.* were strong. Critics in East and West engaged in spirited debates—unique in the history of postwar German literary criticism. A special volume is devoted to the collection and assessment of the most important critiques: Manfred Behn's *Wirkungsgeschichte von Christa Wolfs "Nachdenken über Christa T.,"* 1978 (The Reception of Christa Wolf's "The Quest for Christa T."). In the West Wolf's most severe critic, Marcel Reich-Ranicki, led the overwhelming praise when he judged *The Quest for Christa T.* one of the few significant German novels of the 1960s. The book quickly became the object of serious literary inquiry, which continues to this day.

The East reacted less to the literary value and more to the political implications of the text. Christa Wolf presented issues that had not yet been discussed publicly. Her antiheroine, merely by her unorthodox character, had called into question the convictions of her fellow citizens and, by extension, the regime of the GDR. At the Sixth Congress of Writers in May 1969 Wolf's novel, which was the focus of discussion, was generally rejected on ideological grounds. In essence the author was accused of inadequate observance of dogma and reminded that it was not the mission of socialism to erect memorials for individuality. It must have been a bitter pill when the Mitteldeutsche Verlag, her own publisher, in an act of self-criticism, stated publicly that Christa Wolf was incapable of distancing herself from her heroine, that pessimism is the aesthetic tenor of this book, and that Wolf's ultimate answer is generally humanistic (not socialistic). She was told that *The Quest for Christa T.,* like *Divided Heaven,* was a failure and that she should quit writing.

Not surprisingly, Wolf switched to the publishing house Aufbau-Verlag Berlin and Weimar, because even in East Germany there were unequivocal words of praise for the book and admiration for the author—the socialist as moralist and therapist. The conflict depicted in the novel, subjectivity versus conformity, was, with unintentional irony, mirrored by its critiques. Fortunately, in the end the book's reception was a happy one: the accolades soon silenced the ideologues, in East and West. Wolf's readers responded to Christa T.'s quest more sympathetically than Wolf could have wished. Feelings associated with illness, death, mourning, and loss could finally be discussed publicly, a therapeutic process indispensable to personal and social health. The Theodor Fontane Prize for Art and Literature in 1973, conferred by the GDR, officially acknowledged Wolf's accomplishment. For Christa Wolf personally, writing *The Quest for Christa T.* conveyed a new freedom as an author; according to her former teacher Hans Mayer (a West German citizen since 1963), Wolf had come to herself.

CHAPTER SIX

"Curiosity Is a Vice of Women and Cats"

"The Reader and the Writer"

When the Aufbau Verlag published Wolf's collection of essays, *Lesen und Schreiben. Aufsätze und Betrachtungen (The Reader and the Writer: Essays, Sketches, Memories),* in 1972, it was hailed as a groundbreaking event, although at that time a number of authors, such as Volker Braun and Günter de Bruyn, were voicing similar ideas. The book contains a variety of essays on literary theory, political milestones, and reflections on the work of writers such as Brecht, Seghers, and Bachmann. The centerpiece, however, is the essay providing the collection's title. Completed in 1968, it articulates Wolf's experiences writing *The Quest for Christa T.* Aside from putting an end to the controversy over this novel, the essay is evidence of Wolf's continued commitment to reform official literary policies.

Sensing the breakthrough of a new spirit in the GDR—"a new way of being in this world"—and eager to nurture it, Wolf gives it a name: "Unruhe" (unrest). The term barely conceals the still unacceptable idea of individuality which Wolf believes is insinuating itself in the social structure of the GDR. The need to express this new feeling of unrest will be, in the long run, stronger than the temptation to ignore it, she argues, and it will require "a new way of writing" (DII 463). She appeals to the responsibility of writers to respond to the changed spirit with the kind of prose which "is free from the age-old and the brand-new magic spells of manipulation and does not shun experiments" (DII 491). She challenges them "to reject the esoteric outsider position as well as the banal role of the entertainer and to insist on having something to say" (DII 468). This is clearly a call to arms. Cleverly avoiding specificity, Wolf rejects both past and present literary norms and practices, including the widely accepted theories of the genre "novel" of the Marxist literary historian and theoretician Georg Lukács. The influential Lukács derived his concepts from the great novels of the nineteenth century and contemporary prose as well, in which man was depicted as victim of circumstance or as prefigured hero rather than free agent. Instead, Wolf demands new aesthetic principles and narrative techniques appropriate to new social, political, and psychological conflicts. Clearly, she had concluded that her audience was becoming more open and more sophisticated.

Wolf posits that literature is not a simple mirror of reality; rather, literature and reality merge ultimately in the mind of the author. From the amalgamation of life's material and the author's creativity springs the distilled reality of the book, the new reality. The author's consciousness, then, is the "fourth dimension" in any narrative journey, giving it depth through imagination and historical relevance through personal testimony. Consequently, "the author is clearly an important person" (DII 496), provided that he mediates with scrupulous honesty "unique experiences and does not give in to the temptation of forcefully invading the experiences of others, but rather encourages them to have their own experiences." Wolf's audience certainly had no trouble discerning her veiled message: rather than depict characters representative of commonly held values in order to mold individuals in that image, the modern author, by Wolf's design, has to share honestly with his reader—who is also an important person in Wolf's scheme—his subjective experiences, if he is to encourage individual development. Clearly, Wolf recognizes that personal experience cannot be mechanically mirrored, told with complete objectivity. Telling one's experience means "to invent truthfully on the basis of one's own experience" (DII 481). The author's theme, then, is not reality but, rather, his subjective relationship to reality. The goal, finally, is not to persuade or soothe the reader but to touch the innermost core of the individual and stir it into action "to preserve the individual's contact with his roots, to strengthen his self-consciousness," and "to present possibilities to exist as a human being" (DII 502–3).

Wolf's insistence on developing individual rather than collective personality, and on expanding awareness of the individual's role within society, may be rooted in the Enlightenment's concept of the "aesthetic education toward humanity," but she had no intention of opposing or separating from socialist ideals. In fact, she emphasizes that the welfare of socialism is at the heart of her reform efforts. The ultimate goal of prose remains the depiction and "evaluation of structures of human interaction under the light of their productivity." By contributing to our understanding of ourselves, literature expands our understanding of the world and improves society. Consequently, even subjective writing is necessarily a social act and in concord with socialist principles. The concluding paragraph of Wolf's essay speaks about the future, defining a vision of socialism realized in which the dilemmas of individual and group demands might coexist in a manner she calls "brotherly": "Literature can expand the limits of what we know about ourselves. It keeps alive in us the memory of a future which we must not disavow lest we be destroyed. It helps us become individuals. . . . It is revolutionary and realistic: it seduces and encourages us to do the impossible" (DII 503).

The Reader and the Writer is a sort of manifesto that orients Wolf's later work. It typically exemplifies her skill in using the essay as an apologia for a new direction in her fiction. The imperatives articulated here contain the theoretical underpinnings of *The Quest for Christa T.,* which explains the uproar at the time of the novel's publication in 1968. The political and artistic climate in the GDR had not accommodated the changes Wolf argues for in this essay of 1972, when subjectivity was still feared to be the eye of a hurricane. Like George Bernard Shaw, Wolf felt obliged to accompany all her subsequent work by explanatory essays, unless the process of reflection was built into the novel itself, which is the case in her next large project, *Patterns of Childhood.*

Before embarking on *Patterns of Childhood,* Wolf completed (aside from several smaller prose texts) a film story, *Till Eulenspiegel,* for the major GDR film studio DEFA. Her collaborator was her husband, Gerhard Wolf, with whom she had worked on other film projects, among them the cinematic version of *Divided Heaven.* The material for *Till Eulenspiegel* was based on the adventures of Eulenspiegel, a popular figure in German folk tradition, who roamed the countryside in the beginning of the fourteenth century, a turbulent time of transition from the feudal system to a bourgeois society. Eulenspiegel enjoyed playing amusing tricks on everybody and exposing the foibles of humanity: the deceit and callousness of the powerful, the weakness of and discord among the exploited. In his role as jester he presents society's frailties to strengthen it. The Wolfs wanted to demonstrate with their film how a person with nothing but his wits can not only defend himself in times of great adversity but also expand the opportunity of personal freedom for all.

"Unter den Linden"

Among the prose written between 1968 and 1972 three stories have gained acclaim: "Unter den Linden," 1969 ("Unter den Linden"), "Neue Lebensansichten eines Katers," 1970 ("A Tomcat's New Views on Life"), and "Selbstversuch," 1972 ("Self-Experiment: Appendix to a Report)" (the three stories appeared in English translation in 1993 in *What Remains*). They were all published in 1974 in one volume under the title of the feature story, *Unter den Linden.* The subtitle reads, "Three Improbable Stories." The three stories have little in common except that they are "improbable," depicting, as it were, the

71

fantastic, the grotesque, and the utopian, respectively. Thus, they examine the world from a playful, imaginary standpoint. Search for the self was extracted as a common theme, although in the case of the tomcat he has already affirmed his self to the point of extreme arrogance, and the scientific design of a "normal human being" results in a caricature void of any individuality. It has also been observed that these stories are vehicles for the analysis of contemporary problems with a distinct call for change, which, to be sure, applies to all of Wolf's work. Other than Wolf's appeal for freedom and personal courage to express one's individuality, there is little that links these stories together.

The title of the first text, "Unter den Linden," suggests at first glance the famous street in Berlin which was closed to the West by the Wall at the infamous Brandenburg Gate. It also alludes to the poetic spirit of folk songs and the dreamworld of fairy tales, in which linden trees are frequently providers of shade and shelter. The title metaphor strikes overtones characteristic of fiction from the nineteenth-century period of Romanticism—and, of course, of Wolf's story. Romanticism held particular fascination for Wolf. Fantasy and dream, search for the self, love and yearning—all anchored in the very heart of the individual and of Romantic fiction—were considered by Romantic writers to be part of reality and Wolf's distinct sentiment as well. More than any other work of Wolf, "Unter den Linden" celebrates the restorative powers of the imagination.

Anna Seghers had introduced Wolf to several female authors from the Romantic period: Karoline von Günderrode, protagonist in Wolf's later novel *Kein Ort. Nirgends,* 1979 *(No Place on Earth);* Bettina von Arnim, Günderrode's friend, whose residential address in Berlin—"center of independent spirits"— was 21 Unter den Linden, not an insignificant curiosity; and Rahel Varnhagen, author of the story's epigraph: "I am convinced it is part of life on earth that everyone gets hurt where one is most sensitive and vulnerable: how to get out of that is essential." In Varnhagen's letters Wolf must have read about a stroll that Varnhagen took along the street Unter den Linden one day, when she was overcome by "strange, very strange" feelings. Wolf's story starts with just such a walk: "I always liked to walk Unter den Linden. Preferably, alone, as you know. Recently, after having avoided it for a long time, the street appeared to me in a dream. Now I can finally talk about it" (GE 54).

In a discussion with a class of students in 1989 Wolf said that she saw no chance of publication when she conceived "Unter den Linden" in 1969. She wrote the piece strictly for herself, "for the drawer," and it had no message, at least not for a general audience. This story was an exclusive, personal endeavor. Careful analysis of the fiction reveals little or no socialist subtext—contrary to what some academicians have concluded. Wolf also conceded that the story was the most difficult thing she had ever written. Already the mysterious beginning challenges us with many intriguing questions, to which the story offers various mysterious answers. At the very end the narrator provides no solution but simply points us back to the beginning: "Not until much later, today, the idea came to me to account in the accustomed manner for my experience, because above all we treasure the joy of being known. I, the happy one, knew immediately to whom I could tell it, came to you, saw that you wanted to listen, and began: I always liked to walk Unter den Linden. Preferably alone, as you know" (GE 96).

It is clear that the first-person narrator—a literary construct that, as Wolf attests, is not Wolf herself—is telling a dream to a "you." That you could be a friend, a lover, or the reader, or it could also be the narrator speaking to a distanced self, the very self she encounters at the end of the dream: "All of a sudden I realized: that was I. It was I, nobody but I, whom I had met" (GE 96). The destination of her dream walk, then, is her own self, and, unlike *The Quest for Christa T.*, this quest has a happy ending—both typical traits in fairy tales.

But why does the narrator embark on this journey in the first place? The story's epigraph, the quotation from Rahel Varnhagen, provides an answer: the narrator was deeply hurt, and she is trying to recover. It appears that she was wounded by a lover, and she overcomes the pain of this experience in a dream, presented as the medium of healing. Walking along the dream street, encountering her self, and consequently becoming whole again has also enabled the narrator to tell the story. As long as she was walking the actual street, she could not write about her own self because, as Wolf's essay "The Reader and the Writer" declares, reality has to merge with the author's imagination to form a new entity before anything can be truly told. This narrator's dream is the realm in which such a merger takes place and in which speech is found. Wolf defined this kind of speech as "fantastic precision," the kind not tied to facts and which allows her "to speak the truth freely." Revealing oneself truthfully and fully is essential, "because above all we treasure the joy of being known." "Being known" must be read here in the double sense of the phrase: in the sense of "understood" as well as in the biblical sense of "being loved." The narrator rejoices over the gift of language, which she once possessed but lost, and she exults after the cryptic opening: "I love beyond description these confident beginnings, which are only granted to the happy people. I always knew that some day they would be at my disposal again" (GE 54). By reclaiming both her self and a new command of language, the narrator finds happiness and is healed.

One prominent thread is woven throughout the different, seemingly disjointed phases of the dream and the dreamer's many fantastic adventures: she is responding to a judicial order, a powerful arraignment. The narrator undertakes her dream journey because she was "ordered to appear." A mysterious high command, a "commission for conflict" or court of law is expecting her—intimations of Franz Kafka's novel *The Trial*. But, while Kafka's Josef K. is sentenced to death without being able to ascertain his crime or identify the law ruling his unknown destiny, Wolf's narrator knows that she was appointed to join the "fraternity of the happy ones." She is not facing a Kafkaesque nightmare.

The dreamer's journey meanders from geographically identifiable places such as Berlin's National Library to the depth of a deep well, giving "*under* the linden trees" yet another dimension. In Romantic and folk literature the bottom of wells, places deeply recessed in the earth, hold the secrets to life. There the individual tends to and restores an alienated self. Tapping this tradition, Ingeborg Bachmann wrote a story "Undine Goes," which Wolf knew. Bachmann's protagonist descends into a well in the courtyard of the National Library to be protected from the entanglements of society. In Wolf's story, too, the surface of the water separates the narrator from the faces above, allowing her to be not "concerned" about them. But her submersion is just a cleansing phase in the dream experience, from which she ascends again "to cast into the wind all old experiences, mingle with other people again and violate the taboos" (GE 61).

Among the people she meets, strange and familiar, two stand out: her old friend Peter, the history professor, opportunist, and philanderer; and, most important, the girl, his student, who suffers from her unhappy love for him. She "was aware that she had seduced him and was demanding but one thing: he should make her forget. But Peter could not do that because he was indifferent" (GE 87). The girl's story unfolds in erratic but realistically detailed sequences, and we soon realize that it is the narrator's own story projected onto the dream characters of Peter and the girl. Their relationship is "made known" to the dream walker "for her edification." Through Peter and the girl the narrator is forced to face her own unhappy past, a therapeutic process that will "get her out of" the pandemonium of rejection, shame, pain, and fear. These emotional residues from her own love affair can only be conquered through forgiveness. Thus, the culprit, a man "who wants to be unnamed," is summoned to the dreamworld so that the dreamer may absolve him, and, when he dutifully requests his sentence, she says, "Not guilty." After acquitting the man and her own conscience, the narrator is hungry for a fulfilling love: "I cannot postpone love. Not to a new century. Not to the next year. Not by a single day." Reminiscent of Christa T.'s "When if not now?" this realization is the energizing force toward the imminent encounter with the self. The narrator shortly thereafter meets a young woman, and "all of a sudden I realized: that was I." Through realization of the conflict and forgiveness she has found the potential for love and acceptance of self, which may be the same.

This story reflects Wolf's love of books whose content cannot be told, cannot be reduced to simple messages, to a plot or string of facts. "Unter den Linden" works because of its interdependence of autobiography and imagination. She employs here a technique modeled by Anna Seghers, who had tried to join in her own work two seemingly antagonistic worlds, the personal experience and the fantastic; notably Wolf quotes Seghers: "Narrating what stirs me today and the colorful ambience of the fairy tale, that is what I would have liked to unite . . . " (DI 329). In the act of writing, Wolf transports autobiographical experience into the realm of fantasy and clarifies baffling internal conflicts through the explicating medium of dream. Through these therapeutic processes the experience paradoxically is objectified, delivered to the narrator's consciousness, and then resolved.

"A Tomcat's New Views on Life"

Wolf is not known for her humor. Yet "The Tomcat's New Views of Life" is a witty satire about a strictly rational approach to life, which is championed by the cat Max and, of course, not new at all. Having its roots in the eighteenth century, rationality at the expense of the emotional and spiritual appears to Wolf to threaten our civilization today—thus the satire. The cat Max has illustrious ancestors such as the Romantic Kater Murr, a creation by E. T. A. Hoffmann; the cat with boots from fairytale land; and, especially, the devil's assistant in Bulgakov's *The Master and Margarita,* a Russian novel Wolf admired. All intelligent observers of their masters' behavior, they point their sharp claws at human shortcomings. Like them, Max has exaggerated human characteristics, most particularly arrogance.

Max's ambition is writing, which, unfortunately, is limited to this account of his master's research—a fragment in the Romantic tradition—because he dies prematurely of a mysterious cat disease. His master, professor of applied psychology, is working on "a system for the maximal health of body and soul," the SYMAHE, which in turn is the prerequisite for his ultimate goal, the TOHUHA: "total human happiness." After much research the professor concludes that the soul is an obstacle in the way of human happiness. It therefore should be discarded as a figment of reactionary imagination, along with many other factors that "inhibit achievement": equality between men and women, which gives way to the inferiority of women; literature, which is declared an unproductive branch of the economy; and truth, which is reduced to a utilitarian function. Even creativity, courage, imagination, faithfulness, altruism, mercy, sexuality—in short, all individual characteristics, everything that makes us human, is to be eliminated from the professor's design of the new human being. The improved "normal" person will be controlled by a single central computer system and programmed to respond predictably to stimuli within a range of "deviation of plus/minus zero." Max in his role as naive commentator remarks: "At this moment I understood that human beings use their language not only to make themselves understood, but also to hide from themselves that which has already been understood" (GE 115).

Not content with observing the proceedings and eager to apply his own view of humanity, Max wreaks havoc with his master's note cards by rearranging them creatively. His credo, not unlike that of the professor, is rationality, the guiding light for understanding and shaping human life. He removes the card "adaptation," for instance, from the box labeled "Social Norms" and places it in the box labeled "Pleasures of Life," a change that the professor attributes to his own genius and uses for the basis of his invention. Max's random interventions in the scientific plans and the professor's own personal failings—ulcer, impotence in marriage, a passion for a young girl—complete the absurdity of the research project. Behind the grotesque exaggerations and biting humor of satire lurks the ironic if not bitter message from E. T. A. Hoffmann's *Kater Murr:* "The more culture, the less freedom, that is a truism, indeed."

Wolf had always been dubious about the rapid development and unchecked expansion of the sciences. She believed that technology, the sciences, and the economy should not be allowed to pursue overreaching goals for their own sake, because the outcome was dangerous and dehumanizing. Particularly perturbing to her is the tendency to consider "real" only those facts established in scientific laboratories and to consider "existing" only that which can be described in scientific terms. In "Interview with Myself" she addresses this conflict: "But our scientific age will not be what it could be and must be—if we are to avoid a terrible catastrophe—unless the artists start asking their fellowmen, for whom they do their work, pertinent questions and continue to make their demands; to encourage them to become themselves, that is, to change all life long through creative productivity" (DI 34).

In "A Tomcat's New Views on Life" Wolf issues a stern satirical warning against uncritical adherence to rational scientific thought at the expense of all else. Filtered through the sharp pupils of a cat (related to the narrative technique of the fable), buffered by fanciful imagination and witty rhetoric, Wolf's grievous commentary on human foibles appears at once trenchant, humorous, and palatable. One wished that she would sharpen her satirical pen more often. It is a rare and cathartic experience to laugh out loud about the world of humanity which Christa Wolf unfolds in her work. Adding a last hilarious twist to the story, a short note by the "editor" of the cat's manuscript, Wolf turns satire against herself and her readers: "As is usually the case when one has known an author personally, one is struck by the peculiar, not to say distorted world view of his works. Our Max, too, has taken the liberty to invent. We even believe we know him differently and better than the narrative 'I' of this text" (GE 123).

"Self-Experiment"

"Self-Experiment: Appendix to a Report" was a commissioned piece. Edith Anderson, an American author who had been living and publishing in the GDR for many years, had invited Wolf, along with four other female and five male writers, to contribute to an anthology a story about a reversal of sex. The question was: What if I were a man? What if I were a woman? Wolf liked the project because psychology as well as biological and medical research are of great interest to her. But she found it problematic having to flesh out and illustrate a given idea, since her working mode is one of discovery rather than presentation of a predetermined issue. She chose to approach the subject matter as science fiction, exposing the perverse nature of the common notion that a woman has to be like a man in order to have success in the world of men and, ironically, to realize herself. The result was labeled "supermodern" when it appeared in 1974. A female scientist prepares to have herself changed into a man by means of the formula "Bepeter Masculinum 199," which was invented and developed by the chief scientist, who is male, along with the antidote that can reverse the metamorphosis. The woman participates in this extraordinary experiment because she wants to prove her worth in the male-dominated world of science and, ironically, to impress this chief scientist, even make him love her, because she secretly loves him. She has already made serious sacrifices to facilitate entry into the scientific community by leaving a good man who loved her and by forgoing her own desire to have a child. The story develops the paradox that, to assert herself as really a female, she has to become a male.

As the woman slowly turns into a man named Mr. Anders (the German name makes a pun meaning "different" or "other"), she keeps a scientific record of her transformation. Constituting our story, however, is an attached appendix, an antidote, in a manner of speaking, against the official report. She insists that this report is factually correct—"But all sentences in it explain nothing" (GE 158). To counteract the "unreal" scientific neutrality of her official report, she adds an appendix containing her "real" memories, a subjective report in which she reveals, often in a sarcastic tone, her motivations to participate in the experiment and the emotional changes she undergoes during the metamorphosis. But, most important, she reveals the reason for her decision to reverse the process before it is finished. Retrospectively, the woman can evaluate the experiment from both the female and the male perspective—an extraordinary view, indeed. Ironically, having been a man gives her courage to be a woman fully. Therefore, to describe her experiences she decides to avail herself of female tools: "unvarnished language," a privilege women too rarely use, and the truth, a word men would rather avoid.

The female scientist's appendix reveals that men and women live in quite different worlds. Neither is enviable, although the ledger of female attributes is by far richer than that of males and is spiked with many privileges men do not enjoy—the reasons for her returning to her female self. On the woman's side she contrasts curiosity, smiles, compromises, guilt feelings, propensity to be hurt, instincts, interest in matters of the soul, to masculine characteristics, which she reconnoiters during her short sojourn as a man in the world of men: thirst for knowledge, impenetrable faces, tendency toward absolutes, indifference, callousness, blindness, interest in matters of physical reality.

Toward the end of the experiment, while she is still Mr. Anders, the chief scientist asks her a question that would ironically be considered typically female because it reveals compassion: "Well, Anders, how are you feeling?" Anders's answer: "Like in a movie theater." "You too," her superior exclaims unwittingly. And those two words reveal to the female still curled up like a cat inside Anders men's secret or, rather, their defect: "That they cannot love and know it." Man's distance and indifference to the world, his observing and reigning rather than participating role in social interaction, makes him incapable of enjoying love and all its ancillaries: imagination, dreams, feelings, sensitivity— in short, all exclusively female characteristics. The woman scientist is not willing to sacrifice her gender's most valuable virtue: the ability to love. She did not have to change to gain the ability to love, but she did have to become a man to realize that she possessed it. And this is the next experiment she will dare, "the attempt to love. Which, by the way, can also lead to fantastic inventions: the invention of the one person one can love" (GE 185). Thus, "Self-Experiment" is another imaginative portrait in Wolf's continuing story of self-realization.

While the other female contributors to the planned anthology of stories about gender transformation exposed, in feminist fashion, patriarchal structures and male dominance in all areas of political, social, scientific, and cultural life, Wolf chose to examine women's compulsion to imitate men, to internalize male values. In this story she does not complain that women are victims of men, but she does complain about the willingness of women to sacrifice their female traits and to conform in the search for recognition and equal opportunity. Wolf's essays frequently raise the question of whether the goal of female emancipation should be equality; whether women should try to secure the same rights and obligations men have, since men live in definable prisons themselves. She wondered whether women were not identifying with an obsolete male ideal. Why demand rights and duties that should be fundamentally revised? Furthermore, in view of documented increased insecurities in the male community as a result of women's liberation, Wolf fears for the problematic consequences of women gaining self-confidence at the expense of male self-confidence. Unquestionably, Wolf sympathizes with the situation of her female contemporaries, but she distances herself from feminist groups who "believe that they have to fight men with the same means, with which men have fought them for centuries; but— fortunately—they [women] do not possess these means; they possess a keen feeling of powerlessness; deprived of rights, they try to obtain their self-confidence by depleting that of men; their path to self-realization often retreats to their own gender; it has to be difficult for them to devise visions that include all of society" (DI 205).

Wolf believes that women must ask new and radical questions about the equality of men and women to overcome the alienation between the two camps. With increasing material, economic, and legal equality—which she considers to be imperative—both sexes should be given "the possibility of differentiation." We need to recognize that men and women have different needs and, a crucial point in Wolf's thinking about emancipation, "that the model for the human being is not the male, but man *and* woman" (DII 801; emph. added).

In the fall of 1989 "Self-Experiment" was released as a film made for GDR television, the first time that this medium presented Wolf's work to a mass audience. Almost two decades after the story's conception, when science had rendered the futuristic fiction a real possibility and grassroots demands for social and political change were churning mass upheaval in the GDR, its subject matter was more relevant than ever. Wolf's criticism of the science institutions' dominance of "male thinking" (not criticism of science per se, as Wolf would insist), which comes out more strongly in the film than in the story, her warning against conformity to inhumane male values, and the call for gender-specific emancipation seemed particularly pertinent at a time when the public's resolute demands for change, once again, did not address women's concerns. At the time Wolf could not know that her appeal would be swept aside by the tide of unification. Perhaps in years to come it will prove pertinent again.

79

CHAPTER SEVEN

"Running into Knives"

Patterns of Childhood

Not surprisingly, Wolf has struggled all her adult life to come to terms with her own and her country's past. Many times she and others of her generation, such as dramatist Heiner Müller, had expressed concern about the official GDR policy of delegating responsibility and atonement for the Nazi past solely to West Germany—a past that all Germans shared and whose impact everyone still felt. She believed that people who had lived through this period understood how pervasively it affected everyone. The GDR's blame shifting and mental paralysis regarding the Nazi period was not, in Wolf's view, the same as reconciled peace. Therefore, everyone, especially writers, had a certain responsibility to analyze and describe what they had witnessed: "What one cannot speak about, one has to stop being silent about" (KM 167). She was disturbed by novels whose heroes living in the Third Reich remained untouched by Nazi indoctrination, heroes who were magically empowered by appropriate insights to resist the fascist ideology or who were quick to change and acquire the desired characteristics of "the new socialist man." Those were hardly Wolf's experiences. In both plot and character all such novels owed more to political correctness and expediency than to truth. In her estimation false witness to the past only propounded problems inherited from the past.

Wolf did not want to practice *Vergangenheitsbewältigung*—"coming to terms with the past"—as it was understood in West Germany, in the sense of describing as objectively and fully as possible the historical phenomenon of the Third Reich. People in West Germany believed that they were absolved from national guilt by articulating it and then making collective amends. But Wolf believed this had to be a very personal endeavor, a "confrontation of the individual with his very own past, with things he himself did and thought and cannot blame on others and for which he cannot excuse himself along with masses of people who did the same or worse" (DII 811). She wanted to investigate how fascism could shape the individual's consciousness, erode one's conscience, and continue to exert its insidious force into the present. Wolf sought to examine personal and social morality and the conditions that rendered both defunct.

At the same time she wanted to explore the past's impact on the present, to "hone the perception of what we call 'present'" (KM 14).

In the early 1970s Wolf's interest in the Nazi phenomenon and the war became more urgent. Aided by a loosening of the government's attitudes toward the German past, which she acknowledges as "a new mood that is in the air," she began preparations for what should have been, in terms of historical sequence, a precursor to *The Quest for Christa T.* In this new novel Wolf did not plan to answer the questions "How could it happen?" or "How did they [the Nazi perpetrators] live with their conscience?" Instead, she intended to answer questions that continued to trouble her generation: "How did we become what we are?" and "What kind of circumstances causes such massive loss of conscience" (KM 295)? Although "it is so much easier to invent the past than to remember it," Wolf's book was to be based on her memories, starting when she was approximately three years of age. She wanted her memories to be authenticated by archival materials and historical documentation. To that end she read biographies and diaries, studied various authentic personal materials, researched numerous historical and psychological studies, collected songs and pictures, and visited the sites of her childhood. It was an unusually arduous process. Only after one year of thirty-six false starts did she discover the appropriate narrative entry into the project.

Her husband, Gerhard Wolf, is said to have provided the title, *Kindheitsmuster,* which signals Wolf's agenda in regard to theme, content, and form. In the novel she explains the derivations and meanings of the word which made this title appealing to her: "'Muster' comes from the Latin word 'monstrum,' which literally meant 'sample' and that is just fine. But there will also be monsters in today's sense of the word" (KM 39). The word *muster,* as in the English translation *Patterns of Childhood,* also describes the patterns inscribed in a child's mind and soul by its environment. Thus, as in previous novels, her title is programmatic. For the novel's epigram she chose a poem by Pablo Neruda contained in *Book of Questions;* its concluding verses delicately reflect the profundity of her agenda:

> Where is the child I once was,
> is it still within me or gone?
> When does the butterfly in flight
> read what's written on its wings?

On 3 November 1972 Wolf wrote the first line, quoting William Faulkner: "The past is not dead, it is not even past." She ended on 2 May 1975, with a final recognition of "the limits of what can be said." Suspended between these meaningful lines is an intricate web of rich, thought-provoking stories and intriguing reflections. The stories interweave the growth of a child within the stranglehold of an authoritarian society with an adult's attempt to recover memories of childhood. The narrator's reflections illuminate both experiences. They uncover the subconscious behavioral patterns instilled in the child and the problematic nature of the adult's labor: retrieval of the past and its preservation in the writing process. It is almost as if the narrator were the curator of the museum of herself—one rapidly built then traumatically abandoned and now reclaimed.

Patterns of Childhood is, therefore, a bildungsroman, although not in the linear narrative tradition following biographical chronology. Wolf's work invokes both senses of the verb *bilden:* to educate and to form. It chronicles the education of a child named Nelly, her conflicts between socialization and self-preservation. On another level it also describes the narrative techniques used to re-create childhood, culminating in a process that liberates the adult. The strength of this unusual work derives from Wolf's clear demonstration of the power of authority over a vulnerable child and also the ultimate triumph of the persevering adult who returns, embraces, and celebrates that child.

The description of Nelly's maturation is one of the most sensitive, comprehensive, and compelling in German literature—a tribute to Wolf's courageous willingness to share her most intimate experiences. This portrait necessarily elaborates an unflinching study of the nature of dictatorship; Wolf sensitively explores the processes coercing the individual to integrate within an authoritarian system. All of this is accomplished with an extraordinary and moving prose style. *Patterns of Childhood* is, therefore, an important and powerful book, not only for the author as an act of delayed maturation but also for Wolf's audience. The novel, while describing a traumatic and horrifying past, confronts current and later generations with the often unexamined forces that control the present and the future.

The novel is thematically divided into eighteen chapters with schematic headlines; chapter 6, for example: "Memory Gaps. 'Peace Time.' Training in Hate." But the essential structural devices override the chapters. After much experimentation Wolf decided to employ two narrative tools to reflect her basic themes: childhood and adult reflection about its recovery. The first of these is a division of perspectives; the second is a manipulation of time. The narrator—Wolf calls it "the voice"—divides herself into two people: the child, always referred to in the third-person *she;* and the adult, always referred to in the second-person *you.* The "she" was a young victim of a strict home and a fascist dictatorship; the "you" endeavors through writing to retrieve and make sense of her childhood. By using these two forms of address, she and you, Wolf establishes a necessary aesthetic distance from her highly personal subject. We are made to feel the child's estrangement by her relationship to the narrator. The child is a stranger from the past and, consequently, has to be addressed as a stranger. Wolf even assigns her a fictional name, Nelly, thus giving the narrator power over her subject and allowing her to create "a person whose life can come to you like that of a stranger; whom you can control, whom you can penetrate—like a murderer. A doctor. A lover" (KM 145). The adult you, as well as the narrator, needs to be distanced from Nelly, so that her endeavor to meet the strange child can be critically observed and evaluated and so that not only the discoveries but their impact on the adult can be described. Occasionally, the narrator will interject an opinion, perhaps admonish the adult for evasion of the complete truth: "You did make note of the fact that Doctor Leitner was a Jew, didn't you?" (KM 76). The narrator reminds the adult (and also the reader) that the adult you is not talking about her own self but about Nelly, the child: "Then suddenly you sat—not you: Nelly, the child—in your parent's house" (KM 122). Wolf's brilliant stratagem was to make the narrator an equal character along with the adult you and the child she.

This narrative invention is designed to satisfy the narrator's "curiosity" about the nature of both child and adult. In the inevitable climax they are united in the first-person *I*. There is nothing wrong with playing "a game with oneself about oneself," the narrator muses—"A game in and with the second and third person for the purpose of their unification" (KM 149). "When will the you and the I come together? Signal the end of this account?" (KM 368) she asks. The tension of this question is realized in the middle of the novel, when the adult doubts that a merger is possible. No less than the narrator, the adult is an invasive stranger pursuing the child's most intimate and confidential secrets. Therefore, it seems that adult and child could never be united. At the end of her odyssey the narrator, affirming her identity with the adult, concludes: "The closer we are to people, the harder it seems to say anything conclusive about them, that is a known fact. The child that was hidden within me—has it emerged? Or did it, frightened, find a deeper, less accessible hiding place" (KM 377)? "I do not know" is the narrator's (and probably Wolf's) answer, curiously overlooking the fact that she is no longer using the distancing you. She has, after all, found her own, first-person voice *I*—Wolf's inconspicuous acknowledgment of her quest's healing powers and an overt admission of the autobiographical nature of *Patterns of Childhood*.

The other important structural device is manipulation of time. Wolf intertwines three different temporal strands: the immediate present; the author's recent visit to her childhood home "L.," which is now Polish "G." (the first letters of the town in which Wolf was actually raised); and, finally, her distant childhood past. Each strand follows a different story line. But frequent crossovers, inconsistent use of tenses, and the absence of clear transitions obstruct easy negotiation from one story to the other. It is therefore helpful to unravel each of these strands in the (reverse chronological) order given here.

The world of the novel's present spans the period between November 1972 and May 1975, during which Wolf wrote the novel. Here we observe the author at her desk and share her thoughts. Occasionally, we hear bits of news used to demonstrate how the past affects matters today or how history repeats itself. We meet the author's husband, H., and her teenage daughter, Lenka. We hear also about their oldest daughter, Ruth, who does not live at home any longer. Most crucial, the author provides reflections about her craft, her progress and setbacks, the hazards of her profession, the limits of language, and numerous personal and professional fears.

Wolf deplores the "immorality" of her profession, especially of the writer who tries merely to capture experiences rather than invent them: "That one cannot live while describing life. That one cannot describe life without living" (KM 282). Reminiscent of Thomas Mann's ideas about the artist's destiny, she claims that one can either write or be happy (apparently not both)—a questionable proposition in her case, since few of her characters are happy. The writer's objective, in Wolf's opinion, is to make the structure of narrative coincide with the structure of experience. She calls this "fantastic precision." But there is no technique that can untangle the intricate web of life and recast it into the linear form of speech without distorting it. Is there, then, she wonders, only the alternative between silence and the popular, mass-produced prose? Is there no alternative between silence and "pseudo" speech (*pseudo* meaning, in Lenka's idiom, "false, not genuine, not true")? Demurring, Wolf conceives of writing as a process that approaches its subject in small, incremental, deliberate steps, whereby honesty is not a singular action but, rather, part of the process itself. The author's moral commitment to truth is reflected in the individuality and utmost precision of language. Wolf also recognizes, however, that her idealistic conception of writing has certain limits and is vexed with many messy preconditions: since truth is contained in words, she argues, it is encumbered in many ways—by the speaker, by his environment, by the subject about whom or which he speaks, and by his perceived or likely audience. Any narrated truth is necessarily tainted; moreover, the audience will corrupt it further with its members' prejudices. "Thus, how useful is truth?" (KM 296). But the writer must remain undaunted by the complications and perils of writing to proceed. As an observer of reality, a role to which he is born, "or else he would not write but fight or die," he fears the moral and artistic burden to communicate only what he believes to be true.

Because memory both aids and obstructs the quest for truth, the properties of memory are a prominent theme in Wolf's reflections. In fact, one of her drafts of *Patterns of Childhood* started with the attempt to describe the work of memory. She supplements her own observations with psychological and other scientific studies, including a cogent interpretation of Salvador Dali's painting *The Persistence of Memory,* which she studied in the Museum of Modern Art in New York. She concludes that, without memory of ourselves and of our past, we would be strangers to ourselves. But Wolf's interest goes beyond the commonplace rationalist objection that memory is not reliable, that it stores and retains experience selectively, that it falsifies and changes its content, which sometimes results in the very same event being recollected differently by all witnesses. Instead, Wolf insists that memory "is not a solid block locked in our brain for good; rather it is, pardon the big words, a *repeated moral act"* (KM 135; emph. added). Wolf means by those "big words" that every act of remembrance is filtered through our consciousness and our concurrent perspectives—in a sense through our soul—thus conferring a moral value to it. This process is demonstrated by the differing ways in which Nelly's mother responded to the question of what she thought when she heard the phrase "prewar years." "Prewar years? Happy times, indeed! she would have answered first. Later perhaps: lots of work. And finally: one hell of a fraud" (KM 135). That our memory is tainted with our current view of life is of great concern to Wolf, because it is an obstacle to meeting honestly with our past self: "Because your sober retrospection from today's vantage point, which just recently was obscured by antipathy, not to say hate, is filled to the brim with injustice. At least equal to the amount of justice. Objects, helplessly imprisoned under glass, without contact with us who seem to know everything, even though we were born later. And when you ask yourself whether you yourself could take that same merciless scrutiny" (KM 174). What would happen to us, the narrator wonders, if we could open the floodgates of our memory and the entire collection of inaccessible remembrances would pour out? Fortunately, memory is incapable of perfect storage and reproduction; otherwise, Wolf's narrator concludes, the novelist would be superfluous.

Throughout the present time strand in *Patterns of Childhood* Wolf chronicles her writing progress—often achieved at night, when one is "more sober, more courageous" than during the day. She includes her frequent setbacks: "Exhausted: from 'to exhaust'? The serious temptation to stop. After all, it is not a story that must lead to a certain end" (KM 322). Most inhibiting to the writing process are insecurity and doubt—forms of fear typically signaled, as in her childhood, by various physical ailments such as sleeplessness, colds, even a cardiac episode. "Fear," Wolf notes, "moves in strange ways. It withdraws when we give it a name, and it comes to the fore with every attempt to evade it" (KM 339). So, rather than dodging her fears, Wolf's narrator tries to name them: "What compels you, you asked yourself—not in words, scarcely, but through headaches— . . . to confront a child . . . to expose yourself once again: to the stare of this child, the wounded defensive stance of all involved, the sheer incomprehension, but above all: your own camouflage tactics and your own doubts. To isolate yourself, which is not unlike going 'into opposition'" (KM 142). While this introspection enumerates the author's primary obstacles to progressing with the text, it also reveals powerful reasons impelling her to write the book—the very reasons, ironically, which help her conquer these anxieties.

First, Wolf fears what she may find when trying to look into the eyes of the child whom the adult "left behind, pushed aside, forgot, suppressed, denied, changed, falsified, spoiled and neglected, was ashamed and proud of, loved with the wrong kind of love and hated with the wrong kind of hate" (KM 12–13). Wolf is passionately describing a process of personal estrangement from her own past which parallels both Germanies' estrangement from the past. The dissociation in either case began with an ideological awakening after the war— in Wolf's case with her conversion to Marxism, in the national context with the mandate of denazification. In order to be able to weave her existence into the social fabric of the newly formed GDR, the child had to cut the ties to fascism. That meant having to disown what she had been. This is the process, then, in which "the past is not dead, it is not even past." Disowning a part of the past does not end anything; rather, the disowned part lives on underground. Wolf said she began to feel as if she were no longer the person who had thought and done the things she had done. The child in her had become a stranger. Thirty years later the adult was eager, yet afraid, to meet that stranger. The more the adult approaches the child, the closer in time the child moves toward the adult, the more strained reconciliation becomes: "Or do you believe," Wolf asks, "that it is possible to understand the one of whom one is ashamed? To protect the person whom one abuses in order to defend one's own self?" (KM 197).

Second, Wolf fears the "wounded" and "defensive" rejection by the people of her own generation who dare not shake hands with a contemporary German for fear what these hands may have done, people who cannot shed guilt feelings, who downplay, ignore, or deny, or who just want to put an end to what Wolf calls "the obligatory exercise of Auschwitz." In any case those of her generation would prefer to ignore rather than confront in themselves the fascist roots of behavior such as the tendency to conform, lack of personal courage, and fear of authority. These are precisely the patterns of conduct which Wolf alludes to (with a touch of cynicism) on the first page of her novel. She begins with a disclaimer that any of the characters are real people but adds the cautionary advice that readers who nevertheless recognize themselves or others consider the "peculiar lack of individuality in the behavior of many contemporaries. Circumstances should be blamed for creating patterns of behavior that we can recognize." It is an engaging stratagem. The opening simultaneously exonerates the people of her generation: they were all too young to become guilty of evil but old enough to be shaped by fascist ideology and to know the burden of shame. But, most important, Wolf's generation, *and only hers,* was old enough at the end of the war to have witnessed much of the Nazi past yet young enough to be converted. Thus, when the new era of socialism was proclaimed, they had to swear by a "totally different creed." Two creeds in one lifetime Wolf considers an "imposition" that is probably unique to her generation. The announced goal—expressionism repeated—was of course "the new man." Wolf, socialist of the 1950s and 1960s, had eagerly embraced this goal. Wolf, novelist of the 1970s, however, believes that pursuing the vision of the new man is as hopeless as it is necessary and that her generation is once again destined to fail. Nevertheless, it is their responsibility to come to terms with these experiences, to reconstruct the formation of their generation's collective personality for the sake of the youth and the nation's future.

Third, Wolf fears the "sheer incomprehension" of her younger audience. She had already observed their lack of historical awareness and sensitivity in many different contexts. She had seen teenagers eat and turn on their portable radios while touring the concentration camp Buchenwald—shocking signs of indifference to the Nazi horrors in a monument intended to preserve the memory of the country's fascist evil. She found it disturbing that Adolf Eichmann, the notorious Nazi "desktop murderer," was not mentioned in GDR textbooks and that her daughter was not taught this embodiment of evil. "Fascism"—Wolf is quoting the Polish writer Kazimierz Brandys—"fascism is larger than the Germans. But they were its classic executor" (KM 39). Clearly, she believes that only if the young understand fascism, if the truth about the German past is kept alive in the collective memory of present and future generations, can similar tragedies be prevented. To sharpen the youth's sense for the fascist dangers lurking in current and future political establishments, Wolf frequently draws attention to contemporaneous acts of political oppression, state-ordered violence, and other symptoms of political derangement in countries such as Chile, Greece, Vietnam, and especially the United States. Wolf has been criticized for rarely mentioning similar incidents in communist countries. When asked during discussions of her book, summarized in "Erfahrungsmuster," 1975 (Patterns of Experience), if fascism could happen again, she declared unequivocally: not in the GDR, but the world as a whole was terribly endangered by such influences (DII 827). Wolf's bias against Western nations may be seen by a sympathetic reader as a symptom and deliberate demonstration of political attitudes ingrained in childhood. But Wolf's prejudicial and simplistic view of capitalist societies resonates through many of her works—an inexplicable failure of honest perception and depiction which most readers would resent and which will haunt her now, as a new member of the Western community, more than ever. Nevertheless, Wolf's intention in *Patterns of Childhood* is to convey a set of values between generations to reclaim the past, bear witness to the painful truths, and ensure a brighter future.

Additional worries that plague Wolf during the writing of *Patterns of Childhood* are her shortcomings as a writer. She has observed that writers, in autobiographical matters, have the tendency either to "lie like a novel or get tongue-tied and hoarse" (KM 14). She acknowledges good reasons for not wanting to know anything about oneself. The possibility of concealing rather than discovering the truth agonizes her, and she confesses self-doubt rather than self-confidence in her ability to perform the task she has set for herself—which is daunting, indeed: a book about the relationship between past, present, and future. Is she probing honestly and meticulously enough into the past? she asks herself. Has she chosen the proper tone and the kind of language which can speak clearly and persuasively to the present to help secure the future? In the middle of her book Wolf expresses alarm over weakening perceptive faculties. Her consciousness—which should be drifting along vigilantly like a balloon casting its own shadow on terrain below—seems to be getting entangled in the events above which it is intended to rise. As a result, consciousness is partly responsible for the eclipse that obscures what it was supposed to illuminate (KM 203). Wolf's metaphor of the balloon defines both the novelist's and historian's dilemma.

Finally, Wolf fears the consequences of isolating herself from society, not in the sense of physical seclusion but in the sense of extricating herself from the ideological network that is designed to hold in delicate balance the thoughts and activities of all citizens. Wolf knows that she is placing herself "in opposition" to the political system. Not with impunity can one explore the most intimate phases of childhood or the subconscious, which contains sociopsychological mechanisms ignored or suppressed by society. Any attempt to explicate social history through self-analysis rather than according to Marxist theory will surely be censured by state authority. Wolf's experiences in the wake of *The Quest for Christa T.* warrants her anxiety. But, beyond the author's attempts to protect herself, naming the fears that temporarily impede her writing is Wolf's way of identifying, recognizing, the symptoms of emotional distress from childhood. Such fears come "from far away and from when one is little," and they are "a wretched legacy" (KM 346)—patterns of childhood which the author is tracing in order to overcome them.

To trace her childhood as precisely as possible the narrator takes a trip, "a return trip," to her birthplace, the town of L., "now Polish G.," on an unusually hot weekend in July 1971. This trip constitutes the second time strand woven through the novel. She is accompanied by her husband, H., her brother, Lutz, and her daughter, Lenka. The journey across the border and the sightseeing tours through the city are described in some detail, rendering a pleasant picture of contemporary Polish life in this formerly German territory. The narrator had not wanted to make this trip, thinking that she could rely fully on her memory, but she yielded to her family and to her own subconscious pressures. Visiting the city of her childhood powerfully stimulates her memory, often in unexpected ways, as she returns to her parents' grocery store, the school where she met Christa T., the marketplace where she witnessed her first Nazi rally, and the cemetery where some of her relatives are buried. Revivified memory reconstructs the places that no longer exist, then removes the Polish inhabitants and populates the entire town with the specters of her past.

As the narrator journeys back into the past, she is accompanied by several companions. Her husband, H., as indicated by the abbreviation, is not an important character. He seems to be a practical man of the present; he drives the car, providing material and psychological support and serving as a sounding board for some of the author's reflections. He encourages her in times of self-doubt and mediates between mother and daughter (similar to the role the husband played in *June Afternoon*).

Lutz, her brother and four years her junior, shared much of her childhood and, therefore, has been given a more detailed profile. He understands his sister's nostalgia, guards her interests, and is attentive to her needs and ideas, but he balks at putting his memory to the test. Lutz does not want to provide his "madam sister" with "emotional details" of their common past. As an engineer, he is a realist who recognizes the limits of human behavior and believes in limits: the improvement of humanity has reached its limits because, in our industrialized societies, "the good human being" could not possibly become "a mass phenomenon" (KM 302). Disapproving of the intensity with which his niece is being introduced to the Nazi past, Lutz gently suggests to his sister the need for limiting the demands made on children. He regards as hopelessly anachronistic his sister's vision of a world in which human beings will pursue only those physical and spiritual needs that benefit humanity. Our materialistic world is geared to satisfying needs that are not all "humane," and he warns her not to stick her nose into humanity's affairs lest it be cut off. Lutz as brother is his sister's ally, but as political contemporary he is the writer's antagonist.

The character of Lenka, surely based on Wolf's youngest daughter of the same age, is crafted in greater detail and fulfills several important functions. She represents the generation for whom *Patterns of Childhood* is being written, although the narrator soon realizes that Lenka cannot possibly understand the child Nelly; her survival mechanisms and beliefs are not useful in Lenka's world. Furthermore, Lenka's attitudes and experiences are invariably contrasted to those of her mother or Nelly to illustrate the generational differences Wolf wants to bridge with her novel. Both Lenka's curiosity and her indifference force her mother to look at the past from the perspective of Lenka's generation. Thus, Lenka is vital to this journey to Poland.

At age fifteen Lenka is still awkwardly suspended between adulthood and childhood. This is indicated when we are introduced to her: although used to travel abroad, she immediately falls asleep on her mother's lap, like a child. Until just recently she thought all grownups were the same age and everyone over fifty was senile. But now she admits to some interest in her mother's concerns, and, for the last two years, her repertoire of ideals contains fairness and justice. She is showing signs of an irreverent, self-confident, broad-minded, and independent personality, the opposite of Nelly at the same age. Her beliefs and values are also opposite. Lenka is not encumbered by bias against other nationalities such as the Poles, a bias held by her mother's generation and delicately indicated in derogatory phrases containing the adjective *Polish*. Lenka, who never lost "home," has no sense of home as place. Home is where her friends and family are, whereas Nelly associated home with her parents' house and her hometown L. Lenka has no standard to measure her mother's longing for her childhood home, on the one hand, and craving for radical change, on the other. Lenka does not even identify with the concept "German." She had removed it from her vocabulary because it meant nothing to her, and now she doesn't care for it at all.

Lenka demands unconditional commitment because she knows no fear. She becomes furious at the sight of a photo of an American GI holding a gun to the head of an old Vietnamese woman. The photographer should have intervened rather than shot the picture. Lenka believes in self-expression and the rights of the individual and regards conformity and fear of authority as "perverse." People who consider normal what the majority thinks and does "get on her nerves." She is not afraid to think differently from the masses, and, if they threatened her, she would "scream." To believe that they could be right just because they are in the majority is "suicidal." Of course, she doesn't obey mother's curfews and ignores her housekeeping rules. Lenka considers Nelly's obsession with the truth and her attempts to please certain teachers "total insanity," and she is capable of lying without the slightest doubt that she is basically an honest person; it is just a matter of priorities. The teenager doesn't understand Nelly, but she sees hope in Nelly's rebellious giggles and spontaneous mischief behind the altar during her confirmation. But both Lenka and Nelly at age fourteen did not say anything they didn't wish to, in contrast to the narrator. In spite of the seriousness of the generation gap laid out in the mother-daughter discussions, they are usually quite amusing because of the linguistic gap with which Wolf plays skillfully. Mother's deliberate, sophisticated, rather dusty rhetoric collides refreshingly with Lenka's trendy jargon, which is spiked with words like *cool, phony, crazy, perverse,* and expressions like "So what?" Ironically, Lenka, like Nelly, must experience exploitation of the innocent, and she asks incredulously: "Would you believe that anyone can do such a thing to people?" This precisely echoes her grandfather Bruno Jordan after his return from the war: "I can't believe what they did to us" (KM 42, 253).

Nelly's world is populated by friends, neighbors, teachers, classmates, and town folk of all kinds—a congenial community all in all. Now and then it is pierced by the distant radio voices of Hitler or Goebbels. But most prominent is her family, including both grandparents, a host of aunts and uncles, their spouses and children—"a collection of people of different ages and gender for the purpose of hiding shared embarrassing secrets" (KM 77), to quote H.'s facetious definition of family. All characters are distinct, vivid, and memorable, such as Nelly's "little muzzle grandma," who supported her three children with her sewing, gardening, and one milking goat and who would threaten them with severe punishment if they did not bring in enough hay for the winter—altogether the prototype of a German mother and emulated by her daughter Charlotte. Uncle Heinrich, who possessed a bald horselike head and yellow teeth, once guided Nelly's finger slowly through a candle flame to teach her that suppression of pain is not bravery. No, bravery was daring to tell him that she is now furious at him and that he is ugly. The narrator recalls Horst Binder from Nelly's school, who "imitated in an almost blasphemic fashion the hair style of the führer" (KM 190) and whom Nelly found at once mysteriously attractive and repulsive. Horst Binder shot his parents and himself when the Third Reich capitulated. Frau Dr. Julia Strauch was Nelly's history teacher and the first intellectual she met. Neither in appearance nor in deed corresponding to the image of an Aryan woman, Dr. Strauch was nevertheless a persuasive coach of history according to Nazi ideology. Nelly, craving and laboring for Julia's personal recognition, experienced for the first time that love can be a form of imprisonment. Army officer Richard Andrack was a hypnotist who entertained at Nelly's confirmation with his magic skills. He hypnotized everyone successfully except for Nelly, who defied the temptation to be manipulated—ironic in view of her manipulation by the fascists. These and other characters in Nelly's life stitched a section of the pattern that would determine her personality. In one way or other almost everyone bears some responsibility for Nelly's conversion from uncommitted innocence to willing dedication to Hitler.

In the family dynamics Nelly's parents, Bruno and Charlotte Jordan, play the crucial roles, although her father is the supporting character, like all males in Wolf's novels, with the exception of Manfred in *Divided Heaven*. Bruno had fought in World War I, and it was his firm opinion that he would never repeat a similar horrid experience. He ran a successful grocery, rather untypically assuming a subordinate role behind his wife, Charlotte, who held jurisdiction for business and family matters firmly in her hand. Not a keen supporter of any cause, Bruno eventually became a member of the National Socialist Party by default, when his rowing league, like all sports clubs, was incorporated by the Nazis. He would probably have fallen prey to the lure or the pressures of the party had not Charlotte pointedly changed his bed to the living room couch one day when he returned home in the early morning hours after a raucous all-night meeting of the Association of Grocers, an organization also ruled by the Nazis. She was not going to tolerate in her bedroom a "vagabond," who strayed from the home base either physically or ideologically. When he was drafted for the second time in his life to serve in World War II and assigned guard duty at a POW camp, Bruno Jordan to his credit treated French prisoners with humanity. He always accommodated every customer who came to his store, regardless of political persuasion or race, even when Nazis threatened him for keeping a ledger for a communist and demanded that he conduct his business more selectively. Not until fourteen years later, after returning from brutal internment in a Russian camp, a broken man and forever a stranger to his family, did he meekly express an opinion about the Nazis: he called them "jerks." It was then that he said: "I can't believe what they did to us."

Nelly's father had no noticeable impact on her development, except, perhaps, by his conspicuous absence in decisions concerning the children and lack of constructive interaction with them. Nelly was already an adult when he could manage only a monosyllabic discussion with her about whether any human being could be turned into an animal. He tended to think yes. The adult daughter perceived the tragic element in Bruno's inability to communicate, because this kind of "verbal impotence, which imprisons a person within his own self, deprives him of the chance to get to know this self" (KM 176). In Wolf's view honest use of language and self-knowledge—self-realization—are inextricably linked. Sluggishly adhering to the norm, Bruno lacked independent perception and judgment. Even if his instincts guided him to do the decent thing and may have helped save his physical life, his verbal impotence rendered his basic humanity moot in the larger social context and ultimately took his inner life. Bruno Jordan embodies the pathology of the "Mitläufer," the person who follows along without much resistance, although not fully in agreement with being led. It is a mark of courage that Wolf uses Bruno to represent millions of Germans—people "who were there and yet not there at the same time" (KM 42).

Mother Charlotte, in contrast to father Bruno, plays a pivotal role in *Patterns of Childhood*. The force of her personality and convictions do much to explain not only Nelly's development but also "how we have become what we are." Her strengths and Bruno's weaknesses represent the factors that determined Nelly's character and, by extension, that of an entire generation. Considering the effects of Charlotte's character and deportment on the development of her daughter Nelly, it is surprising that scholars, who want to align Wolf with the feminist cause, present Charlotte as exemplary. Considering her authoritarian and loveless reign, it seems, she should not serve as a model of virtue but, rather, as a figure of cautionary significance.

Charlotte's portrayal caused the narrator considerable anxieties and acts of procrastination, because mother would be hurt if she read this. Yet mother, depicted with a great deal of color and substantial detail, is given as important a role in the novel as Nelly. Charlotte Jordan was a woman who "could eat more than bread," as the chief surgeon said with admiration after she had talked for two hours straight through her thyroid operation, a measure employed to save her vocal cords from being damaged during the hazardous procedure. She was intelligent, brave, and determined. A leader and a survivor, she maneuvered her family with amazing agility and common sense through the dangerous period of Hitler's ascent and Nazi hegemony over all German society. She stood strong and alone during the war years without Bruno, and, perhaps the hardest challenge of all, she managed to keep her family alive during the immediate post-war years. A bookkeeper by profession, "known for her efficiency and firm principles" (KM 85), Charlotte became a storekeeper after marrying Bruno, but she always dreamed of being a doctor or a nurse. Having no chance to fulfill this dream, she nonetheless took charge of her family's physical and mental health and frequently looked after the downtrodden unfortunates in her community, including women from the East conscripted into forced labor. Assisting these women was politically dangerous, so her deeds of mercy required both circumspection and courage.

Charlotte was also a master of German idiomatic phrases, proverbs, and epigrams—terse, pointed, and often satirical expressions that typified her attitudes. A collection of her favorite sayings would reveal in concise terms her view of life and her endearing, if somewhat subversive, bluntness. Although translation diminishes their sparkle, a few examples do help to reveal her character: "You can't milk a bull by force," was one of her favorites, because it expressed her belief in reason and adaptation to reality—not an easy belief during the 1930s. Therefore, Charlotte, a socialist and not a Nazi, would nonetheless raise the swastika on holidays. She would also tolerate Nelly's joining of the Hitler Youth, although she resented all the fuss about the uniform, because she did not think that loyalty to the führer had to be demonstrated through appearance. She believed it prudent and respectable to conform and be "normal." "That has never killed anyone" (KM 236), she would add—unable to foresee either the irony or the tragedy of an epic of death which resulted from accommodation of what the Nazis considered normal. To Charlotte normal was identical with order: orderly behavior, order in the house, order in all one's affairs. Charlotte's large collection of sayings attests to her compulsive striving for order: "Never put off till tomorrow what you can do today" or "What little Hans doesn't learn today, big Hans will never learn." Wolf grimly affirms this arch-stereotype of German order with rare cynicism: "It seems easier to transform a few hundred or a thousand or a million of people into non-humans or subhumans than to change our concept of cleanliness, order, and comfort" (KM 186).

But Charlotte's insistence on conformity was also balanced by her sense of fairness, which occasionally surfaced in courageous defiance and civil disobedience. She sent her children to the Lehmanns for tutoring in English, even though they had been suspended from their teaching jobs because they were suspected of Jewish ancestry. Those people are no danger to my children, Charlotte declared, willing to swear on the Bible that she had seen proof of the Lehmanns' racial background. Charlotte adjusted her behavior quickly when survival was endangered. In front of her customers in 1944 she recklessly said: "We lost the war, even a blind man can see that." This pronouncement could have put her in jail, had she not vigorously denied it: "Never! said Charlotte. Never did I say such a thing. Losing the war. Someone must have misheard, I tell you, misheard" (KM 155). A short lie was preferable to a long jail term. A year later, trying to secure her family's survival in the presence of the American occupational forces, she sternly reprimanded Nelly for her sassy attitude: "I want no nonsense now. Losers can't be choosers. They are in the driver's seat now. You better get used to it, the sooner the better" (KM 303).

Charlotte "could hear the fleas cough," meaning that she knew what was going on before others did. This intuition and shrewdness gave her a decided advantage in most endeavors and explains her successful business ventures even in very hard times. Her husband dismissed her as a pessimist, but Charlotte smelled war in the air years before it broke out: "There's something rotten in the state of Denmark" (KM 140). All matters political were whispered in the family, barely touched upon by "half sentences," and so the outbreak of the war was kept in the far corners of familial consciousness until Bruno Jordan was served a draft notice. Then Charlotte, who normally did not permit any unseemly language, declared: "I shit on your führer" (KM 156). After surrender, in 1945, Charlotte would not hear of consolations and false promises of better times. This was not the time for illusions: "Our fatherland is finished, she said, and so are we all: that is war. You are the victor, we are the losers. We have nothing to hope for" (KM 305). Charlotte resorted to no epigram, no clever phrase behind which to hide; that these were bare unvarnished words made this moment all the more remarkable.

By then, of course, pretense for the sake of preserving order and normalcy was impossible. Order and normalcy had ceased when the Jordans had to leave their home and when "the war had laid bare the intestines" (KM 161), a phrase from Kazimierz Brandys which Wolf uses several times. The view of most Germans and some foes, that Hitler was solely to blame, did not suit Charlotte either. She had her own idea about guilt, which she stated indirectly yet clearly in her typical fashion: "I do not kick anyone who is already down" (KM 305). Repudiating what she always said—"we are only chess pieces in the game of the mighty" (KM 310)—she believed that everyone had a responsibility for the fate of their country. Charlotte was ready to accept and cope with the consequences of her country's collective guilt: this is not the smallest indication Wolf provides of her mother's heroic resilience and acknowledgment of the real world.

Only once did neither Charlotte's good sense nor her intuition prevail. The event, which became legendary in the family's history, has remained a puzzle to this day. When the Russians threatened to take the town, Charlotte Jordan refused to join the general exodus. To everyone's surprise she "let her children, about whom she had always worried excessively, leave for so-called points-unknown, notwithstanding that they were accompanied by relatives" (KM 262). Charlotte may have felt that she could not abandon everything; that she was still responsible for her children's inheritance while her husband was at war. Denying the patent reality she needed to straighten the house—an absurd and wholly uncharacteristic retreat into disbelief and despair. Having to remove the führer's picture from the wall above the desk ("that felt good, I tell you" [KM 29]) is not a sufficient excuse to leave her children. Not until Charlotte saw with her own eyes German soldiers fleeing westward did she regard herself as "completely crazy." Then she set out to find her family and make sure that they would survive the dreadful aftermath of the war.

When she was dying in 1968, Charlotte Jordan, always dedicated to the service of others, often at her own peril, and always firmly rooted in terra firma, refused all reading matter and radio news. She had completely lost interest in the world. "There are more important things," she said (KM 278). For once she was only concerned with herself and, perhaps, with matters of the soul.

Her daughter Nelly's life from age three until eighteen grows within this world of petit bourgeois domesticity, in which the need to conform to commonly held moral concepts governs all behavior and education. Specific values are never articulated; they are inferred under the aegis of normalcy. *Normal,* or *not normal,* was Charlotte's favorite word, one of those "Glitzerworte" (glittering words) which make "adults' eyes glitter." This was a sign that a child should not ask for the meaning of such words. But early on Nelly knows that "not being normal" is terrible and that being normal is the prerequisite for happiness. The most crucial principle that keeps the Jordans' world in its destined orbit of happy "normalcy" is obedience. It is the first observation given about Nelly—"she has been accustomed to obedience" (KM 11). Receiving motherly love, in the child's perception, follows from her unconditional obedience, because mother Charlotte will award or withhold affection in proportion to Nelly's compliance or disobedience. Only the good child receives a good-night kiss. So strongly are these principles ingrained that Nelly later remembers "that obedience and being loved are one and the same thing" (KM 20) and that happiness results from fitting in. Nelly's compulsion to please her teachers and Hitler Youth leaders with exemplary behavior has its roots in these early childhood lessons.

Quickly, Nelly begins to develop notions about justice and guilt. Once she hurt her little brother's arm—not exactly an accident—and Lutz has to be taken to the hospital. Mother is rightly furious, but, using one of her colorful phrases, she exaggerates: "It is all your fault if his arm stays stiff" (KM 23). Nelly winces under the sudden and new feeling of guilt, a feeling that she will always associate with mother's heavy hand on her shoulder and the urge to hide. Fortunately, her brother's arm turns out to be fine, and Nelly's fright goes away after some consoling hot chocolate and little egg sandwiches. The mixed lesson is learned, however: bad behavior with pleasant consequences is not so bad, after all, and one can rejoice in false praise. But feeling the heavy burden of guilt is a different matter; it becomes Nelly's curse from then on. Although she tries to absolve herself of bad behavior with cleverly reasoned justifications and outrageous lies, "in a deeper, darker corner of her self the problem always raised its head again . . . until all certainty about herself seemed to sink into a bottomless pit" (KM 59). And so Nelly's sense for the subtle shades of right and wrong is inevitably compromised.

The child's conscience is put to a memorable test when, at approximately age seven, she finds herself severely punished, although she is the victim in the incident. Nelly had witnessed three boys torturing their little brother, who then blamed his friend Nelly for throwing a rock that was actually thrown by one of his big brothers. She was crushed by this first experience of betrayal, but she also took action—the first and last time—by reporting everything to the boys' father. Charlotte gave her a harsh beating for squealing, a questionable penalty only illuminated by her woeful comment: "Did you have to make this man mad, of all people?" (KM 26). Nelly does not understand that this beating was a parent's overreaction to fear and intended as a gesture of amends to appease the father of the boys, a mean-spirited Nazi collaborator. She regards this penalty as grossly unfair. She does not say a word. Instead, she invents ways "to scare her mother to death by hurting what she loved most: herself" (KM 27). From then on she responds to injustice by getting sick. This time she puts a pearl in her nose which has to be removed by a doctor. Mother reads this act of revenge as an accident, and, instead of a spanking or a reprimand, which would have been appropriate in Nelly's opinion, she receives praise for having been "brave." Nelly comprehends that her mother derives satisfaction from calling her daughter brave, but there is sadness and loss in realizing that her mother has no interest "to know how she was deep, deep inside . . . that even the good Lord himself preferred the brave, honest, smart, obedient, and above all happy child" (KM 27)—and, of course, the orderly child as well. Not surprisingly, Nelly becomes a messy procrastinator. She does not always clean her shoes carefully before entering the house or save her leftover school sandwiches for supper. Charlotte struggles to find effective means to teach her daughter how to behave like a "normal central European" (KM 186).

To accommodate her mother's insistence upon order and normalcy, on the one hand, and her own deep-seated sense of self, on the other, Nelly invents a new role: the "afternoon child" who cheerfully appears when mother calls. She is, of course, the "brave, honest, smart, obedient, and above all happy child." Subconsciously, she associates the "afternoon Nelly" with pretense, because, when asked in school to provide a noun of emotion (an exercise to remove confusion about the capitalization of all nouns in German), Nelly spontaneously suggests *pretense.* Her answer is another pitiful failure in the eyes of a teacher whom she wants so desperately to impress favorably, but it reveals great emotional confusion. There is, of course, also a "morning child," who is safe from the outside world, especially parental interference. The "morning Nelly" can create "hiding places within herself into which she can retreat to be alone" (KM 58). In these spaces "secrets" are safely kept and not shared with mother, even though she continues to probe at bedtime: you have told me everything now, haven't you? ("The invasiveness of others is the origin for the secret which can develop into a need, finally into a habit, and create beastly vices and magnificent poetry" [KM 58].) Nelly's interior spaces are where feelings are developed and soothed which have no name—not yet, because, as a child of a "happy" family, Nelly does not use words like *sad* or *lonely.* The morning child acts out needs of the inner self which, if unleashed, would collide with her mother's expectations. She lives out fantasies in games, books, and in the local children's theater. She metamorphoses herself into fantastic creatures, family members into witches, and dolls into real people—a game she plays with her brother Lutz called "the pretenders." To expand her range of personal freedom Nelly pressures her mother into the purchase of an old bicycle, and she roams the neighborhood after school, free from mother's apron strings.

Nelly's internal division into two children, signaling her separation from home, continues into high school and even into adulthood. As a teenager, "one part of Nelly would speak to the other, because it had become a habit to watch herself walk and speak and act, and that meant that she had to judge herself continuously" (KM 214). This self-preserving schizophrenia often hindered her to speak freely or to take decisive action. Wolf shows how it helped preserve some innocence of perception and enough of an unspoiled nature to allow the child, if only subconsciously, to discern and reject the worst elements of Nazism. Thus, Nelly could not transform her compassion for the weak and dejected—as she perceived the Jews and Gypsies—into the officially sanctioned feelings of hate or fear. She did not even know any Jews, and "hate toward unknown groups of people doesn't work on command—a defect one must conceal" (KM 122). After the infamous "Crystal Night" of 9 November 1938, when 177 synagogues and 7,500 Jewish businesses were destroyed in the German Reich, Nelly went to watch Jews—in her memory men without legs, because of their long caftans—carrying objects from a burned-out synagogue to their modest homes across the street. They are saving these objects, Nelly thought vaguely. And she would have felt sorry for the Jews had she not recalled the indoctrina-

98

tion lessons from school: "Jews are different. They are spooky. At least one should be afraid of Jews, if one cannot hate them. If Jews were strong, they would kill all of us" (KM 151). In her fantasies Nelly tries to practice hate, tries like the other children to hit this little Jewish boy, but the "film" always stops when she stands in front of him. She never finds out whether she would be able to do "her duty." But she knows that she never wants to be in the position of having to do her duty, because she cannot hate this little boy. "'Blind hate,' yes, that could work. 'Seeing hate' is simply too hard" (KM 128) is her conclusion.

Nelly's conscience—nothing less is the urge "to judge herself"—causes major conflicts with the outside world. Since they cannot be resolved, she invariably responds with illness, ranging from headaches to tuberculosis. Charlotte, who explains her daughter's "breakdowns" with late reading or too much work or too much heat, treats her expertly with home remedies. It never occurs to Charlotte that her daughter's frequent physical ailments could be symptoms of internal dissent or external strife, of her inability to harmonize social demands with conscience. Not surprisingly, Nelly's habit of falling ill in the face of internal discord has a parallel in the adult self. The narrator reacts with painful stiffness when recalling her childhood experiences during the Crystal Night of 1938: the Jews in front of the burned synagogue, the mysterious fire and scorched wicker chair in the children's room that same afternoon, and Nelly's subsequent killing of a matchbox full of ladybugs, her favorite creatures, during which she had spoken a horrifying incantation: "You are evil, damned, disobedient." As the emotional dissonance of the past resonates in the present, so do its symptoms. This is but one example of the narrator's proclivity for an acute physical response to mental anguish.

Nelly's private sense of justice continues to police her experiences, often throwing her into conflict with her chosen community of Nazi youth, although she wanted nothing more than to belong. Her notion of fairness tells her, for instance, that the young Gerda Link, when deprived of her membership in the League of Girls for a minor theft, is penalized too harshly. Rather than actually falling ill, she feigns illness to keep from participating in League activities until Gerda Link is readmitted. Such pretense is Wolf's pattern to show how Nelly's private system of ethical checks and balances is the instrument by which she is able to liberate herself ultimately from the fascist ideology. After the war she finally learns the harsh truth that "she lived for twelve years under a dictatorship without realizing it" (KM 365).

It was not merely her youth that caused Nelly not to understand fully the political circumstances in which she grew up. To preserve a normal and happy family life, her mother, Charlotte, went to great lengths to shield the children from bad news and unpleasant incidents, not just to protect them from harm but mainly to uphold the image of a wholesome world. The intrusion of Nazi politics into town affairs, such as storm trooper violence in a local meeting hall and expulsion of Jews from their homes, were described only in discreet half-sentences. Charlotte did not discuss in front of the children family scandals such as adultery or divorce or tragedies such as the death of a mentally sick aunt at the hand of the Nazis. Certain general topics such as sex were taboo altogether. Because Nelly had "above-average inquisitiveness," she was scolded for asking questions, and she soon learned to curb her curiosity, to target it selectively, and to avoid the "Glitzerworte" and all danger zones. The narrator wonders whether curiosity can be paralyzed if it is never satisfied; whether a child would not eventually lose her ability to distinguish what is dangerous from what is not; and whether such deprivation would not finally cause a child to cease asking any questions at all. Thus, the narrator is preparing her hypothesis that the ability to limit one's curiosity to designated safe areas is a mechanism by which one can survive under a dictatorship. If so, such a mechanism might explain how Nelly, and millions like her, could so innocently walk into the arms of fascism.

The story of Nelly's indoctrination is complex, insidious, and elusive. Because it started in the child's home, its residue can still be acutely felt in the adult's attempts at self-discovery. This story defies simplification; therefore, details from experience must be used to trace the path of Nelly's induction into the Nazi community. When Nelly entered school, she had already learned obedience, so she accepted all socialization methods without overt resistance. Like most children, she was an easy convert because of her desire to liberate herself from her parents' rule, because of her tendency to please authority figures in order to gain their affection, and because of her need to belong to a social network to develop her many talents and interests beyond the confines of the home.

Elementary schoolteacher Warsinski was Nelly's first love. She employed all her talents to get his attention and to please him. But her accomplishments did not seem to matter to Mr. Warsinski, while every one of her shortcomings was reprimanded. Against her mother's better judgment Nelly took ice-cold baths to toughen up, as a German girl should, so that Mr. Warsinski would not be disappointed with her the next time he inquired which girl in his class washed her body with ice-cold water. Nelly extrapolated lack of recognition by her teacher to mean lack of acceptance by her peers. As a result, she felt like an outsider, but that changed dramatically when she lied shamelessly one day about her ownership of a certain cork. This cork had been imbued by Nelly's imagination with magic powers; it had become a talisman that solved problems, dispelled fear of Mr. Warsinski, and made a child popular. The powerful cork was making the rounds in class when Mr. Warsinski discovered it. Soon Nelly would be scolded, and everyone would laugh about her, Nelly thought. And that's when she heard herself say: "No, this is not my cork." Such an outrageous lie impressed everyone; during recess she found herself surrounded by admirers. Even Mr. Warsinski allowed her to shine with the recitation of a poem. Nelly discovered that it was easy to lie, that it was an effective method to feel superior, and, most important: "To lie is to win!" (KM 111). God did not seem to mind, although pleasing God seemed to require many more lies.

Mr. Warsinski was fond of quoting the führer, and Nelly responded powerfully to Hitler's admonition that the citizen of the future, regardless of gender, should be trained in mind and body. Developing the mind came easy; steeling the body was another matter. She began riding her bicycle all over town and training in track and field events until she was one of the ten best athletes in her league. At tournaments she enjoyed seeing the masses of contestants all dressed in black and white with a swastika in the middle of the shirt and the colorful crowds cheering winners like her. Such ceremonies whet her appetite for more. Lured by the camaraderie and attention she craved and by the challenge of competition but also feeling the pressure by teachers and trainers, Nelly joined the Hitler Youth.

The role Nelly played in this group of peers and the increased respect from admired adults were extremely gratifying. Dr. Julia Strauch, her beloved high school teacher, who fed her endless intellectual curiosity with books—the sanctioned variety—and gave her satisfying personal attention, praised Nelly for joining. In the ultimate gesture of acceptance and respect by a superior, Dr. Strauch even invited Nelly to her house. Nelly participated conscientiously in all league activities, especially sport events. Much to her mother's dismay, Nelly even attained a respected leadership position. Her success in the youth organization satisfied her ambitions and need for recognition. Not only a distinct reprieve from fear and guilt but also the joy of belonging and the thrill of liberation from home were associated with her membership in the Hitler Youth: "An elevated existence lay before her, beyond that little shop crowded to the ceiling with cans of fish, sacks of sugar, loaves of bread, barrels of vinegar and sausages; beyond and away from the white figure in her shop coat, who had stepped out, no doubt looking out for her, Nelly" (KM 177).

Nelly had become not just a member of a local Hitler Youth group but a link in the fate of her country. Although she had no clear understanding what that meant, the mystery of it all thrilled her. She felt her heart beat faster when she heard over the radio voices from distant places in Germany, including the fateful announcement on 1 September 1939: "As of this morning we will shoot back," the starting shot for the invasion of Poland. She wholeheartedly shared her teacher Gaßmann's sentiments that these were the words from the stern mouth of history itself. In short she belonged to the Nazi youth movement with body and soul: "She had become addicted" (KM 161).

Nevertheless, she also felt a nagging doubt whether all these wonderful experiences justified the price of hard work, boring hikes, willful intimidation by leaders, and, above all, subjugation to authority. She caught herself finding a counterpoint to every episode in her life, whether enjoyable or frightening. The führer had said, however, "Every trace of weakness has to be chipped away from the old block," and so she suppressed her uncertainties and misgivings. Yet a vague sense of deception, of others and of herself, stubbornly remained, as did her longing for honesty, causing the adult narrator to wonder whether this might have been her saving grace. Perhaps honesty was a critical vestige of self providing a basis to begin again after everything was over. This assertion of self was powerfully affected when Nelly read about the *Lebensborn,* an organization that promoted the union of Aryan men and women selected for the sole purpose of procreating racially pure offspring. "No, not that," she thought: "It was one of those rare, precious, and inexplicable moments where Nelly found herself in conscious opposition to the required creed which she would have liked to share. As so often, her bad conscience caused the imprint of this moment in her memory. How should she have known that a bad conscience under the prevailing circumstances was a prerequisite for inner freedom?" (KM 208).

Soon the effects of war began to intrude upon the eastern provinces of Germany, as floods of refugees and wounded soldiers arrived from the Russian front. Nelly, now a teenager, was old enough to work in hospitals and refugee camps and to observe the victims of the war. In retrospect she believes that she should have been able to read the signs of despair in their eyes. But she had assumed only that they were exhausted after a long journey: "It was as if a wall was being pushed between her observations and the attempt to interpret them" (KM 258). This is the occasion when Nelly is handed a little bundle to pass on to a woman: her baby frozen to death. The mother's scream pierces Nelly's ears. But before she could succumb to a breakdown Dr. Julia Strauch's encouragement sent her back to the trenches.

Not long afterward the Jordans were refugees themselves, fleeing westward along with thousands of others. Nelly registered the desolate faces, the stench of the constantly changing sleeping quarters, the thin coffee from the tin pots of Red Cross assistants, the strafing planes from which one had to scurry to hide, the separation of families. She knew that she would never return home. Yet she still clung to her belief in the *Endsieg,* the "final victory." She held on to the führer's promise: "Berlin will remain German." Better to escape into absurd thought than permit the unthinkable. Her other self understood, however, and once again she reacted to the irresolvable internal conflict by getting sick: "The ultimate sign that she knew deep down . . . came from her own body which, since she had no other language, found expression in its particular way" (KM 259). Yet perhaps it was this desperate delusion that helped her endure. It gave her the strength to turn off all thought about herself or the reality of a lost war, to reject all despondency and to be brave—"You are really brave for your age," she was told (KM 274). Single-mindedly, she pursued only the task at hand: survival. She accompanied her mother on dangerous excursions into the country to find food or safer shelter, helped to maintain a semblance of decency and order in single rooms housing entire families, and tried to obtain information about her father, who was reported killed behind enemy lines.

For Nelly and her family the end of the war was simply marked by a curt announcement: "Have you heard? Hitler is dead" (KM 297). But the Jordans' trek continued westward as if nothing had changed. Only the bureaucracy was different: one had to report to the Americans and later to the Soviets. When the Jordan clan found more permanent shelter in a small village, Nelly, now sixteen years old, assumed a full-time job at the mayor's office in return for a daily meal. Eventually, Charlotte made it possible for Nelly to live in the nearby town and resume school. Her new teacher, Maria Kranhold, had not been a Nazi like Gaßmann or Strauch; she had not "worshiped the alien gods" (KM 362). But she reminded Nelly of her beloved history teacher, and the painful but inevitable question burst forth: Could a teacher like Julia have willfully lied to them all these years? Maria Kranhold answered thoughtfully with another question: Can one lie if one believed in lies oneself? Kranhold added that Julia Strauch could not be exonerated for having sent "her thinking on vacation." She had made Nelly turn her conscience against herself, so that Nelly could not be good, could not even think good thoughts, without feeling guilty. That was inexcusable.

This impetus to reflect on herself and to reevaluate her past released the paralysis that had held Nelly so completely throughout the triumph and collapse of the Third Reich, the finale of her childhood. Not surprisingly, Nelly finally broke down: she contracted tuberculosis. Her slow but steady recuperation is a symbol of her internal change, as Wolf ironically uses the onset of illness to signal the regeneration of Nelly's spiritual health. Her transformation is launched when she assumes the role of nurse and caretaker of terminally ill fellow patients—just as her mother would have done. It is aided by books that Maria Kranhold sent her. They are not the kind of books Dr. Strauch used to dispatch to her sickbed but, rather, books that have the power of healing: books, Nelly thought, for which she contracted this disease that takes so long to heal and gives her so much time to read. Among them are Dante's *Divine Comedy* and the poetry of Goethe. The adult Nelly still remembers two significant lines: "The hand of truth weaves poetry's veil / Out of dawn's fragrance and lucid sunlight" (KM 367).

But clarity and truth would be a long time in coming, not only for Nelly but for her entire generation. Only her adult self understood how they were so involved with their transformation "that there was not enough strength left to look back" (KM 291). It took Wolf a quarter of a century before she was ready for retrospection. To use the language of Wolf's quotation of Ingeborg Bachmann, Nelly had to learn how to write about the nature of fire with her burned hands.

CHAPTER EIGHT

Romanticists
"Precursors, You"

No Place on Earth

The year 1976 was a watershed in cultural politics in the GDR. Since Erich Honecker had given permission to expand the parameters of socialist realism at the Eighth Party Congress in 1971, literary activity had become more diverse and provocative, testing the bureaucratic limits. Many writers stretched them to a degree unacceptable to the Socialist Unity Party, the SED, and a period of severe repression set in. Measures ranged from expulsion from the writers' union to incarceration and even to expatriation. For over a decade Wolf Biermann, poet and songwriter, who had emigrated from West Germany to the GDR in 1953, was officially barred from performing his unvarnished satirical verses. But he could not be silenced, and, finally, in November 1976 Biermann was prohibited from returning to the GDR after a concert tour in West Germany.

Biermann's expatriation is notable for causing the first public protest in the cultural history of the GDR. A group of intellectuals, artists, and writers, among them Sarah Kirsch, Stephan Hermlin, and the Wolfs, signed a petition, the so-called Open Letter, urging the government to lift the sanctions against Biermann. The regime responded predictably by issuing a number of reprisals against the petitioners, "enemies of socialism." With renewed dogmatism the authorities immediately imposed more stringent publication requirements and barred writers from the media. This led to a flood of applications for exit visas, which were quickly granted—better to let the dissidents leave than allow them to remain and corrupt socialist unity. Christa Wolf was expelled from the Executive Committee of the writers' union, a comparatively minor penalty. But her subsequent banishment from any television appearances had teeth because it prevented her from reaching a broader audience who preferred television to books. For many years television remained off-limits to Wolf and many of her outspoken colleagues: it was a "nonexistent medium."

Probably for the first time Wolf and her husband, Gerhard, seriously considered leaving the GDR. They pondered the possibility for a long time, but they had many compelling reasons for rejecting emigration: they did not want to leave behind their two daughters and their families; Christa Wolf's father was still alive and dependent on her assistance; the many letters she received from her readers told her that she was needed in the GDR. Finally, the Wolfs really did not know where to go; no country seemed to offer an acceptable alternative: "Moreover: I had an ardent interest in this country only. Only here could I feel the strong friction, which causes productive sparks, with all the despair, the rejection, the self-doubts associated with life here. That was my reason for writing. . . . It was clear to me that I had to enter a difficult and morally dubious situation. That was very hard for me" (ID 148).

For all writers who chose to stay because they wanted to continue to work on the realization of socialism, such as Hermann Kant, Franz Fühmann, and Volker Braun, the government's intransigence raised the existential question about their role in socialist society more poignantly than ever. Christa Wolf felt the crisis keenly. She saw "the rug pulled out from under" her; she felt like an "outsider" who was no longer needed. To be able to publish she had to try "not to run into every knife" (T 262) and be particularly circumspect. In an interview published under the title "Projektionsraum Romantik," 1982 (Projection Space Romanticism), she described her situation: "At that time I had the powerful feeling of standing with my back to the wall, unable to take a real step. I had to survive a period in which there seemed to be absolutely no way to be effective" (DII 878).

Many honors were bestowed upon Wolf during this period, including the Literature Prize of the City of Bremen in 1977; she was a distinguished guest lecturer at Oberlin College, Ohio, in 1976 and at the University of Edinburgh in 1978. But such honors did not erase feelings of betrayal and uselessness. Being celebrated abroad did not compensate for being suppressed at home. As is typical for Wolf in times of crisis, she invoked the healing powers of writing—"a sort of self-rescue." This time her remedy took the form of a new novel, *Kein Ort. Nirgends,* 1979 *(No Place on Earth).* In it Wolf sought "to examine the conditions for failure, the connection between social despair and failure in literature"—a theme of alienation. But she did not want to explore the subject in contemporary context, because "that would have been impossible for me, that would have been naturalistic and banal and flat" (DII 878). To give her indignation the necessary distance (and defuse official objection to the treatment of volatile issues), she turned to Romanticism, a guise that other writers such as de Bruyn and Seghers had also chosen for similar reasons. As a result, these authors rehabilitated Romanticism, an ignored literary period because it had been officially declared unsuited as a proper model for socialist society.

In her studies of writers from the early phase of Romanticism, those who followed Goethe in the decades after 1800 such as Hölderlin, Novalis, Arnim, and Brentano, Wolf observed that many had experienced the alienation from their society which Wolf had experienced herself. She was forced to weigh certain questions: "How come that after the generation of Classicism so many young authors turn up who obviously cannot 'cope' with their time, their talent, with literature, with their personal life? Who fail according to bourgeois concepts as well as to a certain kind of Marxist literary theory?" (DII 881). Indeed, German writers in the early nineteenth century did face a new era. The failure of the French Republic to realize the ideals of the French Revolution—*liberté, égalité, fraternité*—and the utilitarian and rationalistic ethos associated with the beginning of industrialization caused profound disillusionment among Europe's literary elite. The historical parallels also caused a profound discomfort, if not disillusionment, in Wolf and among the GDR's intelligentsia, who were quite capable of appreciating the historical and political ironies linking GDR authority to French postrevolutionary retrenchment. Unlike the generation preceding them, who, in Wolf's assessment, were still able to live in a "utopia" and whose greatest representative was Wolfgang von Goethe, the Romantic writers experienced as irreconcilable opposites a profusion of fundamental dualities: reality and ideal, life and dream, intellect and emotion, man and nature, society and the individual. Wolf passionately recognizes their internal discord in an essay about Karoline von Günderrode, "Der Schatten eines Traumes" ("The Shadow of a Dream"), a title taken from a passage in the poet's letters. According to Wolf, the early German Romantics

> are the first to experience it [the conflict] unmitigated: they are not needed. . . . The idea of utopia is completely expended, faith is lost, any kind of support gone. They feel alone in the face of history. They hope in vain that others—their people!—could relate to them. One cannot live from self-deception. Isolated, unknown, cut off from any possibility to act, relegated to the adventures of the soul, they are helplessly exposed to their doubts, their despair, the increasing feeling of failure. (DII 516–17)

Unable to cope with an alien and often hostile social environment, unable to exercise their calling and infuse reality with the spirit of the imagination, and unable to make their disillusionment heard, the early Romantics often escaped into other worlds: exile, insanity, illness, death. They seemed to personify Goethe's dictum, which is quoted in *No Place on Earth*: "The Classical is healthy, the Romantic is sick."

In German Romanticism Wolf detected the roots for this "terrible conflict between individuals and society." At the turn of the nineteenth century, she thought, society started to disown literature as a vital element of its own identity, which made it more difficult for the creative artist to integrate life and work. Estrangement of the individual and renouncement of the writer were the inevitable processes of alienation, which Wolf painfully experienced in her own era. She intended to come to terms with those conflicts through writing.

For the centerpiece of her novel Wolf devised a fictitious meeting of two real Romantic authors having different literary careers but similar fates: Heinrich von Kleist (1777–1811), whose prose and plays are a vital part of the German literary canon; and Karoline von Günderrode (1780–1806), an unknown poet. Both impoverished aristocrats, they were frustrated with their declining position in society; they were also unhappy in love and both committed suicide at a young age. Impressed by Günderrode's work, Wolf made it more accessible by an edition of selected poems, prose, and correspondences as well as reminiscences of her contemporaries, entitled *Der Schatten eines Traumes,* 1979 (The Shadow of a Dream). This book was accompanied by Wolf's lengthy essay about Günderrode's life and work under the same name.

To this legendary meeting Wolf brought a third figure, Bettine von Arnim, the sister of the famous poet Clemens Brentano and wife of the equally prominent poet Achim von Arnim and a friend of Günderrode's. Bettine began writing after having raised a family of seven. For the new edition of Bettine von Arnim's biography of Günderrode, first published in 1840, Wolf wrote an extensive essay, "Nun ja! Das nächste Leben geht aber heute an! Ein Brief über Bettine," 1979 (All right! But the Next Life Starts Today! A Letter about Bettine). Both this essay and the one about Günderrode not only demonstrate Wolf's sensitivity toward the fragile work and fractured life of obscure women writers; they also provide valuable background for any study of *No Place on Earth.*

Wolf's novel preserves the authentic individuality of the authors by adhering in detail to their documented life stories and by surrounding them with their actual relatives and friends. Most notably, Wolf provided her protagonists with their very own words: throughout the novel appear some ninety authentic passages from both writers' works (scholars have identified the sources). Wolf freely lifted these citations from the period before 1804, when the fictitious meeting occurs. The borrowed passages are not earmarked in any way. While enhancing the protagonists' authenticity, this technique conforms to an established custom of the Romantic period. Many writers, among them Clemens Brentano and E. T. A. Hoffmann, frequently appropriated texts from fellow authors. Wolf acknowledged "internal citation," but she insisted that the whole is still her own narrative, because she had made the poets' words fit into a story and a world of her own creation. Thus, the characters of the novel are at once both document and fiction, permitting history to speak through art.

Owing to Wolf's adaptation and emulation of poetic material from almost two centuries ago, the tenor of this novel is strikingly different from that of any of her previous work. A conversational rhetoric and a distinctly lyrical tone prevail in *No Place on Earth*. The first two sentences read like lines of a poem: "The strong spoor in which time runs away from us. Precursors you, blood in your shoe" (KO 5). How carefully Wolf crafted her material is apparent when one places the last two lines next to the beginning: "Let us simply go on, they think. We know what is coming" (KO 119). Wolf's entire novel is, in a sense, a great prolepsis completing the poetic image of continuity, kinship, and shared pain between the early Romantics, to whom she alludes as "precursors," and the artists of the late twentieth century, whose fate is implied in the last sentence.

The language as well as the composition of *No Place on Earth* are reminiscent of lyrical drama rather than the novel. The text's structure is dictated by the nature of the scenario that Wolf devised for her protagonists' meeting—"desired legend": a tea party on a June afternoon in 1804 at the summer home of Merten, a merchant living in the small town of Winkelon on the Rhine River (where Günderrode took her life two years later). Not unlike Wolf's short story "June Afternoon" from 1965, the drama unfolds in a small space within a few quick hours: a tea salon (the stage set), furnished with period pieces and appointed tastefully with the obligatory landscape painting, parquet floor, and a delicate clock on the fireplace mantle marking time every half an hour. There is virtually no plot. Instead, Wolf pays meticulous attention to the intellectual and psychological life of the characters and their interaction. It is as if the reader is sitting in a theater watching the guests milling about and hearing their conversations and interior monologues. In the second and final act there is an abrupt scene change. The party has moved outside and is taking a stroll along the Rhine River—a richly evoked sunset with sights and sounds of country life. In this Romantic setting Kleist and Günderrode separate from the others and exchange intimate ideas, their losses and personal pain, which forms the climax of the novel.

Another guest at the tea party is Kleist's physician, Wedekind, who has been trying to cure Kleist from the serious breakdown he suffered after burning his latest unfinished work, "Robert Guiscard." Wedekind, a rationalist who believes in free will, practices medicine with the belief that every illness contains its own remedy and that it is merely a question of will to activate either one, the illness or the remedy. He does not believe it is good to look too deeply into the psyche. Wedekind's prescription for healing Kleist's deep despair is adaptation to circumstances and, if that fails, distraction—hence, Kleist's attendance at the tea party.

Other significant guests include the Brentano siblings: Clemens, the successful writer who is not encumbered by self-doubt although, perhaps, by self-delusion; Bettine, a young free spirit but a perceptive and devoted friend to Günderrode; the scientist Esenbeck and wife, espousing optimistically the idea of unfettered economic progress and of science as the savior of humanity; and, most important, the lawyer and soon-to-be Prussian Minister of Justice Savigny, who "has a male mind" and "only one kind of curiosity: the curiosity for what is indisputable, logical and solvable" (KO 81). Savigny's role is pivotal in this constellation of characters because he represents the "counterpoint" to Kleist and is the object of Günderrode's unrequited love, because he is already married to Brentano's sister Gunda.

This circle of intellectuals is designed to cast Kleist and Günderrode in their destined role as outsiders. Unlike Kleist and Günderrode, the rest of this cast believes in order, progress, and the power of rationality and seems unconcerned that the course of culture is fated "to expand more and more the realm of the rational mind and to confine more and more the realm of the imagination" (KO 80). They all agree wholeheartedly with Kleist's facetious supposition that the poet "is assigned the administration of our illusions" (KO 81). Savigny's proposition—that the neat separation of the realm of thought from the realm of action is actually a benevolent arrangement—represents the prevailing belief of his time. Yet it is abhorrent to Kleist and Günderrode. Wolf's protagonists, on the contrary, believe that ideas—the fruit of the imagination—must infuse reality, the arena of action, in order that our humanity be preserved.

Much of the charm and power of this novel derives from the way Wolf has maneuvered her readers into being party crashers from the twentieth century. She makes us feel obligated to apply constant attention to discern who is speaking or is engaged in quiet thinking, because she does not always clearly identify the speaker. As in the theater, no narrator marks the beginning of speech by "she says" or "he thinks." Narrative is chronologically layered because Wolf must present in linear time conversations and monologues that, in real time, as marked by the little clock on the fireplace, occur simultaneously. Wolf obligates the reader to identify and superimpose the various strains of thought and conversation. Moreover, she deliberately distorts the structure by embedding in the interior monologues other bits of remembered dialogue. Sometimes she unexpectedly switches the perspective from first person to third, as if the narrator had suddenly taken over direction of the character's internal drama. To facilitate identification of speakers Wolf plants various clues into the text, such as personal pronouns, names, forms of address, biographical facts, and, for those readers thoroughly versed in the poets' work, unmarked quotations.

Yet untangling the web of party conversation from passages of unspoken personal contemplation requires the reader's constant vigilance as well as active participation. Wolf clearly intended this process to be a challenge, because the reader's attention is frequently jolted by various questions: "Who is speaking?" (KO 6, 113) or "What were they speaking of?" (KO 114). Such questions could also be addressed to the narrator, the other twentieth-century voyeur, because both reader and writer are included in the narrative process. Wolf often fashions statements in a way that allows us to assign them to one of the twentieth-century characters as well as to a present-day witness: "The word was finally spoken" (KO 100), "We all know everything" (KO 79), or the brief interrogative "Why?" when it is placed on a line by itself. Wolf always implies the narrator's and the reader's tacit agreement when she has the character address a general "you" or speak in the royal "we." Here, as in all her novels, Wolf uses the technique of meshing personal pronouns in order to target several characters at once. She calls it "grammar of multiple simultaneous relations" (VEK 129). In *No Place on Earth* she generally uses this technique when broad social or political issues are being discussed pertinent to the present: "Or are you really unwilling to see the restrictions that would be imposed on all thought, if we had to fear that our fantasies could find entry into the real world? Heavens no: *not* to take philosophy by its word, *not* to measure life by the ideal—that is the law" (KO 50–51). Or "Whatever we fear will surely come when we lose hope" (KO 117). Converging the perspectives of character, narrator, and reader invokes the close relationship between the past and the present, summons our judgment, and stimulates a commitment to change—Wolf's ultimate goal.

For *No Place on Earth* Wolf chose two epigraphs by Kleist and Günderrode which epitomize the theme of the novel; if elided and read as one continuous text, these describe the fate of both poets:

I contain my heart like a northern land does the seed of a tropical fruit: it
   sprouts and sprouts, and it cannot bear fruit.

Kleist

Therefore, I imagine myself lying in a coffin and my two selves stare in bewilderment at each other.

Günderrode

Because both poets are unable to realize their individuality and are broken in two by internal conflict, they seek death. But Kleist and Günderrode have much more than this in common. Their kindred spirit as well as their individual dispositions, although different in vital ways, conflict sharply with societal rules and expectations. Both suffer from an inability to live by the conventions and demands of society, which they call "the law of all laws" (KO 51) and which clash fatally with the laws they carry in their hearts. The poets' internal or personal laws are more binding than all "external ones, even if signed by a king" (KO 68). Androgynous in mentality—"He not quite man, she not quite woman" (KO 95)—they both feel male and female principles within themselves, "two selves" struggling against each other. When Kleist agonizes over the form of address to use when he will finally be introduced to Günderrode, he invents the word *Jünglingin,* which means a young man-woman. Aware of instincts within himself associated with femaleness, Kleist senses in the woman her need to assert impulses that are traditionally assigned to men. Both Kleist and Günderrode have what he calls "the innate bad habit" of being in places where they don't live, or living in a time that is either past or yet to come—they are, in his view, anachronisms incarnate. Hence, they constantly wish they had not come to the party, that they could either leave or be by themselves. Kleist's most ardent wishes, "Freedom. A poem. A house" (KO 87), cannot be fulfilled because they are irreconcilable, as Günderrode points out. But these are also her own wishes. She, too, would like to expand the boundaries of her existence, overcome the shortcomings she perceives in herself as a writer so that she could create the perfect poem; she, too, longs for emotional and physical security. But both Kleist and Günderrode know that their vision of life is utopian and believe that there is "no hope for an existence suited to their needs." Consequently, they are condemned not to find a place on earth—"Unlivable life. No place. Nowhere" (KO 108). Wolf's protagonists subscribe to a bleak vision of life reminiscent of the anomie and stalemate found in Samuel Beckett's universe.

This conflict between self and society and its impending consequences are illustrated in Kleist's comical story about Wedekind's dog. Bello, a willing and obedient dog, is called by his mistress to guard her child; at the same moment Bello is called by Kleist to take the daily walk. Plagued by indecision over which order to follow, Bello finally curls up between the two callers and goes into deep sleep. Kleist and Günderrode, faced by irreconcilable conflicts magnified by personal shame, wished they could "sleep all life long" (KO 63), a universal metaphor for death. Not surprisingly, they both talk frequently about death: "The most dreadful thing, Kleist says, is this inner command forcing me to turn against myself." Günderrode phrases this idea more paradoxically: "Giving birth to what kills me" (KO 97). Günderrode carries a dagger with her at all times which she is prepared to use against herself; she has already learned how to strike effectively. She derives consolation from the knowledge that she does not *have* to live. For Kleist death is less of a comfort, more of a penalty that, he fears, he is destined to execute with his own hands. There is a tone of sarcasm when he calls such a death "a fate after his own heart" (KO 31).

At this tea party the kinship between Kleist and Günderrode inevitably draws them together in a soul-baring conversation. It occurs—seemingly *has to occur*—during their stroll outside, in the infinite space of nature, far away from the confinements of the salon. Only when they are outside in a natural setting can they share their deepest secrets. It is then that the pronoun *we* replaces the *I*, signaling the spiritual union of the protagonists but also a new bond with the reader. This union at the novel's climax justifies Wolf's technique of maintaining ambiguity regarding the identification of speakers: it is not important who speaks, if the words issue from a common weltanschauung.

Aside from the poets' common destiny their differences are also captured in the epigraphs quoted earlier: Kleist's imagination yearns to pick the fruits of metaphor in distant lands, whereas Günderrode's poetic space implodes into the ultimate confinement. He appears to be restlessly moving about, but she exhibits an imprisoned existence. These contrasting poetic images indicate their personal situations, which are amply revealed in the course of the novel.

In the exposition setting up the tea party, Kleist is described as a restless wanderer who, "afflicted with this acute sense of hearing, flees under pretexts he is not permitted to understand. Aimlessly, it seems, he charts the torn map of Europe with his bizarre spoor. Happiness is where I am not" (KO 6). Beginning with his service in the Prussian army at age fifteen, Kleist has traversed Germany and the other countries of Europe hoping that he could "pluck the flower of happiness somewhere" (KO 67). On the occasion of his first border crossing he learned "how one's home country looked better and better the farther away one moved; how the pressure of obligations to his country slowly abated, which, although self-imposed, could not be fulfilled" (KO 66–67). But he also realized that, in spite of his "good will, fearful trust," no country offered what he needed, and nowhere could he find what he was looking for. Perhaps these laments make veiled reference to Wolf Biermann's expatriation, but they also describe a dilemma that affects Kleist even as he speaks: he regrets sincerely having followed Wedekind to the tea party. Unfortunately, Kleist's financial situation does not allow him to indulge his restlessness. In fact, soon he will be forced to terminate his sojourn on the Rhine with Wedekind and return home to Prussia to pursue a degrading civil service career that "would run counter to his vocation" (KO 64). Such a career would not allow him to write—an activity he ardently desires and fears at the same time.

Incapable of constraining either his external restlessness or his internal turmoil, Kleist regrets that he is not master over the thoughts and pains within him (there are several intimations that the source of his shame may be an incestuous relationship with his sister Ulrike). He knows he would be cured if only he were able "to rein the voice within that teases and mocks him" (KO 12). But silencing this voice, he fears, would mean his death. Kleist's constitution is riddled with similar conflicts that defy solution. If he tolerates dependencies—such as his reliance on Wedekind for his mental health—they suffocate him, but, if he tears himself away, he is destroyed. He agonizes over the choice between a civil service position, which is debasing but affords a modest income, and literature, which guarantees dire poverty but a wholesome feeling of self-worth. Kleist believes that mankind has an irrepressible drive toward enlightenment, or else we would be only animals. Yet, as soon as we convert our knowledge into action, it turns against us. Insight and technology are no saviors but only instruments threatening our security. In the throngs of such fatal alternatives Kleist has little left but his writing, although it, too, seems to be doomed by quandaries.

By 1804 Kleist had not yet written his great works. In fact, he had just burned the unfinished manuscript of his play "Robert Guiscard." The epigraph's metaphor about fruit evokes his frustration over his inability to write. Several times in the course of the novel Kleist articulates his phobia: "Only never having to write again. Everything, but not that" (KO 44). Kleist had painfully experienced the inadequacies of language when his doctor, Wedekind, had probed into the source of his unfathomable anguish. Pressed to the limits of pain by Wedekind's relentless questions, Kleist realized "that words cannot paint the soul, and he believed he would never find it within him to write again" (KO 40). At the height of his suffering appropriate words fail him—then he feels mute like an animal—and afterward, when words do come, he curses because they seem riddled with falsehood and vanity. The severity of his anguish leads him to the brink of psychosis. During conversations he has visions of toads jumping out of his and everyone's mouth. Rarely has anyone made the depiction of a writer's pain more vivid.

Günderrode sensitively recognizes Kleist's creative impasse: "What he needed years to understand, the woman understands in minutes." She is supportive and helps him realize that his Guiscard project failed not because of him but because of problems inherent in the material: "Wanting to expose one's worst enemy and at the same time one's own self is an endeavor bound to fail. The material is immense; failing at it no disgrace" (KO 116). In spite of his inhibitions, Kleist has literary ambition. He desperately wants to be famous. The idea that his contemporaries and generations after him could ignore him as a marginal literary figure is unbearable. Günderrode has detected this drive in him: "You don't live without secret securities, do you? Without the hidden hope that at least generations later you will be needed, if your contemporaries happen to do without you? And don't you, nevertheless, long for fame right now?" (KO 114). Kleist begs her to stop. He knows she is right. Wolf shows us that Günderrode's wise counsel exerts a comforting and crucial influence on Kleist's self-confidence as a writer, instilling hope when she says, "Whatever we fear will surely come when we lose hope" (KO 117). Wolf is suggesting that Günderrode's intervention and friendship were quite powerful because Kleist was productive and successful in the seven remaining years of his life. Both his prose and his plays have maintained relevance to this day.

Because Günderrode is female, her life moves in a different world. Wolf's essay "The Shadow of a Dream" describes succinctly the conflicts embodied in the novel's second epigraph:

> She wants to unite what cannot be united: to be loved by a man and to create a work which can be measured by absolute standards. To be wife and poet; to establish and care for a family and to go public with her own daring productions: unlivable wishes. Three men played a role in her life: Clemens Brentano, Savigny, Friedrich Creuzer—three variations of the same experience: what she desires cannot be. Three times she experiences the most insufferable: she is made into an object. (DII 529)

Restless like Kleist and desiring to be where she is not, Günderrode is nevertheless trying to live within her physical and emotional confines. As she says, "I train myself to want what I must do" (KO 101). In the novel's exposition she is introduced as "sequestered in a narrow circle, reflective, clairvoyant, unaffected by transience, resolved to live for immortality, to sacrifice the visible to the invisible" (KO 6). This small circle delineates the social limitations imposed on women in the nineteenth century, especially women without any financial means of their own. The restraints are painfully felt by Günderrode the woman as well as the writer. As a woman, she cannot bear men's preconceptions and the liberties they take against women. Even Kleist, the kindred spirit, expresses certain prejudices against her, that she is destined to suffer because women are of the suffering gender or that she could not possibly know the meaning of ambition, a male trait. Practiced in self-defense, Günderrode counters sharply, "She observed, she says, that the ambition of the talented hones itself on unfavorable conditions, the ambition of the untalented on their distorted self-esteem" (KO 101). She shrewdly does not specify the category that applies to Kleist. As a writer, Günderrode has to publish her poetry under a male pseudonym, Tian, and she must suffer the indignities of a condescending review when her identity is revealed.

Forced by impoverished family circumstances, Günderrode has lived since the age of nineteen in a *Stift,* a home for poor single females of the upper class, similar to a convent. The small room, narrow bed, strict rules, and few privileges—confinements alluded to in the epigraph—are hard to bear for a free spirit. Having become an autodidact because her family could not afford to give her a formal education, Günderrode attempted to break through the limitations of her circumstances by intensive and wide-ranging, if solitary, study. Ironically, her intelligence, knowledge, and insight, not expected and accepted in a female, isolate her even more. The effects of her extraordinary self-development are instinctively recognized by others: "An invisible circle is drawn around her which one hesitates to cross" (KO 10–11).

Not surprisingly, Günderrode's emotional life is painfully constrained by her physical and social situation: "She has the misfortune to be passionate and proud, thus, to be misjudged. So she holds herself back, with reins that cut into the flesh. That works. One lives. It would be dangerous if one let go of the reins, charged ahead and ran into that obstacle which the others call reality and which she does not quite understand—as they would impute" (KO 10).

Presumably in keeping with her resolve to restrain her passions, Günderrode broke off her relationship with Clemens Brentano—an action still unforgiven at the time of the tea party. Likewise, although she loves Savigny deeply, she resigns herself to his marriage to a woman who possesses, as Savigny remarks, "the right mixture of independence and devotion" (KO 59), not the kind of provocative independence which characterizes "his little Günderrode." Education, circumstances, and vulnerability have taught Günderrode the art of pretense. Thus, she professes abhorrence at the idea of being dependent on anyone and distances herself from Savigny, proclaiming to live her "own, isolated, happy life" (KO 50). "Where my home is, love exists only at the price of death," she explains (KO 37). Yet in her real life, as her letters to Savigny reveal, Günderrode was not quite so reticent about her feelings for him. Nor did she resign from love. In the last year of her life she carried on an unhappy but passionate affair with Friedrich Creuzer, professor of comparative mythology and a married man, on whose account she is thought to have committed suicide.

In contrast to Kleist, for whom the vocation of writing seemed to be a curse, writing is an imperative for Günderrode: "I can fail in both, living and writing, but I do not have a choice" (KO 37). Poetry gave her wings to soar above the confines of her existence. "That I have to write is certain. There is a longing within me to express myself in permanent form" (KO 25). Writing poetry, according to Günderrode, is a balm laid upon life's wounds. She also likens it to a mirror in which she gathers and sees herself and through which she extends herself (KO 36). Not for Kleist, but for Günderrode, writing is a form of self-realization, and, thus, it is life sustaining. She does not write for fame or for future generations. Sensing her fate in literary history, she resigns herself to being unknown: "The territory between eras is obscure, one strays easily and gets lost mysteriously. That does not frighten me. Life is taken out of our hands, anyway. I do not have to exist forever. Does this make me invulnerable?" (KO 118). Günderrode's desire to express herself, to come to terms with her fate through the writing process, links her to Christa Wolf—"precursor, you." Wolf has succeeded in drawing a poignant portrait of a female mentor distant only in time.

Wolf called her novel *Kein Ort. Nirgends,* which means "No Place. Nowhere"—an apparent redundancy separated by a period. Aside from underscoring the utter futility of finding a sanctuary on earth, the deliberate tautology indicates that *both* protagonists are afflicted with spiritual homelessness. Furthermore, the nature of their tragedy is illuminated by the skillful turn of phrase implied in *no place.* The Greek root of *no place* is *u-topos,* "utopia," which means either a place of ideal (thus not attainable) perfection or an impractical scheme of social engineering. Both definitions apply to Wolf's novel. Kleist and Günderrode must perish because they measure life by an ideal, a utopia, which their society cannot possibly attain. Nowhere, be it in other countries or in love relationships, can utopia be found. Günderrode's and Kleist's idea of regenerating their society by infusing it with poetry, the spirit of the arts, is utopian as well. Once again Wolf captures in precise words the universe of her novel.

Toward the end of Kleist and Günderrode's conversation, while walking toward the sunset, Günderrode, in a motherly gesture to soothe Kleist's despair, says: "Men and women who do not deceive themselves will extract from the foment of any era something new by expressing it" (KO 83). With rigorous honesty voicing their insights, the two writers extracted the malaise infecting their lives and their era. They left a heritage from which Christa Wolf wrested a poetic yet provocative proclamation about the upheavals within her own life and era. Using the words of Kleist and Günderrode, she speaks directly to us:

> So we, too, are responsible for dividing mankind into doers and thinkers. Do we not realize that the actions of those who usurp the right to act become more and more ruthless? How the poetry of the thinkers is beginning to correspond to the purposes of the doers? Must we, incapable of practical activity, not fear of becoming members of the effeminate gender of the complainers, incapable of the smallest concession necessary in daily life and stubbornly clinging to a claim no one on earth can fulfill: To act and, in doing so, remain ourselves?
> Who is speaking? (KO 113)

CHAPTER NINE

"Books Are Deeds"

Cassandra

As an author of privilege during the year of the Wall, Wolf was able to travel to Western countries. After Biermann's expatriation and Wolf's protest, the authorities may have granted her travel rights in the hope that she would not return. At any rate, in 1980 she took a journey to Greece. Her experiences there spawned the Cassandra project, a series of lectures and the novel *Kassandra (Cassandra)*, which she presented in 1982 as a guest lecturer in poetics at the Johann Wolfgang Goethe University of Frankfurt. This coveted position was first held by her idol, Ingeborg Bachmann (1959–60), and later by Heinrich Böll, Martin Walser, Uwe Johnson, and other distinguished authors. Like Bachmann, Wolf did not lecture on poetics, the theory of poetic systems. Instead, she delivered five presentations composed of travelogue, work diary, a letter, and the draft of her new novel about Cassandra.

In the first four lectures Wolf ruminated about her growing fascination with this Trojan prophet and her travels through Greece to explore details about the myth. She described her subsequent studies of Greek mythology and archaeology undertaken at home in Berlin and their summer house in the northern state of Mecklenburg. She also reported extensively on current world affairs that seemed relevant to the themes treated in her studies. Most significant is her discourse on women as victims of a male-dominated world and the adverse conditions affecting female writers throughout history. In essence these lectures describe Wolf's discovery of Cassandra, her creative transformation of the mythological figure into a flesh-and-blood woman, and her interpretation of the myth as a prefiguration of our nuclear age, which Wolf perceived as the final phase of our civilization. Thus, the lectures served as an exposition to the fifth presentation, the reading of the novel's draft. After revision and expansion, the four lectures and the novel were published in 1983. In East Germany they appeared as one volume; in the West they were divided into two separate volumes, *Prerequisites for a Story: Cassandra* and the novel itself entitled *Cassandra*. Wolf touched a sensitive nerve in readers on both sides of the Wall.

Cassandra enjoyed wide popularity and generated much correspondence and vigorous debate. In East Germany every new printing was immediately sold out, and in West Germany it remained on the best-seller list for more than a year.

Wolf's four lectures illuminate the dense and demanding text of the novel. She explicates parts of Aeschylus' *Oresteia,* the plays that inspired her interest in Cassandra, and she retells a composite of different versions of the myth, uncovering the male point of view which, Wolf believes, determines the characters of Greek mythology. She brings to life the historical places where Cassandra lived three thousand years ago and unearths, in a manner of speaking, the city of Troy, whose annihilation by the Greeks, hidden in the Trojan horse, Cassandra had predicted. We travel with Wolf to the fortress of Mycenae, where Cassandra was taken by her captor, Agamemnon, and killed by his wife, Clytemnestra, who, it will be remembered, had already killed her husband to avenge his sacrificial murder of their daughter Iphigenia. Clytemnestra in turn is killed herself in revenge by her son Orestes.

Wolf examines Cassandra's family according to Homer's epic: her parents, Priam and Hecuba, king and queen of Troy; her brother Paris, who caused the Trojan War by kidnapping Helen, wife of the Greek king Menelaus and reputed to be the most beautiful woman on earth; her brave brother Hector, who died at the hands of Achilles, killer of the Amazon Penthesilea; Aeneas, who leaves the ruins of Troy to found the city of Rome; and, of course, Cassandra herself, to whom Apollo gave the gift of prophecy in exchange for the promise of love. When, however, Cassandra did not keep her promise, Apollo added the curse that no one would believe her prophecies. The Trojans soon grew irritated by Cassandra's constant predictions of doom and silenced her by imprisonment.

Wolf's lectures reveal her efforts to gain "sovereignty over the material" (VEK 7), a subjective assimilation of seemingly "objective" popular notions of the past. Through them we can trace how the mythological figures are absorbed and transformed in Wolf's imagination and how, as a result, her views about the myth change. When looking for psychological reality behind the tale, Wolf says, an author will project a contemporary ideal onto the mythological figure. This operation is informed by the author's imagination and the collective knowledge of the time. The resulting metamorphosis of the myth "reflects the subconscious, therefore particularly potent wishes of the interpreter" (VEK 58). Aeschylus, for example, proceeding from a male point of view, presents a Cassandra horrified at and weeping for Agamemnon's fate at the hands of his murderous wife, Clytemnestra. Wolf knows Cassandra better: her protagonist would not shed a single tear for the last in a series of men who had violently abused her. Wolf wanted to remove Cassandra from the metaphorical realm of myth "into the (perceived) social and historical coordinates" (VEK 111); in other words, she provides Cassandra with a realistic contemporaneous context appropriate for a woman of her elevated station.

Intending to provide a credible physical environment for her protagonist, Wolf immersed herself in ancient Greek history, art, and archaeology and studied models of other authors who had adapted antiquity to contemporary purposes, such as Goethe and Thomas Mann. Equally important in this process of re-creating and modernizing ancient material are Wolf's own observations during her travels through present-day Greece, which she describes in minute and often tedious detail. Wanting to resurrect Cassandra's life as faithfully as possible, Wolf utilizes numerous details unaffected by time: landscapes, the sky, faces, art forms, and ancient customs. The features of the Syrian women, for example, whom Wolf saw on the plane to Athens, all dressed in plain black clothes as they might have appeared centuries ago, serve as models for Cassandra. The "magical light" of the evening sun bathing the sky over the harbor of Piraeus, when Wolf's ship departed for Crete, illuminates a love scene in *Cassandra* then fades away at the end of the novel. And the headless stone lions still guarding the ruins of the palace of Mycenae are haunting images dominating the beginning and end of the novel—vivid reminders of our connection to civilizations long gone: "Here it is. These stone lions looked at her. In the changing light they seem to move" (K 160). By animating the past with impressions from the present, Wolf gives form to her conviction that neither human beings nor circumstances have changed much over three thousand years, either internally or externally.

Not surprisingly, then, Wolf discovered that Cassandra's life and society teem with parallels to Wolf's own. Unquestionably, Wolf found in the Trojan War a perspective for examining contemporary conflicts. "In Troy, I am sure, people were no different than we are. Their gods are our gods: the wrong ones" (VEK 95). Wolf developed two major themes in her novel: the dynamics in a society she calls "prewar," including the motivation and preparation for war and its impact on the individual, and achievement of individual autonomy in spite of oppression. Appetite for war and social oppression are endemic in our society, Wolf contends; these themes can easily be traced back to the dawn of occidental civilization, "the seam" between matriarchal and patriarchal social systems. By studying how destructive forces emerged in antiquity, Wolf hoped to illuminate the present and the future. In 1983 she acknowledged: "In my later books—*No Place on Earth* and *Cassandra*—I remember something: the origins of the symptoms of alienation in our civilization. This has been my interest in the last seven years. And the last, farthest step into early history makes it possible, strangely enough, to probe into the future, which is, after all, the actual subject matter when I tell about things past" (DII 928).

While Wolf worked on her Cassandra project, the German writers' associations in East and West both got actively involved in the European peace movement. Alarmed by the possibility of a nuclear confrontation between the two superpowers on European soil, they issued a joint appeal to stop the worldwide arms race and work toward global peace. In 1981 over one hundred authors from East and West, among them Christa Wolf, signed the document. The initiative was followed by a number of peace conferences that Wolf attended. In one of her speeches she rejected as absurd the argument that excessive nuclear armament by both superpowers creates a "balance of terror" and, consequently, mutual safety. The devastating effect of a constant nuclear threat exerts a terrible pressure on anyone's personal life, including her own. Wielding her pen in support of peace efforts, she warned against continued war preparations and demanded immediate peace negotiations. Asked about the role of literature in such, Wolf expressed doubt about its impact on the political process, but she cast fiction in a supporting role: "It is probably true that it cannot change anything. But the least it can do is articulate what so many people feel, support them in their fear, their depressions—and, of course, in their resistance, or else they would feel very alone. I think that it is important to articulate positions of resistance" (DII 922). An "aesthetic of resistance," however, against the logic of escalating nuclear arsenals has yet to be developed, Wolf said; it is unimaginable to compose a hymn on the beauty of nuclear missiles similar to panegyrics formerly used to extol ancient battle gear.

In *Cassandra* Wolf conceived a "position of resistance" against the destructive elements of power. Cassandra, the Trojan citizen who learns to break the "taboos"—finding and revealing shameful secrets—and to fight for the life of her country, personifies Wolf's notion of civil courage and reasoned opposition. She would no doubt applaud Wolf's urgent directive: "In order to avoid war, people in their respective country have to issue criticism of the defects in their own country. The role of taboos in preparations for war: the number of disgraceful secrets grows incessantly. How insignificant are all censorship taboos and the consequences of breaking them when life is threatened" (VEK 114).

In the history of external and internal forces leading to Troy's destruction, Wolf documents the emergence of such taboos and secrets, the typical patterns of a society's compulsive drive toward war. "We can tell when war begins, but when does prewar begin? In case there are any rules, one should pass them on. Etched in clay, in stone, they should be handed down. What would they say?

Among other things: do not be deceived by your own people" (K 78). Wolf articulates some of these "rules" in *Cassandra:* the furtive steps and overt preparations that lead to war with an external opponent and also the insidious internal mechanisms, the political and social controls, which, to use a phrase from *Patterns of Childhood,* "expose everyone's intestines" (K 25). During an extended time of distress such prewar repressions corrode the social fabric as well as the spiritual bond of any community.

In her attempt to extricate and refine the mythological framework and establish "social and historical coordinates" for her version of the Trojan War, Wolf converts the battle for recapturing a beautiful queen into a struggle for economic advantage—a reversal of the common notion that the Greeks were the sole culprit. The crucial issue becomes control of the Dardanelles, the shipping lanes to the Hellespont. While the Trojans can claim a traditional right to control access to the waters at their front door, the Greeks can boast military superiority. Wolf contrives the escalation of this underlying economic struggle with three ships, which King Priam and the Royal Palace, seat of Trojan power, send to Greece. Each fails to accomplish its true but covert mission. Priam's royal propaganda machine transforms, however, each failure into a success in the eyes of the gullible Trojan citizens, and, thus, the war fever accelerates.

The first expedition, called the First Ship, under the leadership of Lampos, is unable to negotiate a settlement with the Greeks. The Trojan public is made to believe that the ship was sent to consult the famous oracle of Delphi about Troy's security. The Delphic priest Panthous, a Greek, had fallen in love with Lampos and followed the Trojan expedition home. A willing defector, he is nevertheless exhibited with great fanfare as war booty to the cheering population. Thus, a miscarried enterprise seems successful, and the populace derive a false sense of national purpose and strength.

The Second Ship is sent to retrieve Priam's sister Hesione, supposedly held captive by a Greek king, Telamon. The argument that Telamon made her his queen falls on deaf ears, since the real point of the mission is to inflame the citizens' hate against the Greeks. This is arranged by forcing the popular prophet Calchas to make a favorable prediction about the Second Ship's objective. When King Telamon refuses to let his wife go and the mission has to be aborted, Calchas defects and remains in Greece. This is a reasonable act considering that unreliable prophets are traditionally put to death. The Royal Palace pronounces Calchas a hostage of the boastful enemy and whips up even more hatred for the Greeks.

The assignment of the Third Ship coincides largely with established mythology. Paris, Priam's prodigal son, pretending to attempt the recapture of his aunt Hesione to restore his father's honor, sets out to abduct Helen, the most beautiful woman in Greece and a prize promised him by the gods. He returns empty-handed because he lost Helen to the mighty king of Egypt. The Trojans are led to believe that Paris, failing to get Priam's sister, had instead apprehended Helen. They come to cheer the returning ship and a heavily veiled woman on Paris's arm. In the public's eye the king's humiliation is avenged and his honor restored. Of course, it follows that the Greeks will try to retrieve Helen and that war will ensue—ironically, not for beauty but for a phantom, a false proxy of beauty.

Cassandra pleads with her father to tell the population the truth about Helen, because a war waged for a phantom will surely be lost. "Why? The king asked earnestly . . . . We just need to make sure that the army does not lose faith in the phantom" (K 82). Cassandra seems to be the only one who recognizes the destructive force unleashed by the cynical invention of the motive for war: "It couldn't be, I thought, to base the entire war and our whole life—for wasn't the war our life?—on an accidental lie. . . . In the Helen we invented, we defended everything we no longer had, and the more it disappeared, the more real we had to proclaim it to be. So that a different Troy arose from the words, gestures, ceremonies, and silence, a ghostly city in which we were supposed to live and feel at home" (K 100).

The Trojan political powers knew that there was no chance of victory against the Greeks' military might. Had Troy been powerful, there would have been no need to negotiate for a right they already possessed. Nevertheless, King Priam emphatically rejected all propositions to prevent a confrontation with the Greeks, especially telling them the actual location of Helen or arbitrating a settlement: "The honor of the royal house is at stake," he proclaimed (K 83). He also was gullible or vain enough to believe his troops' assurances that they could win. To incite the proper fighting spirit, the Royal House manipulated the motives for war and designed inflammatory demonic images of the enemy. Under false pretenses and ill prepared, the citizens of Troy were led to die for a phantom and for the deceitful honor of their leaders. But Wolf did not exculpate the people of Troy. They colluded in shaping public perceptions "in order not to have to see the frightening reality behind the bright façade" (K 44).

The parallels to modern warfare and its official incantations are obvious: the use of military rather than diplomatic means to resolve conflict, escalating demands and an arms race, the exploitation of moral and psychological considerations such as national honor, fear of losing face, self-delusion, and the mindless willingness of the people to be deceived and to follow their leaders blindly.

While the Greeks besieged Troy and decimated the Trojan troops, the city was slowly destroyed by an internal enemy as well. The erosion of the social and moral substance of the community was engineered by an evil bureaucratic policeman named Eumelos. Initially a member of the "King's Party" and of Priam's council, Eumelos was appointed chief officer of the palace guard. "A competent man at the right place at the right time" (K 66), Eumelos quickly turned a mere ceremonial sentry into an omnipresent "security force" that terrorized the population. In the process he assumed a position of menacing power over the Royal Palace and eventually over the entire city.

Eumelos effectively polarized the citizens, dividing them into those who supported the power structure and those who did not. In order to defeat the Greeks, Eumelos tried to change the Trojans "to be like the enemy." So they were instructed to think like Greeks in antinomies, such as victory or defeat, life or death. They should only believe in what can "be seen, smelled, heard, or touched"; to "do what has to be done" quickly, thoroughly, and without moral scruples; and, most important, to "obey" authority (K 37). Eumelos insulated the royal house from possible dissent by screening every visitor, including the king's own children. Even Cassandra had to obtain permission to have an audience with her father. The queen, Priam's most competent right hand in matters of government and an opponent of Eumelos' machinations, was banished from the council. "Whoever is not on our side now is working against us" became the official motto (K 83). Many citizens were inducted into the service of the security forces, and suspect citizens were spied upon, among them the Greek priest Panthous. Even members and friends of the royal family became victims of Eumelos' terror tactics. In gaudy ornate uniforms his troops patrolled the streets of Troy. Covertly, they followed Cassandra on her excursions through town. When she objected to being "watched," her father, already under Eumelos' dominion, explained that her guard was merely a "protector" assigned to ensure her safety.

This linguistic finesse is one of the first signs of the ensuing inflammatory "language war" waged by Eumelos' propaganda machinery: the Greeks were already being called "enemies" even before they launched their ships. King Menelaus, as a guest of King Priam, is no longer a respected visitor in the old tradition of hospitality but an "informant" and "provocateur" and, therefore, caught in the vigilant "security net." Use of the word *war* is punished severely. Priam reprimands his own daughter for using it: "What do you mean, war? Such big words. I would say, we will be attacked, and I would say, we will defend ourselves" (K 82). *War* is replaced by euphemisms such as *surprise attack.* With every passing year and increasing casualties, traditional language as well as secular and religious rituals change to conceal a certain defeat. The memorial celebrations of dead heroes turn into festivities for living warriors. Priam's title of king is first replaced by "Our Mighty King" and then by "Our Almighty King." The purpose behind this inflation is persuasion by repetition: "In the end, one believes that which one says often enough" (K 77). Few realize the almost imperceptible change in the social and spiritual order of Troy, considered inviolable by most. But Cassandra is one of the few: "The new time respected neither the living nor the dead. It took a while before I understood it. It was already in the fortress before the enemy came. It penetrated every crack, I don't know how. We gave it the name Eumelos" (K 90).

The name Eumelos begins to stand for fear. "The Eumelos in me forbid that," says Cassandra (K 81), suppressing her urge to tell the Trojans that there is no Helen within the walls of Troy. The polarization of the population through distrust and its demoralization through suppression of truth aids the external enemy in the destruction of Troy. Eumelos, however, is indestructible; everything he stands for did not perish and never will. His spirit lives to this day: "He, to be sure, survived. And the Greeks would use him. Wherever we would happen to go, he would already be there. And he would surpass us" (K 158).

Western commentators frequently accused Wolf of having supported the corrupt authoritarian regime of the GDR, if not actively then through conspicuous and persistent silence. These critics either did not read or, more likely, ignored *Cassandra.* Through the metaphor of Troy Wolf clearly predicted the demise of the GDR under the system of the SED. Eumelos and his security force represent the GDR's Ministry of State Security (Stasi)—a realistic, candid depiction of Stasi activities. Except for pointing a direct finger at Stasi terror tactics, which would have been cause for immediate expulsion or incarceration, Wolf could not have been more explicit. But it would be a mistake to limit an interpretation of the character of Eumelos and his security force strictly to the GDR's pervasive system of civil control. Wolf is portraying the character of any internal authority that oppresses its citizens by means of deception and intimidation sowing fear and distrust among the population. Eumelos could also have been a perfect chief of the Nazi Gestapo and the Trojan War a precursor to World War II. *Cassandra* thus also demonstrates that humanity does not learn from history and repeats catastrophic mistakes again and again.

In the context of these external and internal Trojan conflicts Wolf develops the character of Cassandra, the voice of criticism and resistance, a model of self-realization and hard-won independence. Wolf characterized her as follows:

Cassandra, the oldest and favorite daughter of King Priam of Troy, a vivacious girl, interested in social and political matters, does not want to marry and be keeper of the house, like her mother Hecuba, like her sisters. She wants to learn something. For a woman of rank, the only feasible profession is that of priestess, seer. . . . This position, a privilege, is assigned to her: she is to fill it according to tradition. But she has to refuse it—at first, because she believes she can best serve her people, to whom she is closely connected and dedicated, in her own way; later, because she realizes that "her people" are not her people. A painful process of detachment, in the course of which she is first pronounced mad and then thrown in the dungeon by her beloved father Priam—for telling the truth. . . . In the end, she is alone, prey of her city's conquerors. (VEK 96)

Wolf tells this story in Cassandra's own (first-person) voice and frames it with a third-person narrator's brief description of the place in front of the palace at Mycenae where Cassandra reviewed her life a few hours before her death:

Here it was. There she stood. These stone lions, now without a head, looked at her. This fortress, once impregnable, a pile of stones now, was the last thing she saw. . . . Close by the giant stone walls, today as yesterday, directing the path: to the door—no blood seeping through from below. To darkness. To the slaughterhouse. And alone. With my story I am approaching my death. (K 5)

Thus, Wolf beautifully fashions the transition from the narrator's viewpoint in the present, "Here," to Cassandra's situation in the distant past, "There." With the last line—"With my story I am approaching my death"—Wolf establishes not only her identification with Cassandra but also their kinship to protagonists from other novels who struggled to achieve self-actualization, such as Günderrode, who utters essentially the same lament: "Giving birth to what kills me" (KO 97).

Captured by Agamemnon, Cassandra had been taken to Mycenae to die. While she waits in front of his palace door, Agamemnon is being murdered by his wife, Clytemnestra, and Cassandra reviews her own life from the time she became aware of her wish to predict the future to this moment at death's door—"so close to myself" (K 6). Occasionally, she interrupts her recollections to engage in a brief exchange with her maid and friend Marpessa, who responds to Cassandra's silent musings as if she had been addressed directly, a sign of their mutual understanding. Now and then Cassandra's consciousness merges so completely with the past as to blend it with the present, and she imagines she is in Troy rather than on enemy territory. Sometimes she becomes cognizant of reality, such as when Greeks approach her, the famous seer, to have their fate divined. Reminded of her dire situation, she feels fear, which she tries to dispel by thinking. All her life she had practiced controlling powerful feelings including love with her mind. This habit serves, and is skillfully represented by, Wolf's narrative scheme.

Interior monologue, silent reminiscence, is a technique that appears in most of Wolf's previous novels. For *Cassandra,* however, Wolf orchestrates a diction that captures both the ancient past and the present. To accomplish this she styles long passages of prose employing the metric rhythms of Greek epics. Unfortunately, the passages of pure hexameters and pentameters embedded throughout the novel suffer when translated into other languages. Considering that Wolf offers her version of Cassandra's story to contrast the male versions, it is ironic that she should use poetic devices of a tradition dominated by men such as Homer. At any rate Wolf's narrator insinuates startling modern counterpoints into the staid classical tone. These often appear as derogatory appendages to honored names such as Achilles "the beast" or Agamemnon "the dope" and as prosaic or colloquial expressions such as "dumb," "nothing to be sneezed at," "neither fish nor fowl," or "the topic itched so much, I was hot for every splinter of conversation" (K 40). The more Cassandra liberates herself from familial and social ties and achieves personal autonomy, the more she asserts her individual voice. Concomitantly, Wolf relaxes the measured formality of language and uses far more casual rhythms and speech. Character and diction are inseparable concerns throughout the story.

Wolf's prose can be alternately poetic or cryptic almost to the point of silence. When Cassandra recalls her first intimate encounter with Aeneas, a turning point in her life, she reaches the limits of speech: "We went into a distant corner of the temple and, without noticing it, crossed that threshold behind which speech ceases to be" (K 21). Often Wolf uses rich pithy syntactical fragments; usually, they contain a large complex of uncertainties that can no longer be resolved but need to be stated. When Cassandra recalls one of her first foreboding dreams, she says: "I can still see this dream-image through the many other, grimmer images superimposed by reality. I would like to know (what am I thinking: *would like? know? I?*—yet, the words are appropriate), I would like to know what kind of anxiety, not known to me, in the midst of peace, of happiness (this is how we talked!) caused such dreams" (K 22; emph. added).

Wolf's narrative style is not always transparent. The paratactic structure, at once classical and modern, clear and enigmatic, prosaic and poetic, requires constant explication. The recollective narration, which at times seems like the free association of ideas, ignores the chronology of Cassandra's life and, instead, vacillates among the descriptive, the immediately emotional, and the reflective modes. Cassandra's tale is often unexpectedly interrupted by brief reports about her present situation. Wolf once again requires the active participation of her readers, asking us to fix in our minds the sequence of events, to separate past from present, to assign dialogue to the proper speaker, to respond to layered poetic rhetoric—all without traditional narrative markers. Wolf would agree with Hugo von Hofmannsthal's and Samuel Coleridge's observation that, when we read the poem and use the full range of our imagination, the vision is so completely shared that we become the poet.

When Cassandra starts to recount her story, she has already freed herself from external constraints and achieved the highest degree of self-realization possible. Wolf calls it a "process of liberation, in which she has freed herself from *all* beliefs, including (first and foremost!) her own" (VEK 90). Furthermore, separated from her country and her past, relieved of all obligations (she has even handed her children over to Marpessa's care, never to see them again) and facing imminent death, Cassandra is able to contemplate her life from a position of utmost self-knowledge and insight. Her curiosity, she says, is totally free, even when directed toward herself. As a result, she can trace her development from the perspective and with the wisdom normally reserved for a third-person narrator. "At the end of her life," Wolf said, "she can pick her experience like a ripe fruit, which is why I do not consider her a failed person" (DII 915).

Although Wolf cannot see her protagonist as a tragic figure (VEK 89), Cassandra is caught in two tragic dilemmas: one, she has to choose between life with Aeneas and her independence and death at the hands of the Greeks; and, two, while having achieved individual autonomy and, concomitantly, the ability to articulate her journey, she is restricted to silence and cannot communicate her experiences to future generations. Briefly, she wishes that a witness could record her tale—the female version of the Trojan tragedy: "So that next to the stream of heroic epics this tiny rivulet could also reach, if laboriously, those distant, perhaps happier human beings who will live then" (K 96). But Cassandra cannot write, and no one is there to listen and preserve her insights. She has no Horatio who has witnessed all. Her wish is not fulfilled until three thousand years pass. Consequently, neither the lessons learned from war nor those from oppression can be transmitted to benefit future generations. Cassandra becomes a memorial for the tragedy that civilizations can destroy and can be destroyed without passing on the memory of the nature of destruction. The central tragedy of this novel, then, is the tragedy of obstructing or killing a *legacy*. Wolf writes from the knowledge that a civilization without its legacy has no soul.

Since Cassandra was not a man and could not hold formal positions of power, she wanted to be a priestess and prophet. Thanks to the collusion between royal and religious powers, Cassandra became priestess at the temple of Apollo. Panthous the Greek, her instructor in priestly matters, alleged that she chose this career to be able to influence people. In accordance with Trojan tradition she believed at first that she had been chosen by Apollo, the god of the seers, to receive the gift of prophecy (a gift later amended by the curse that no one would believe her). This belief seemed confirmed by Apollo's appearance to her in a dream. Both her wishes were now fulfilled: she had become a priestess and a prophet. Unfortunately, she had not yet understood that a priestess of Apollo would be required to adapt and conform to secular political demands at the expense of her inner calling. As a novice, she thought that to grow up meant "to lose oneself" in obeying a sacred tradition rather than in developing one's nature. Only later did she realize that she merely "played" the role of priestess and prophet. Consequently, she "saw" nothing; she was a blind seer.

Plagued by guilt and fear of failing, she but slowly realized that she was serving both secular and divine gods who dominated a *"verkehrte Welt,"* a world turned upside down, a wrong and bad world that she could not accept. The conflicts between her tendency to conform to the power structure and her longing for knowledge and independence, between actual circumstances and recognized truth, caused her "desperate self-estrangement," which culminated in frightening episodes of insanity. The first one happened when Cassandra finally faced the truth she had sensed all along: that the official explanation of the outcome of the Second Ship's mission was a ruse; that the seer Calchas, who willingly defected to the Greeks, was a victim of political intrigue. The outbreak of Cassandra's second episode of insanity occurs when her body recognizes the truth about the Third Ship's stratagem even before her mind registers the facts. Ostensibly to recapture Hesione, the ship actually sailed off to abduct Helen. "I alone saw it. Or did I 'see?' How was that exactly? I felt. Experienced—yes, that is the word; because it was, it is an experience when I 'see,' 'saw '"(K 70). Following her instincts, Cassandra issued a passionate foreboding and warned not to let the ship sail. Had her warning been heeded, a civilization might not have been destroyed. Wolf is earnest in showing how the search for truth is not an abstract bloodless business.

Although there are indications that Cassandra masterminded her episodes of insanity, she insists that she "could not stop making them" (K 71). But after each recurrence she emerged a more enlightened person and a more capable seer. "You changed," her lover Aeneas observed (K 78). In the last episode Cassandra received a helping hand from Arisbe, mother of her favorite brother, Aisakos, and female counterpart to Anchises. A wise old Trojan renegade, Arisbe told Cassandra to quit feeling sorry for herself, come out of it, open her inner eye, and look at herself. This initiates Cassandra's slow but steady liberation from the secular and divine authorities, symbolized by the Royal Palace and temple, and the beginning of her journey to self-realization. She found that she did not want to be a prophet to gain power any longer but rather: "To speak with my own voice. The ultimate. I wanted no more, nothing else" (K 6).

Achievement of autonomy within an authoritarian culture was an arduous process for Cassandra. It required the painful recognition that she had been "a prisoner" and that she had allowed others to take control of her. "Why did you let them become powerful?" asked Arisbe, betraying her sympathy, when Cassandra complained about her dependence (K 74). To effect change Cassandra had to shed misconceptions and comforting but false emotions, especially her love for her father. She finally did cast Priam off "like a stranger" when he became like Eumelos and gave her sister Poluxena to "the beast" Achilles in a crude political deal.

But, paramount on her journey to emancipation, Cassandra had to acquire knowledge about the world and about herself. "I needed much time. My position of privilege was an obstacle between me and the most necessary insights," Cassandra admits (K 64), but "the strange creature that wanted to know had already permeated me so deeply, I couldn't get rid of it" (K 58). So she began to pursue consciously and deliberately what had always interested her: the affairs of Troy. As a child on her father's knee, she had eagerly learned about politics and the economy. On her strolls through the palace grounds she had listened to the conversations of the slaves. Now she gathered information in the streets of Troy—from trusted friends, from people of all classes including her nurse; her maid, Marpessa; Arisbe; Aeneas' father, Anchises ("a free man"); and the women who had sought refuge from the war in mountain caves and established a communal antitoxin to the male-dominated city of Troy. But she also collected information about the enemy, the Greeks, and in retrospect she wonders what compelled her to learn about them, since she had "to keep the shock: they are like us!" to herself (K 16). Finally, Cassandra discovered that the ability to predict the future is no divine gift but, rather, a function of knowledge and experience: "Whoever lives shall see," she observed when she finally acquired the skill of seeing "what is not" (K 42).

Cassandra teaches that clairvoyance, although hard to earn, is accessible to anyone. Yet most people are partly or wholly blind. They are like the Greeks asking Cassandra to forecast their fate: "Everything they need to know will unfold in front of their eyes, but they will not see a thing. That's the way it goes," she charges (K 11). She reflects on the hazards of her profession: if the prediction does not coincide with expectation, the seer will not be believed, will be called "insane," or will be killed. As Cassandra says: "It is the same old story: not the crime but its revelation makes people pale, even mad, I have experienced it myself. And we prefer to punish the one who proclaims the deed rather than the one who commits it" (K 18).

In her famous speech delivered at the Büchner Prize award ceremony in 1980, Wolf likened growing up to "seeing." Her observations about this process apply to Cassandra's maturation: "In the concrete circumstances in which we live and write, grow up—which also means: become seeing—get involved, fail, rebel, and crave new experiences: in these concrete circumstances, innocence devoid of responsibility was not planned in. Today and here! is the slogan, and while we proceed, the masks are torn from our faces" (DII 611). One could argue that, in the throngs of her last bout with insanity, Cassandra sheds her "innocence," assumes responsibility, and sets out to grow up and earn her office of seer. Less and less encumbered by prejudice and wishful thinking, unaffected by political pressures, she learns to see the realities around her and to conjecture accurately the path of the future. Inevitably, the imposter is revealed, and Cassandra discovers her true self: "Rather late and with effort did I learn to distinguish the properties one knows about oneself from those that are inborn and almost unrecognizable. . . . But the good fortune to become myself and thus more useful to others—I was able to experience it" (K 15). Individuation has enabled her to serve her society by raising her voice in the service of truth and in opposition to the destructive forces within, climaxing in the word *no*, the ultimate syllable of resistance.

Although Cassandra loves Aeneas more than her life, at the bitter end she cannot follow him to safety and be his because she cannot give up her autonomy. She has no opportunity to explain to Aeneas why she prefers capture by the Greeks and certain death to him. "Perhaps he will understand without me what I had to reject even at the price of death: the subjugation under a role which ran against my grain" (K 111). Quite literally at death's door, Cassandra tries to preserve her new hard-won consciousness. She wants to be a witness and "seer" to the very end, although nobody survives who would need her testimony. Being conscious is being alive, and being alive means "not to evade the most difficult thing: changing the image of oneself" (K 26), or "having to bring forth what will destroy us" (K 771). These powerful sentiments parallel Günderrode's voice: "Giving birth to what kills me" (KO 97).

Cassandra's unending process of becoming herself, of revealing a profoundly personal and traumatic teleology, is fundamental to all of Wolf's mature work. It explains the novelist's eager assimilation of the mythological Cassandra and the modern relevance of her ancient heroine. Cassandra shares "the pain of individuation" with all other protagonists in Wolf's work. One could easily imagine Nelly from *Patterns of Childhood,* who at the end of the novel was ready to embark on the journey of self-realization, following Cassandra's footsteps.

The Cassandra project was immediately appropriated by feminists as a poignant statement of female emancipation from patriarchal oppression and a manifesto for an alternate feminist way of life. Such an interpretation appears to be supported by numerous programmatic declarations in Wolf's lectures on the situation of women throughout history and by fictional presentations of women's lives in the novel. Wolf's fourth Cassandra lecture deals exclusively with these concerns. Here she expresses her belief that women write differently from men because they experience reality differently and also express their experiences differently. Such differences are partly rooted in biology, partly in history; they are circumstanced by the fact that women have been subjugated for thousands of years and that they were "second degree objects, often enough objects of men who were objects themselves." Wolf laments the abuse of women at the hands "of those one loves the most. Not to be allowed to be I nor you, but 'it': object of alien purposes" (VEK 114–15). And she celebrates female writers who exposed the injustices done to women.

A sharp critic of men's collective conduct, Wolf designed for *Cassandra* generally negative male characters (with significant exceptions). Achilles, "the beast," abuses women violently and kills for pleasure. Wolf attributes his perversions to sexual insecurities. Agamemnon, "the dope," is weak and superstitious to the degree of killing his daughter in order to appease the gods. His military aggressiveness is attributed to sexual impotence. Even the "good" King Priam, in the face of war, succumbs to the corrupt practices of Eumelos, trades his daughter Poluxena to the bestial Achilles for political gain. Priam gives his other daughter, Cassandra, to Euryplos in exchange for a military alliance. Eumelos engineers the moral bankruptcy of the Royal Palace and the corruption of unsuspecting citizens. The four men are or become completely unable to love.

Wolf subjected "male thinking," a frequent theme in her essays from the 1980s, to rigorous examination in the *Prerequisites for a Story: Cassandra*. Dominated by rationalism, the male spirit "counts and measures and evaluates and awards and punishes according to merit" (VEK 129). Characterized by strict dualism, analysis, objectivity, specificity, pragmatism, and order, the male universe excludes things emotional, fragmentary, undefined, sensual, subjective, spiritual. Male thinking "does not want to love but rather understand mother nature in order to dominate her and erect the amazing structure of a world of the mind, estranged from nature, from which women are excluded from now on; women who must be feared, no less, perhaps because they, *too* . . . are the cause of this fear of conscience which knocks awake man's heart" (VEK 75–76). Wolf speculates that, had women participated as equals in the collective thinking process over the last two thousand years, the process itself would be quite different today, because women would have complemented male aesthetics with a necessarily different perspective. Ironically, Wolf admits to possessing herself a mind-set characteristic of men and exemplified by the Greeks in *Cassandra:* she admits "to thinking in antinomies" (VEK 73). Perhaps the Greeks' mode of thinking is not exclusively male, after all.

Wolf's numerous passionate charges against the relentless oppression of women and their exclusion from vital social and cultural processes and her distillation of these practices in the story of Cassandra's life seem to corroborate the feminist perspective in Wolf's work: "Supposition: in Cassandra, one of the first female figures has been handed down to us whose fate prefigures what shall subsequently, for three thousand years, happen to women: that they are made objects" (VEK 86). That women have not been able to contribute substantially to our civilization for thousands of years is not only shameful, Wolf says, but, more important, the absence of equal female participation in the shaping of our collective destiny is the weak link in our culture and the very reason why it is unable to mature.

The female community Wolf created in the novel *Cassandra* as a refuge from the war-torn city of Troy has been hailed as an alternative to patriarchal systems. Presumably, it is a model to be adopted if we are to survive as a species. In the caves of the mountains outside Troy women of all classes, including the Greeks, gathered to establish a community of harmony and bliss. They shared their dreams, learned from one another, made and decorated pots, wove cloth, danced and touched, picked fruit, tended to warriors "wounded in body or soul by the war," worshiped the goddess Cybele, and, unable to write, preserved their experiences in pictures for the generations to come. As a group, they formed a protective and supportive entity, a "we," as Cassandra realized with amazement. As individuals, they were in pursuit of self-realization: "Since our time was limited, we could not waste it on insignificant matters. Therefore we proceeded, playfully, as if we had all the time in the world, toward the main thing: ourselves" (K 154).

It is a fundamental mistake, however, to believe that Wolf intended this as a utopia or feminist paradigm to be emulated. Rather, it is the female antidote to the toxic situation in Troy, "a dream," as Cassandra says, from which she wakes up one morning to find the world "desolate." In the fourth lecture Wolf alludes to this kind of social idyll, rejecting it as unacceptable for our time: "'Back to nature,' thus, or back to early civilizations, which some consider to be the same? Dear A., we cannot possibly want that" (VEK 145). Cassandra herself says that the women of the caves did not see themselves as a "model," although they felt that they were "trying something." They were just grateful to be able "to advance a small sliver of future into the dark present, which occupies all time" (K 156). The women, by responding to their nature rather than to social expectations or male demands, experimented with an alternate form of culture which could possibly improve life in the future but not displace known social systems. Arisbe, a dominating figure among the women, was quietly critical of some practices; she objected to the worship of goddesses as a substitute for "what we do not dare recognize in ourselves" (K 144). Cassandra describes moving from the world of the palace to the caves as a move from "tragedy to the *burlesque,* whose essence is that one does not see oneself as a tragic figure. Important— yes, and why not. But not tragic" (K 64–65; emph. added). In her lectures Wolf stated categorically that "women who retreat to their femaleness as a virtue act essentially as they had been trained to do: they react with a grandiose evasive maneuver to the challenges reality issues to their whole person" (VEK 116)— a trenchant dismissal of the homogeneous culture of the caves.

One problem with a strict feminist reading of *Cassandra* is that its most positive character is a male, Anchises, who in fact appears to be the focus and teacher of this cave community. Tolerant, wise, friendly, even cheerful, Anchises is the only "free human being" in the novel, embodying ideal humanity. He instructs the female novices to the caves "how to dream with both feet planted on the ground" (K 156), a significant statement substantiating the ephemeral nature of the community. And it is also a male, his son Aeneas, who points the way to proper gender identification. After Cassandra has spent months of brutal imprisonment for insurrection, a penalty issued by her father, Aeneas carries Cassandra in his arms to the women. "You had to be carried to us, they later alleged, teasingly. Otherwise you would not have come" (K 142). Ironically, both Aeneas and Anchises survive the war in body and soul. The women do not. Both males personify what is otherwise separated into male and female—mind and soul; they are integrated human beings.

Although sympathetic toward the fate of women and adamant about their inclusion in all areas of public life, Christa Wolf has not defined herself as a feminist. In fact, she is surprisingly critical of many feminist attempts to cope with oppression or to rectify social issues primarily affecting women. In her fiction and lectures Wolf remains as dubious of the way women pursue liberation as she is resentful of their lack of resistance. Wolf rejects both the attitude of passive suffering and the militant posture often associated with feminism. In that sense most of the female characters in *Cassandra,* with the notable exceptions of the protagonist and Arisbe, are negatively conceived, although they are presented empathetically. Either they suffer passively or actively pursue abusive sexual relationships, as do Cassandra's sister Poluxena and Paris's lover, Oenone, or they withdraw into silent resignation, as does Cassandra's mother, Hecuba, after Eumelos takes control of political life in Troy. Wolf is particularly critical of women who behave like men, who choose to act out aggression and try to seize power. Cassandra predicts that Clytemnestra, to whom she feels a sisterly affinity, will, after assuming the throne, eventually be "struck by the kind of blindness associated with power" (K 50) and bring about the demise of Mycenae. Her gender does not make her immune to the seductions of authority. Penthesilea, accompanied by female warriors whom she controls "like a king," battles not only the Greeks but all men. She prefers to die fighting than to live enslaved by men. She argues that the male world has turned with increasing cruelty and speed against women and must be defeated. Anchises, tolerant even of this militant woman, remarks that the world has turned not only against women but against all people—the echo of Wolf's own voice. Penthesilea acknowledges that she does, ironically, what men do, if only to show that she is different. For her killing is not a pleasure, as it presumably is for men, but a necessity to rid the world of evil.

Wolf rejects both destructive strategies and withdrawal into segregated enclaves to gain freedom from oppression. It does not bring us closer to cultural maturity, she argues, "when male delusion is replaced by female delusion and when women, as proponents of a pre-rational phase in human development, throw overboard the achievements of rational thinking only because they were originated by males" (VEK 115). Instead, Wolf proposes that both men and women work on their respective emancipations. For women that means *not* imitating men, because doing so would embrace masculine shortcomings as well. For men she envisions a "gentle revolution enabling men to derive security from gentle feelings" (ID 152). The goal of emancipation should not be equality but, rather, development of one's nature, personal maturation, self-realization, individual autonomy—for Wolf all synonyms of becoming a human being. Autonomous persons and, by extension, autonomous states do not have to make war like those "whose inner insecurities and immaturity constantly demand demarcations and postures of strength" (VEK 115). They can work together peacefully and, by using all their gender-specific resources and individual strengths, find solutions for conflicts and construct an authentic comity. In the figure of Cassandra, Wolf presented a model for gaining autonomy, the prerequisite for peace among people, regardless of sex, nationality, and persuasion.

CHAPTER TEN

"Idyll and Catastrophe"

Sommerstück

The Biermann affair in 1976 affected Wolf's life deeply. Not only did she finally realize the extent to which the regime had veered away from the ideals of socialism, but she also found her political commitment unwanted. Furthermore, she suffered from the continuous surveillance by the Stasi, and, being barred from the media, she was prevented from expressing herself effectively in public. Wolf experienced bitterly the relevance of the observation by the philosopher Friedrich Hegel (1770–1831): "An unhappy consciousness corresponds to a reality broken in two."

Wolf even considered leaving the GDR. To sift through the painful emotions of stalemate and official suppression, she went into inner exile and often retreated to her summer home in Mecklenburg—"to the rehabilitation clinic of nature's peace" (T 39). Her first country home, a farmhouse near the village of Meteln, had burned down in 1983. The second one, an old rectory, is located in the small village of Woserin. Many colleagues and friends feeling equally ostracized escaped to sanctuaries like these to "preserve their integrity" and "think themselves free": "We were looking for a place like this; we experienced Berlin of the seventies and eighties as increasingly taxing and destructive; the demands on us, which many people made with our consent, were more and more difficult to combine with our work; and we harbored the illusion that the powers of the state would observe us less closely in the country. We were looking for free space" (T 214). Wolf found not only solace in the seclusion of country life but also a sense of security. Moreover, she discovered the many pleasures grandchildren bring, and she relished their frequent visits. The two novels *Störfall, 1986 (Accident)* and *Sommerstück, 1987*, both featuring the peace and beauty of life in the countryside, also depict a grandmother's interest and pride in the development of her grandchildren, giving Wolf's protagonist a new perspective into the future. But, as always with Wolf, tranquillity contains undercurrents of pain and danger.

In *Prerequisites for a Story: Cassandra*, when making the transition to her chapter on women's writing, Wolf wonders if one could not create a new language to counteract "today's necrophilia which manifests itself in steel, glass, and concrete" (VEK 124). This new language "would have to be subversive, carefree, 'impressive' in the literal sense of the word, it could not ask whether it reached its goal—indeed, it should not even have a 'goal.' . . . It would not deliver stories about heroes or anti-heroes. It would be rather inconspicuous and would seek to name the inconspicuous, the precious daily life, concretely" (VEK 124–25). *Accident* and *Sommerstück,* published but not written in this order, would employ just such a language. While writing *No Place on Earth,* Wolf also started working on *Sommerstück,* completing an early draft in 1983. She halted work on it in 1986 to write *Accident.* The final version of *Sommerstück* was submitted for publication in 1987.

Sommerstück can mean several things in German: *Stück* means a piece, a portion or fragment, of a larger entity. It also refers to a drama or play, connoting the improvised drama staged by the protagonists at a summer party where the guests are asked to play themselves. The tone of this two-hundred-page novel is wrought with much sophistication. Wolf presents her audience with a pastoral tale of a magical summer in a village in northern Germany. The lyrical virtuosity of the prose causes the narrator to wonder: "But where will this lead? Can beauty be described? A devastating question. What hope remains for a time marked by scorn for beauty; when a strange kind of courage is necessary to declare—repeatedly—that a certain group of oaks is beautiful" (S 10). In the opening the narrator admits that it was not easy finding the "sober tone appropriate to the rare occasions to which life exposes us" (S 7). "The rare occasions" with which *Sommerstück* is concerned are not extraordinary events but, rather, the small details "into which life crawls." They are simple vignettes of everyday life and the short-lived fellowship of a dozen people, family members, friends, and acquaintances from the city, who are spending a summer in the country. There are no heroes, no antiheroes, no outstanding characters. There is no plot, no continuous tale, no discernible sequence—only an extraordinary consciousness of the passing of life represented in prose suffused with sharp, often brutal observations of the human condition.

The narrator, a member of the group, arranges these vignettes into a delicate impressionistic portrait. She functions as a landscape painter lovingly obsessed with all particulars of "this strange summer," which the papers would call the summer of the century for its relentless heat: the picturesque village surrounded by green pastures, grain fields, and forests which the villagers nicknamed "the tomcat" because of its shape when seen from atop of one of the hills; the thatched-roof farmhouses so susceptible to fires and surrounded by colorful flower gardens and shade trees. She records the minute details of the purchase and restoration of old farmhouses; of frequent gatherings of friends on warm summer nights; of cooking crabs, cooling bottles of wine, tending to a litter of kittens, playing with children, weeding gardens; of excursions into the countryside, visits with the villagers, and renditions of their tales; of the dreams and fleeting private thoughts of the characters. No thing is too inconspicuous or banal to be described in precise detail, and no conversation is too trite not to be recorded at length. *Sommerstück* is a paean to the quotidian.

It is the unspoken purpose of the protagonists' sojourn in the country that they claim or affirm the self just as nature around them does: "We were to be as completely ourselves" (S 8). The story records the process of each discrete self slowly emerging from daily minutia. To this end Wolf employs a new narrative technique not previously found in her novels: the narrator's third-person depiction of the internal dynamics of each character is amplified by the observations of other people, and even the characters themselves are given a voice in their portrayal. Yet Wolf does not make it easy for the reader to assemble a coherent composite picture of each individual, whose appearances are quite random. We also do not learn more about them than is typically revealed in normal interaction between well-established friends. No expositions, no flashbacks or other narrative devices, help to provide a context for each character's story or situation. Thus, we know little or nothing that antedates, little about their professions, families, educational background. We do learn much, however, about their interior lives, especially those of the females, who are generally described in more detail than the males.

Not surprisingly, this wispy summer idyll is suspended over an abyss alluded to in the opening paragraph: "Now that Luisa has departed, Bella has left us forever, Steffi is dead, the houses are destroyed, memory is reigning over life once again" (S 7). Along with all its beauty the summer also unfolds the menace that is communal as well as individual. The village struggles with the intense summer heat and the resulting fires, one of which threatens the house of Ellen and Jan, the most prominent couple in the story. Later their house does burn down, as did Wolf's first summer house in 1983. The villagers' lives endure under much misfortune: a farmer's inability to maintain his farm under the socialist precepts of cooperative management, a mentally ill child, an alcoholic wife, the ramifications of World War II on one lonely woman's life, the new generation's disrespect for family and country traditions. In the words of the narrator, "the problems of the world can nowadays be found in every village" (S 61).

Following the call back to nature, which rings from as far back as the Enlightenment, the group comes to the village to recuperate from the stress of modern life in the city. But, unlike the eighteenth-century worshipers of nature's healing power, they don't find the country to be an antidote to city life, nor is nature a healing agent for corrosive urban pressures. Rather, they discover a "distant, alien land" described in vocabulary of warfare: the countryside, which the people had intended to "penetrate," seemed instead to "occupy" them—and it was not clear who "conquered" whom. Nature presented "a challenge," and the landscape "seized" the group. Everything associated with life in the country is unfamiliar and surprising to people conditioned by the environment of the city:

> The weather which we had ceased to take seriously and on which we now depended. The seasons, almost forgotten, which surprised us. The incredulous amazement when blossoms opened whose seeds we had planted in the soil ourselves. What we had searched for instinctively, when the false alternatives had driven us into a corner, does that exist after all—a third thing? Between black and white, right and wrong, friend and foe—simply life? (S 73)

Time itself registers differently in the country—"the time passing now could be felt" (S 187)—and the city people, used to frenetic schedules, resist its steady pace because of a deep fear that they may miss something terribly important. Their sleep is disturbed by nocturnal noises, and their daily activities are directed by the rhythms of nature. They count attentively the cuckoo's persistent calls, yielding to the superstition that the number of calls indicates the number of years one is destined to live. For the younger members of the group the retreat from the city to the country turns out to be "a new illusion"; for others, people of Wolf's age, it is presumably an escape from disappointment and capitulation. Revolutionaries in their youth, opines the adult daughter about her parents' generation, they flee to the country to seek shelter from their later disillusionment. In essence everyone simply moves their personal burdens and conflicts from city to country. Relief and this "third thing," "simply life," are at best temporary. In retrospect the narrator longs for these precious moments of the past: "Today, we seem to know no stronger, more painful longing than to keep alive in us the days and nights of that summer" (S 8).

With surgical precision the narrator scrutinizes the shared as well as the individual conflicts and pains. The eagerness for friendship, which causes everyone to find trivial excuses to come together, is based on the apprehension that a "loneliness would come against which we wanted to stock an inventory of togetherness" (S 10). Thus, the summer retreat not only alleviates troubles rooted in the past but also builds a reservoir for the future. Each person has a particular hidden affliction, an internal pain that is revealed only to the extent that the friends are able to discern it or that the character's self is willing to confront it.

141

Not surprisingly, the women are more introspective than their husbands. We readily recognize their problems because Wolf developed them more explicitly and exhaustively in protagonists of previous novels: dependence on others for their self-image and respect, the halting attempts to break dependencies, inability to express significant insights, emotional deficiencies such as lack of love causing interpersonal difficulties. In characterizing various personal problems, Wolf occasionally lapses into popular psychology. Her analyses are often fanciful and heavy-handed, and they unquestionably detract from the "sober tone" that works so well in the descriptions of landscape. *Sommerstück* is perhaps unique in Wolf's canon for failing to satisfy the psychological demands raised by her subject.

Irene has a dysfunctional relationship with her mother, who was apparently without a husband and had wanted to have a boy. The symptoms surface most perversely in Irene's marriage to Clemens, by her own judgment a kind and compassionate man. She demands that she be the only source of his happiness—not the cuckoo nor the old farmhouse nor the gatherings of friends which he so enjoys. Since she cannot make him love her in the exclusive manner she thinks he should, Irene tries desperately to generate a substitute motive, a "Cinderella-sister of love": his pity. To this end she inflicts painful wounds upon her hands by picking poisonous weeds. And, to relieve her inner torture, she torments him with relentless questions and unexpected bursts of tears, disrupting what he desires most: peace and quiet. Irene admits that she will drive Clemens crazy, destroy him, if she cannot make him love her in the manner she requires.

Aware that her weaknesses form the bond between her and Clemens, Irene expects the same in all other relationships. She therefore tries to discern the "two weak spots that happen to fit together" in Luisa and Antonis (S 53). She will use her knowledge against them to combat her terrifying feeling of *Nichtvorhandensein* (not existing in the awareness of others), to feel less insignificant. Irene cannot accept a person's strength as anything other than a mask for a shortcoming, the *Schmerzpunkt* (point of pain) which she is compelled to detect so that she can turn it against him or her.

Luisa is an unrealized artist, much like Christa T., who seeks the lascivious eyes of men while hiding behind a crafted mask of cosmetics and stylish clothes. She does not allow herself the feeling of sadness about identifying with this strange person she creates with lipstick and mascara rather than with the unfulfilled person behind the disguise, the authentic self. Nonetheless, Luisa tries to make sure "that mask and costume do not grow anywhere into the flesh of her warm, hungry, unprotected body" (S 35) and that no one will discover her painful secret. The divided nature of her personality manifests itself in different ways. She enjoys the beauty and goodness she spontaneously finds everywhere. But at the same time she recoils with an empathetic fear of the evil, often visualized with great intensity, which she imagines will strike others. She is always plagued by guilt feelings and cannot even express her personal thoughts with impunity—the fanciful wish, for instance, that she could be two people: one residing here in the village with the little boy, Jonas, and his mother, Bella, whom she both nourishes and overwhelms with her love; and the other traveling with her husband, Antonis, who is on the way to his native country Greece: "She could not wish, that was her fault. Every wish arising in her was bound to change into guilt before she could articulate it" (S 115). Luisa senses the cruel law of art which requires "that it is fed with parts of oneself." Consequently, she is unable to realize her talent in a completed piece of art, "but she also could not keep from making the effort to want it, to do it; she would have to live with this contradiction, and thus with the constant awareness of her shortcoming" (S 85). Her husband, Antonis, shrewd manipulator of real estate and collector of old furniture, is consumed by homesickness for Greece. We must assume from the opening lines that he does not return from the trip to his home village, which he undertakes as soon as he has received the long-awaited exit visa and is able to travel.

Luisa's friend Bella, hardened and tortured by disappointments, unable to relax, play, and enjoy summer pleasures, can only express her anger over an unhappy love affair, an unhappy life, in letters that she either burns or tears into thousands of little pieces. As mother, too, she is tragically impotent. Her little son, Jonas, frustrated by lack of attention and understanding, is addicted to playing war games, which he often translates into real life to make himself known. Luisa assumes parental duties with Jonas so that Bella can write. But Bella's pain, which is focused on her "pretense of love," as she herself admits, paralyzes her. Yet, as Luisa observes with envy: "Even her misfortune was as it should be, and it would never have occurred to her to blame herself. She was lucky even in her misfortune" (S 147–48). The story provides several inconclusive indications that Bella eventually committed suicide.

Ellen is the most carefully crafted character—a veiled portrait of Christa Wolf. She is a writer who has developed an aversion to the written word: "Apparently, the gods have placed before self-reproach a mute zone—silence," she complains (S 36). It is essentially, although not exclusively, through Ellen's critical eyes that we see the various group members. With her ability "to see everything, from the outside, physically, and, at the same time, be touched by its meaning" (S 164), and with her "compulsion to pass judgment over everything" (S 64–65), she seems eminently qualified to describe her friends and herself. In the city Ellen had felt as if she were in a "net" or "trap," metaphors for something even worse, she fears. She had become dependent in the city but cannot explain upon what or even the circumstances. But Ellen knows that, as a result, she had lost the "ferment" necessary for writing: self-confidence. To prevent her creative well from drying up, she sought refuge in the country with her husband, Jan. In the "fullness" of country life Ellen is hoping to regain if not "naiveté" then at least the "joy of discovery" and to find the words again to describe it. So she and her husband restore a farmhouse "in which they didn't belong," wear skirts and shirts made from rustic material "which they had no right to wear" (S 187), and play hosts to their two grown daughters, their grand-child, Littelmary, and their friends—activities that keep Ellen from doing the writing she had come to do.

In typical Wolf fashion Ellen contemplates the nature of writing. Like many poets before her, but in much the same vein as Hugo von Hofmannsthal's "Let-ter of Lord Chandos," Ellen laments the inadequacy and the perils of language. All words seem inadequate, especially in the face of the fatal illness with which her friend and colleague Steffi is struggling: "How tight the connection be-tween words can become, forming word chains which wrap around us many times and in many ways, an unbreakable band, a word entanglement which gradually replaces the real circumstances instead of simply describing them. Are we obligated, indeed, are we empowered to continue to work on that?" (S 41). Ellen is also prone to complain about the shortcomings of human percep-tion and action, especially her own. "Hundreds of times she herself had said that she felt sharply how incomplete everyone's life is, how it lacked the expe-riences everyone else has" (S 67). But she does not see a solution to this di-lemma, lest she entertain the fate of poets before her who escaped the *Dauerreibung* (constant friction) by escaping life—a not-so-veiled reference to the Romantic poets who sought refuge in suicide or insanity.

Reflecting on a friend's furious accusation of all artists' "damned arro-gance" and their ignorance of life, Ellen articulates at the same time the reasons for her creative impasse:

He is right and he is wrong, Ellen thought. . . . No notion of what life is, maybe. Or too much notion of the kind of life which countless normal lives have been denied and towards which poetry has to continue to navigate, regardless of the insanity by which the person feels threatened, whose vari-ous components are torn asunder tearing toward different goals. And what if she sat here, hidden in this farmhouse, because she did not want to pay the price, not for the one direction, but also not entirely for the other one? Well, one way or another, it would be revealed. If only the unrest would remain. (S 66–67)

This internal monologue contains an explicit, succinct description of Wolf's own history as a writer: her professional castigation by the official critics, her disapproval of the direction society was taking, her view of literature's responsibility to describe the human condition and of the writer's personal risks before an authoritarian bureaucracy, the dilemma of having to satisfy both a political agenda and a contradictory inner calling, and the source of her creative drive—a goading restlessness and unwillingness to acquiesce to the status quo.

There are several incidents that contribute to the eventual restoration of Ellen's creative drive. They address the psychological baggage she has brought from the city: pent-up anger and unexplained fears. During an outing to a nearby city Ellen has an opportunity to vent her wrath, the cause of which her husband, Jan, recognizes but does not reveal. All we know is that it is not the pesky "little man in the loden coat" who screams at Jan for not parking in what he considers a proper manner. This man triggers a deep-seated emotion in Ellen. Recently, she had noticed that "righteous little men had taken on historic proportions," and she determined to resist their petty tyrannies and reproachful profanities. In the spirit of her resolve Ellen steps up to the pesky man and, in a barely controlled tone of voice, tells him politely to shut his mouth or something bad would happen. "No more accommodation. No more not-stepping-on-anyone's-toes. *Ersatz*-satisfaction" (S 78). Ellen laughs with relief when the man retreats in quiet fury. One is tempted to compare this incident with Wolf's own anger over the self-serving control of her country's bureaucracy, of which she had been a victim many times. Of course, it is infinitely easier to confront a stranger on the street than a bureaucrat enforcing the policies of a political authority, such as the officials of the Ministry of Culture who screen manuscripts.

Another important although traumatic event in Ellen's summer sojourn is a brushfire that threatens her house. On the way to report the fire Ellen imagines the house catching fire and burning to the ground: "Ellen was without feeling. Within her the house burned undescribably hot. It was the pre-heat which, when the house really burned, would not occur again with the same intensity. The real pictures and circumstances paled behind the image of the burning house" (S 196). No doubt Ellen's reaction to this summer's fiery threat is based on Wolf's own battle with the flames when her summer house burned.

Ellen's friend and colleague Steffi comes to visit, accompanied by her son and husband, a concentration camp survivor. Steffi is "not in the same sense lost" as everyone else; she is lost because of terminal cancer. These summer weeks are her last reprieve. Ironically, Steffi is one of the few women in the novel whose attitude toward life seems healthy and strong. In spite of her advanced disease, Steffi has hope: "I live as long as I believe in change," she states bravely, adding, however: "Who knows how I will respond later when my life is really at stake?" (S 40). She continues working on a book, taking photographs, and pursuing daily life as if it would never end. Her death, indicated in the opening of the novel, contradicts the doctor's vapid proclamation that hope and life are the same.

The last chapter consists of a long conversation between Steffi and the narrator. Reading more like an appendix to the summer tale, it is a strange mixture of a letter to the dead Steffi, into which Steffi's voice is unexpectedly inserted, and an imagined discussion about life and death between the two women. At the very end of the novel it becomes clear that the narrator actually recorded a real conversation with Steffi which took place on top of the steps in Ellen's house. Although nowhere explicitly stated, there are several indications in this chapter suggesting that the narrator, the character Ellen, and Wolf herself are all the same. In the final chapter, when Steffi encourages her conversation partner to write about the summer, the narrator responds without thinking: "For that to happen, the house must have burnt down" (S 214), intimating not only Ellen's near catastrophe but also Wolf's loss of her summer home. At the end Steffi inquires whether the narrator's retreat to the country's peaceful and beautiful solitude was an "escape." This is a closing reference to Ellen's stated reason for coming to the village and to the narrator's scruples about writing of beauty, expressed in the opening of the novel. The narrator's response is telling: "You must be crazy. Does it look like that to you?" (S 215). "No longer," is Steffi's answer. This exchange clearly indicates that the "restlessness," which Ellen had hoped would remain, is at work again and that Ellen has conquered the "mute zone" of silence. It is significant that Ellen's revival occurs in the company and valued conversation of her brave friend Steffi, whose lease on life is short. Steffi is aware of her impact on Ellen's creative energies; she knows that Ellen will now resume her writing: "I am glad I was here" are her last words (S 216).

Sommerstück is dedicated to "All friends of that summer." Like so many of Wolf's other works, this novel articulates a rationale for its narrative structure and simultaneously preempts any arguments that the friends, who serve as cast of the piece, may summon to protest their portrayal. The language captures the "inconspicuous, precious daily life" in minute detail. Addressing both her friends and the readers, the narrator concedes:

> Details, details. But how other than with the help of these details can we bear witness to the fact that what we long for is present within us as a possibility? As a very fleeting, evanescent possibility—that may be true. Justice? One should let justice prevail? You know that is impossible. It may be that justice would be done to everyone of us if everyone would write their own report about the summer. And perhaps it would be possible, said Ellen to Luisa, to write only good things about everyone. Luisa said to do that, one would have to think only good things about everyone. That afternoon, no one thought that was hard. (S 160–61)

Thinking only good things is not in the nature of a writer who is, by her own oath, in pursuit of the truth and who feels empowered to write about others as long as she evaluates her own self most mercilessly. Nevertheless, we cannot help but wonder how the friends of that summer reacted to this probing and often painful depiction of character. Wolf herself has acknowledged that their reactions were quite varied. Some were tolerant, but others could not accept her account. One of these must have been the model for Antonis, Thomas Nicolaou, child of a communist guerrilla fighter in the Greek civil war, who grew up in the GDR but had his Greek citizenship restored in the 1970s and maintained a home in Greece as well. In that decade he and his German wife, Carola, gathered a number of prominent writers and artists near their home in Drispeth, a small village in Mecklenburg. The Wolfs' summer home was nearby, in Meteln. Others in this circle included Maxie Wander, Helga Schubert, and Sarah Kirsch, whose poem "Bird of Prey Sweet Is the Air" serves as epigraph to *Sommerstück* and who described the same summer experiences in two stories, *Allerlei-Rauh* (Different Kinds of Rough) and *Rückenwind* (Tailwind).

Thomas Nicolaou, however, had many close ties with Wolf. He had been her host during her Greek journey in 1980, which was the impetus for her massive Cassandra project. How would Wolf have conceived the character of Antonis had she known before publication of *Sommerstück* that Nicolaou had long been an informant for the Stasi, delivering implicating details for the secret *Kader*-files of his friends? That allegedly he was responsible for the two-year incarceration of painter and graphic artist Sieghard Pohl, who asked Wolf from his jail cell to contact Nicolaou on his behalf, a request she declined? Such subsequent disclosures punctured the fragile veil of a summer's idyll more diabolically than Christa Wolf could have imagined. But she must have had a sense of the delicate nature of her revelations. She hesitated for more than a decade to publish *Sommerstück*—ostensibly because she considered it her most personal book. She claimed that she gave in to concerted pressure before she submitted it for publication. When it appeared in 1989, a time of political upheavals leading to the overthrow of the GDR government and unification, Wolf was scorned in the press for offering a fluffy "idyll." This attack was certainly not the first of many political ironies to surround Wolf's character and career in the new Germany.

Accident

"We live in this troubling area between catastrophe and idyll, and it will be that way for a long time, if we survive" (DI 457), Wolf observed in 1985 in "The White Circle." She wrote this essay for a catalog of posters by artists from all over the world called "Save Life on Earth" and published in the United States. *Sommerstück,* as we have seen, describes this troubling area in the lives of several individuals. But the tragedies looming in the background do not strike until after the summer (and the novel) has ended. In Wolf's next book, *Störfall,* the catastrophes have already occurred, and Wolf describes their effects on daily life.

Wolf was working on *Sommerstück* when a horrifying catastrophe struck Europe: on 26 April 1986 a reactor exploded in the nuclear power plant of Chernobyl, a small town in the Soviet Union approximately one hundred miles north of Kiev, almost causing a meltdown. High levels of radiation were released which not only severely contaminated the surrounding area of Chernobyl but also affected countries as far away as France and Norway. This nuclear disaster, the worst the world had seen, compelled Wolf to suspend work on *Sommerstück* and write an account of the impact Chernobyl exerted on her life. The manuscript was finished in September 1986, and publication followed in the spring of 1987 in both East and West Germany. This unusually speedy completion was prompted by Wolf's perception of the urgency of the issues, "to save life on earth," and by her mandate that "artists have to have a vision— be it an apocalypse, an ideal, a warning or an admonition. The earth, its perfect form—the shape of a ball—broken by villainous abuse of awesome energies. Or: the earth, peaceful home to man and animal. Who would not reject the former in horror, who would not long for the latter?" (DI 457).

Wolf documented her vision—a warning on her scale from apocalypse to admonition—in a short prose text, which she called *Störfall,* translated as *Accident* and published in 1989. Wolf characteristically employs deliberate ambiguity in the title. The literal meaning signifies a disturbing case or, in scientific jargon, a breakdown, particularly in a nuclear facility. But Wolf extended the connotation to refer to the two catastrophic events occurring simultaneously which form the counterpointed subject of her book: both the Chernobyl malfunction and the brain tumor of the narrator's brother. Both of these are "breakdowns" from an operational perspective, and both are "disturbing" from the narrator's viewpoint, but the irony is that neither case could be called an "accident." The nuclear disaster was the result of reckless human negligence, the brain tumor of nature's indifference.

The novel describes a May day in the life of the narrator: the fifth day after Chernobyl and the day of her brother's brain surgery. The narrator more than ever before resembles Wolf herself, regardless of her denial that any of the characters in the book are real. She admits in several passages that in writing this book she had to play the role of the writer, but at the same time she had to tear the mask off her face and turn her authentic self outward, whether she wanted to or not. She continues: "On a day like this, paradoxical in its effect, we are forced, I am forced to turn personal things inside out, to overcome the resistance" (ST 92). Moreover, there are numerous allusions to experiences recounted in other stories and novels in which the narrator could be identified with Wolf. The house in the country, where the narrator is spending this fateful day alone, the village nearby, where she shops for milk, even some of the inhabitants with whom she chats about the disaster—all closely resemble the location and the characters in *Sommerstück*. No doubt we are in Wolf's summer home in Mecklenburg. References to Wolf's family and events from the past, such as the dislocation of her brother's arm and their struggle with typhus shortly after the war, derive from *Patterns of Childhood*. From "June Afternoon" Wolf uses nearly verbatim references to the scene of the jets overhead breaking the sound barrier and terrifying the narrator. *Accident* is therefore neither fiction nor essay in the sense to which we are accustomed in Wolf's oeuvre. It is an intimate autobiographical account of the author's physical, emotional, and intellectual reactions to the Chernobyl disaster and to her brother's ordeal, which she presents in vivid detail. The narrator of *Accident* is identical to the writer of the essay "The White Circle," which illuminates the novel's purpose and contains similar admonitions.

The narrative of *Accident* vacillates between lengthy scientific investigation, emotional riposte, and intellectual reflection about both events, giving nearly equal time to the significance and impact of the hourly news bulletins about the nuclear disaster and of her brother's operation. The prose structure tries to simulate the actual working of the brain, translating the simultaneity of the mind's activities into the linear sequence of narration. Wolf acknowledges

149

the futility of her attempt, the loss of reality from the mind to the writing pen: "Everything I was able to think and feel exceeded the limits of prose. . . . The loss of immediacy, richness, precision, sharpness, and a series of qualities I cannot name, perhaps don't even suspect" (ST 66). Using diary form and, similar to *Sommerstück,* paying painstaking attention to trivial detail, Wolf records the impact of both calamities on her life. She enumerates her activities, thoughts, feelings, and responses to "A Day's News," which is the book's subtitle. In these accounts and in the imagined conversation with her brother she surveys a great many topics. While this is not unusual procedure in Wolf's work, it is striking that here the characteristic narrative impulse is one of question rather than statement. Normally, Wolf states opinions unequivocally. Here she tends to express herself inconclusively, frequently couching her musings in rhetorical questions. Perhaps this change is caused by the momentous events that dominate this day and have called everything into question, except the ultimate simple truth that rules all life and which is mediated to Wolf in a dream about her grandparents. It states "that we all have to die and that we can accept this" (ST 74). Yet, in spite of all the perils invoked in the novel, it ends with an affirmative sigh: that it would be very difficult to say good-bye to this earth.

After all, there is still the idyllic aspect to life, which is summoned in the beginning. "One could tell, this would be one of the most beautiful days of the year" (ST 25). This poignant irony follows the narrator's approving glance into the "flawless blue sky," "this symbol of purity." The implied contradiction between the brilliance of a perfect spring day and the lethal change of the environment is reflected in the language. "Now they even make a mess of the clouds" (ST 48), said Heinrich Plaack, one of the villagers. Clouds, once consisting of uncontaminated purity, the objects of poetry transformed by children's imagination into fantastic creatures, now conjure up deadly atomic explosions. "That we still call it 'cloud' is only a sign of our inability to keep pace linguistically with the advances in science," Wolf observes (ST 34). Charged with radioactivity, clouds are now harbingers of death, and the author wishes they would sail away to rain somewhere else. The word *mushroom,* once the fanciful embodiment of spirits in fairy tales and children's songs, now represents images of disaster over Hiroshima and Nagasaki and pictures of horribly wounded victims of the bombs. Mushrooms, after a good rain eagerly collected in German forests and pastures, are no longer edible because fungi are prone to soak up more radioactivity than even leafy vegetables. Rays, associated with the sun's light and warmth and the life-saving properties of X rays, have assumed fatal significance. "The Janus-faced language," as Wolf calls it.

As in *Sommerstück,* but enhanced by the impact of the momentous situation, time assumes a special quality: "One day. One day is like a thousand years. A thousand years are like one day. How did the old poets know that?" (ST 65). Upon human history a single day can have the impact of a thousand years. With this altered, plastic sense of time Wolf moves restlessly from one daily activity to another, doing chores similar to those recounted in *Sommerstück.* We watch her toil in house and garden, eat and drink, take a shower, sing and recite poetry, run errands in the village, chitchat with neighbors, talk to daughter and friends on the phone, go to sleep and dream ominous dreams. She also suspends writing on her manuscript *Sommerstück.* "Relieved, if this is the proper word here, I have granted myself a vacation. Not a word today." The pages of the manuscript leave her cold, she says. "They, or I, or both of us have changed" (ST 30), and, as a result, she finds the questions as well as the solutions to the problems posed in her draft "false." It would be useful to know how such insights affected Wolf's revisions of *Sommerstück* undertaken before its publication two years later.

Everything Wolf does that day is reevaluated in the light of "THE NEWS" about the nuclear disaster, which she receives with "perverse joy" on her small Sanyo transistor radio, news "restyled and chopped up by the hour" (ST 11). The more she learns about the repercussions of the nuclear fallout, contradictory and inconclusive as the information may be, the more her view of reality changes. She contemplates how a Geiger counter would register the lush green pastures in front of the house; she wonders when the consumption of eggs from the neighbor's clucking chicken, the spinach and lettuce from the garden, and the milk from the dairy—the lack of which kills thousands of children on other continents—would start killing German children.

The narrator's grown daughter in the city assures her that she is following the latest advice from the experts. She will not let her young children play in the sandbox or give them a bath, as she did yesterday and the day before, knowing now that radioactivity is stored in the sand and washed into the open pores of soaked skin. But she also heard the message "that everything is too late, and there are the two children lying in their beds, and she could not bear the sight and so she just could not sleep" (ST 22). She asks her mother whether there was a better reason for insomnia. Wolf equivocates: yes, no, on the other hand. Apparently, she is less fatalistic than her daughter, perhaps less realistic; at any rate she seems to think like the villagers.

On her trip to the village Wolf discovers their reactions range from skepticism about the severity of the situation to resignation and indifference. Mr.

Gutjahr (Goodyear) declares that he has been in worse predicaments. According to the slogan that "ignorance is bliss," he ignores "all this hoopla" on the radio. The saleslady in the milk store is not surprised that everyone is still picking up their milk, although it is said to be contaminated. "We cannot stop eating and drinking, after all," she argues, and, while all this is "terrible, just terrible," "there is nothing we can do about it, anyway" (ST 41). In view of these reactions Wolf "admires" the seamless manner in which "everything fits together like gears" in the dynamics of society: "the desire of most people for comfort, their tendency to believe the speakers on raised podiums and the men in white lab coats, everyone's compulsion to conform, and their fear to contradict, all seem to correspond to the lust for power and arrogance, the greed for profit, the unscrupulousness, curiosity and egocentricity of the few" (ST 23).

In Wolf's view "the few," "the men in the white lab coats," the scientists and technocrats, are mainly responsible for the threat to human survival. Tragically, the very nature of their activities is linked to universal destruction. This premise is articulated in one of the two epigraphs Wolf chose for her book: Carl Sagan's assertion that there is a connection between killing and inventing and that both are innate in man. According to some interpreters of *Accident,* Wolf places the blame for humanity's catastrophes specifically on males. Only when taken out of context, however, do Wolf's statements support this interpretation. Admittedly, she wonders whether women who feed babies would advance a technology that poisons their milk. She asks her daughter, bewildered, what on earth is done to little boys to make them so tough? She also insinuates that "men of science and technology" would probably not pursue "the kind of technology whose very essence is diabolical danger" (ST 27), had they ever planted a seed or were accustomed to other such joys clearly associated with the traditional female realm—activities such as diapering babies, cooking, cleaning, nurturing. Wolf carefully dissociates herself, however, from any conclusion intimating that the destructive property of science and technology is exclusively the responsibility of males. She consistently frames all speculations of this kind in questions and uses the inconclusive subjunctive and words such as *probably* and *perhaps.* Finally, she adds: "What follows from that? To be honest: I do not know" (ST 27). She quotes her daughter's opinion on the subject, who said that little boys, when made tough, will take revenge as adults, that is certain, concluding: "The person who had the ability to love beaten out of him is bound to prevent others from love" (ST 24). Since women raise these boys, they are clearly accountable for the formation of their sons' disposition. Thus, Wolf argues that the responsibility for the perilous state of the world rests squarely with *all* of us and that the lack of love is a continuing evil for either sex.

To bring the potentially destructive scientific mind into focus, Wolf makes a sweeping allusion to Goethe's Faust, the scholar who sold his soul to the devil, although not for knowledge (as did the Dr. Faust of the folk story) but, rather, for a moment of bliss. Using the American science community as a prototype, Wolf identifies one of the scientists of the Livermore Laboratories ("Peter Hagelstein, not Frankenstein") with "Faust, who does not want to achieve knowledge but fame" (ST 73). Like the other young scientist, Hagelstein has sold himself not to the devil ("The good old devil. I wished he still existed!") but to the "fascination of a technical problem" (ST 70), and he is, although reluctantly, working on the development of a bomb. Like his colleagues, he is isolated in his "star war lab" from women, children, and friends. He derives joy only from work; his emotional life is absorbed by work. "A human being wants to experience strong feelings, and he wants to be loved," Wolf declares in a different context (ST 38). Yet in the absence of human love the scientists like Hagelstein find emotional satisfaction in the interaction with their "dear, beloved computer. To which they are more closely tied, shackled, than a slave to the galleons" (ST 70–71). Where did human evolution go wrong, "to couple sexual satisfaction with the urge to kill," Wolf wonders, or "what kind of fear sequesters these young men from what we normal people call 'life.' A fear which must be so immense that they rather 'liberate' the atom than themselves" (ST 73).

It is notable that, while Wolf asserts the culpability of American technology, she never explicitly associates the nuclear disaster with the Russian town of Chernobyl. Nor does she mention the devastating consequences of the Soviets' deliberate delay in reporting the explosion and of their continued attempts to minimize the damage. Many Western critics understandably reproached Wolf for blatant bias. Others argued that, by not identifying the source of the disaster, she gives the event "proper global relevance." If, however, global relevance is to be gained by anonymity, then why did Wolf put the blame for other devices of mass destruction upon the "star warriors" of the Livermore Laboratories and accuse the "best minds of the United States" of being attracted to the "maelstrom of death" and to "the potential of fabricating the void?" (ST 72). While it is understandable that Wolf refrains from implicating her country's patron, the Soviet Union, it is regrettable that she singles out the West as the culprit in the destruction of the earth, especially in light of recent revelations about the Eastern Bloc's terrible environmental abuses.

Ascribing blame for the world's ills to the United States seems to be a reflex conditioned by Wolf's socialist indoctrination. It completely contradicts her philosophy of both global and individual responsibility for the survival of our planet, expressed in many essays. Especially in the "The White Circle," she pleads for global brotherhood and the eradication of the "blinde Fleck" (blind spot) which, in this context, connotes prejudice toward other cultures. She renounces narrow provincial notions that posit "every member of another tribe as alien, barbaric"—a bias voiced in *Accident* as well. More characteristically, Wolf attributes such notions, and most human shortcomings, to fear:

> Fear is at the root of the otherwise hard to understand, painfully slow pace with which insights, absolutely essential for our survival, are dispersed. Fear directs the defensive, repudiating attitude, this washing-of-one's-own-hands, this blaming of others, this lethal hesitation to act effectively. The white circle: that's the others. The other culture. The other way of being in this world which threatens me. Is it possible that groups of people would rather calculate their own destruction—not only with weapons, by the way—than to consider seriously a radical change in their lifestyle? (DI 457–58)

Ultimately, Wolf places responsibility for our world's situation in the individual and sees the source of hope for improving the earth's fate in the individual. Cain's question "Am I my brother's keeper?"—more pertinent than ever before in history—is, according to Wolf's reading, a genuine and necessary inquiry. The answer can only be an unequivocal yes: We are all responsible for one another. Wolf believes that large mishaps, such as Chernobyl, derive from the sum of many little ones. To substantiate the point she recounts several stories that illustrate the impact of individual decisions on the whole. Heinrich Plaack tells of his brother-in-law's job as chauffeur for the Nazi's Gestapo, something Plaack perceives to have been an innocent occupation, since the man did not know about his employer's sinister activities. This story inspires Wolf to imagine all those cars without drivers, rendering the Gestapo's operations impossible—what if every chauffeur had declined to work for the Gestapo? Then, Wolf recites the life story of a brave Jewish friend exiled in London whose perseverance to survive she considers a model for personal behavior. Finally, Wolf embraces her daughter's suggestion that a culture would have a chance for survival if only its citizens would dare "look their own truth in the eye fearlessly" (ST 104). This means, Wolf reflects, that it is not an external collective enemy who causes the danger in our lives but individual fears.

Wolf therefore embarks on a thorough inquiry into her own culpability, the "blind spot" in her own moral fiber, yielding some surprising results. She realizes that her role as creator of literature is not so different from that of the scientist as inventor of technology. Sagan's linking of invention and killing is mirrored in Wolf's discovery that the joy of writing is coupled with the act of destruction. The kind of writing that "intervenes," which diagnoses the ills of our society—Wolf's own work—may be necessary and beneficial, yet it also victimizes people. As subjects of fiction, "they must feel observed, pinned to the wall, categorized, misjudged, or worse, betrayed, always kept at a distance for the sake of the proper turn of phrase" (ST 109). Unfortunately, authorial silence is not the remedy for this predicament, because that, too, would be an act of self-deception—another of many fatal alternatives in Wolf's work.

Like the inventor who cannot halt the development of an idea regardless of his invention's consequences, Wolf cannot suppress a creative thought and its expression, although she is fully aware of the dangers of words. She recalls a conversation with her brother in which she had admitted that words can destroy like projectiles. In retrospect her brother's probing questions suddenly reveal their gravity: Could and would she determine the point at which her words become hurtful or even destructive? What degree of destructiveness would she consider prohibitive? When would she choose silence? At this moment of her reflections, precisely at midpoint of the book, Wolf is struck by their historic significance. Wolf the author and the "men of science and technology" face the same dilemma: pursuit of one's vision or fatal inactivity. "This was the turning point of the day," she declares (ST 55), marking the moment with a startling expression of emotion: she hurls things around the kitchen.

For Wolf silence is not an alternative. Therefore, she has to find a justification for continuing her craft in spite of its perils. In the slightly altered words of Friedrich Hebbel from his tragedy *Gyges and His Ring,* Wolf indicates that one should not apologize for pursuing a vision, provided it is the truth: "You are not supposed to excuse yourself, / You are supposed to just say what happened" (ST 109). The extensive examination of her role and responsibility as writer, however, eventually turns into an apologia that includes the science community. Yet even the realization of her own culpability is couched in questions rather than unequivocal statements, and, thus, she ultimately leaves the moral verdict to the reader: "(So are we to blame, or share in the blame, when we say what we believe we know, and—although it may be hurtful—feel satisfaction in the process? Because we know it? Because we can express it? And when silence would be just as miserable? In what kind of fix are we all, pray tell, dear brother?)" (ST 56).

While Wolf examines the meaning of the Chernobyl disaster, her brother lies in the hands of surgeons who are removing a brain tumor—successfully, as we learn during the "turning point of the day." Directly addressing the absent brother, she sends her thoughts via the restorative "rays" of psychic communication to his brain, "penetrating effortlessly the dense defenses" of his unconsciousness, searching "for the glowing, pulsating core" (ST 10). Similar analogies to the world of nuclear science establish the common features of the two events. But they betray the fact that the surgical procedure, described in tedious physiological, anatomical, and technical detail, represents the antithesis to the reactor's malfunction. The technology that can lead to our destruction can also save human life. And it is precisely this contradiction inherent in science and technology which impels the author to be circumspect in her assessment of the forces unleashed in Chernobyl.

Wolf's silent monologue directed toward her brother is the vessel for reflections on many disparate themes that the narrative process knits together: an exposition of the fire in the fourth reactor, the responsibility of a surgeon, recollections of the past. She imagines the surgical procedure, her unconscious brother's vital signs, his eventual return to consciousness. She speculates about the surgeon's unilateral decision about which part of the brain to save and, consequently, which of the brother's sensory capabilities to preserve—another demonstration of personal responsibility and impersonal scientific jurisdiction over fate. By sending long psychic cables of encouragement to her brother, Wolf shows her belief in mental and spiritual forces that cannot be explained scientifically or controlled through will. Such forces are implied to be potent when Wolf spontaneously and inexplicably breaks out in song—the "Ode to Joy"—at the very moment the operation is pronounced successful.

Wolf's frequent but cursory and inconclusive references to spiritual powers is a unique phenomenon in her work, although the extent of her interest in matters of spirituality is yet to be established. She speaks about "a spirit of nature responsible for the larger connections" (ST 32); about an "anti-god" who did not create the world, who does not rule it and cannot be perceived by the senses yet is making his presence known to her. She describes, partly using biblical phrases, an "experience lasting mere seconds" that approaches the spiritual: "I felt that, with tremendous, possibly self-destructive effort, I could induce the power or force or energy or potency suddenly surrounding me (an atmosphere concentrated to the point of pain) to materialize: to show its face. Quickly, quickly, I reduced the tension just before it became unbearable, and I had great fear" (ST 46). Yet Wolf terminates and minimizes this experience by claiming to be close to a collapse and to lack adequate words. She strikes a more cynical note when she ascribes a religious basis to people's compulsion for fashioning gods to be dominated and subjugated and when she associates the need for a god with terms such as *escape* and *emergency exit*. The extent of spiritual experience in Wolf's work may change in the future.

156

Among the many topics touched upon in the rambling narrative of *Accident* are surprising confessions about her loyalty to socialism. While wondering whether scientists who defend their utopia are "monsters," she confronts the question of her own utopia, framing a justification for her earnest adherence to socialism: "Were we monsters when, for the sake of justice, equality, humanity for all—a utopia not to be postponed—we fought those who had (have) no interest in this utopia and those who dared to doubt that the purpose justifies the means—although we had our own doubts?" (ST 37). This rhetorical question is illuminated by a later lengthy review of the history of her disillusionment with the GDR regime. The candor with which she reveals her dissociation from the system is extraordinary at this time. It could have led to her total excommunication. Not until after the Wall fell could Wolf openly admit that the disenchantment began when the Soviet troops invaded Czechoslovakia in 1968 and that the last glimmer of hope was extinguished with Biermann's forced expatriation in 1976. In *Accident* Wolf herself remarks upon the wisdom of "risking one's life" in the attempt to express oneself "more and more precisely, recognizably, identifiably." The phrase "born again" triggered her recollection of the slow and painful recognition that her belief in the GDR system of socialism had been betrayed:

What a word. Can you hear it, brother: born again. Yes, I can still remember the time when I myself used such words and associated meaning with them. A short, sharp painful longing tore open before me this very period of time, along with the abyss in which it disappeared. I understood that there was a time—perhaps not all at once, perhaps not until today—when the ropes tore which tied our life's net to certain poles. Ropes which could be called securities, but also shackles. The generation before us would be held by them and bound by them forever. The generations after us cut the ropes and find themselves, relieved and free, to do as they please. We would never again be able to rely on these ties, but also never quite be rid of them, if only as a longing for them. (ST 88–89)

In this passage Wolf faces for the second time in her life the betrayal of an ideological conviction that had structured her thinking and her professional activities for nearly four decades—a third *Störfall*, a personal tragedy of major and lasting consequence. In 1990 she was forced to abandon altogether the dream of socialism realized in her lifetime.

Shortly after *Accident* was published in 1987 the GDR Academy of the Arts awarded Christa Wolf the highest honor, the National Prize First Class.

She was not happy being offered this award. Since Biermann's expatriation Wolf had severed ties to the SED organizations and withdrawn from political involvements insofar as possible. She did not want her acceptance of the prize to be misunderstood as a sign of reconciliation with the regime. But she chose not to refuse it. Perhaps her motive for accepting the award can be partly seen in her decision to give the prize money to three needy young writers whom she did not name. Even catastrophic changes can yield small individual acts of grace—in life and in art.

CHAPTER ELEVEN

"Returning Home to a Foreign Land"

What Remains

In the fall of 1989, through peaceful but persistent demonstrations and massive escapes to the West by way of Hungary and Czechoslovakia, the East German population brought about a series of profound changes that dissolved the country's authoritarian government. The hermetically sealed border to West Germany was finally broken: the Berlin Wall crumbled. Wolf had predicted this collapse of her country in *Cassandra* with the fall of Troy. Now she celebrated along with some seventy-five million Germans. She hoped that these events offered a unique chance for the restoration of socialism as it was conceived at the birth of her country. In October 1989 she envisioned the promise and "real possibility to develop structures in the GDR which can productively move towards a socialist society" (ID 85). What Wolf perceived as a national dream could perhaps be fulfilled after all: "Just imagine, it is socialism realized, and no one is leaving!" she exclaimed on 4 November 1989 (ID 120)—only five days before the Wall fell—at a rally on the Alexander-Platz in East Berlin, where one million people had gathered to demonstrate for basic human rights: freedom of the press, free elections, and the ability to travel abroad.

Wolf and her fellow citizens had good reason to feel exultant. On 18 October 1989 Erich Honecker, the secretary-general of the governing party, the SED, a rigid man who had dictatorially ruled the country for eighteen years, had been forced to resign. On 8 November the SED's politburo of party bosses was dissolved. The SED's exclusive hold on power had been shattered. This change was formalized on 1 December 1989, when the Volkskammer, the council representing all political parties in the GDR, abolished the law that established the SED as the only legitimate political authority. That all these revolutionary upheavals occurred so rapidly and without bloodshed is, to say the least, remarkable. Very few periods of fundamental change achieved bloodlessly in any Western country during the last century can parallel this astonishing moment in Germany's history.

It is, therefore, virtually impossible to summarize adequately the political and spiritual energies released in both Germanies, especially during the eleven months between the fall of the Wall and unification. The sudden dissolution of the SED's stranglehold on power, the departure of Honecker, the falling away from Moscow, the option of true self-governance and democracy in the East, the lifting of travel restrictions, and, of course, the possibility of unification with West Germany—all these manifested themselves suddenly and powerfully to a people not used to much change or even the *possibility* of change. When unification was contemplated by the citizens of East Germany, it is safe to say that only a very small percentage of them clearly grasped the long-range implications. The same might also be said of those in the West.

Wolf herself hoped in the fall of 1989, in the wake of the SED's demise, that the social and political changes demanded by the people were a revolutionary call for restoration of socialist principles. Later, when she was blamed and ridiculed for stubbornly adhering to a failed system and demanding its preservation, she responded: "When we made this appeal, we really did not think of the old GDR . . . of its continuance or its resurrection. For a very short historic moment we thought of an entirely different country which none of us would ever see. I knew then that this was an illusion" (T 292). Nevertheless, to prepare for such a country she enthusiastically participated in the planning sessions of citizens' forums and political groups. When the slogan "We are *the* people" began to change to "We are *one* people" and the political impulse to unify the two Germanies became stronger, Wolf was alarmed. She wished for the continued independence of the GDR, at least for a time sufficient to resurrect the socialist values on which her country was founded. She believed that these values had been suppressed, abused, and discredited by the "ruling power structures" and that now they could and should be restored. Wolf clearly understood the attraction the West held for people deprived of basic material needs, but she argued passionately against unification because she doubted "that the capitalist system, in the long run, would be able to solve the problems facing us all, facing humanity—if it does not also change greatly. It seems to me it could also be in the definite interest of the Federal Republic if an alternative to the structures developing there, which I do not want to criticize by any means, could be established on German soil" (ID 88–89).

It is difficult to assess now the extent to which the people of the GDR favored unification. In the period between Honecker's departure and unification the country was governed by a group of shifting and uncertain alliances with many referendums and elections. While there was not anarchy, neither was there a clear mandate for any person or group to lead the country decisively. Regardless of political process, or the lack of it, Wolf regards 3 October 1990, the date of political unification, as the day when East Germany was *annexed* by West Germany. Because Wolf believes it was an unmandated political fiat rather than the result of popular consensus, she considers unification a defeat—one not less painful or demoralizing because it can be explained or because it had been experienced before.

At a reading that year Wolf was tremendously moved by an East German woman's response to the moderator's plea to speak up: "We did not learn that," she said timidly. This reply inspired Wolf to wield a belligerent and passionate pen in defense of her fellow citizens. In numerous interviews, newspaper articles, speeches, and essays, collected in *Auf dem Weg nach Tabou,* 1994 (On the Way to Taboo), she relentlessly analyzed the process of unification—or, rather, the process of further "estrangement," as she preferred to call it: "A scary, increasingly speedy process of the reevaluation of all values is under way, in whose course those members of the intelligentsia are or were bound to be run over who were looking for ideological alternatives to capitalism's consumerism and practice of estrangement" (T 75). Wolf was determined she would not be "run over." Ignoring the detriment to her artistic reputation, she proceeded vigorously to expose the failures and dangers of the capitalist economic system under which those of her country were now compelled to live. Her list of grievances included its ruthless competitiveness and pursuit of efficiency to the physical and psychological detriment of the human being, capitalism's exploitation of developing countries for the sake of expansion, and the appropriation of East German real estate, businesses, and cultural institutions by Western entrepreneurs at the expense of their insolvent and inexperienced Eastern colleagues. She objected to the "demonization" of the former GDR, whether it was merely the result of ignorance or intentionally deceitful. She deplored the "monster shows" of former GDR citizens in the media designed to affirm false GDR stereotypes. Responding to the reluctance of West Germans to get to know their new brothers and sisters and to make a sincere effort to inform themselves about GDR history, she uses a moving image: "Do you believe that you can learn what is essential about the nature of life—let's say of a society of ants—if you turn over the stone, under which it has made a living of sorts, in order to draw significant conclusions from the manner in which it scurries in all directions under the eyes of slightly repulsed observers, recklessly betraying its identity? An inappropriate comparison? The cool glance of the voyeurs has forced it upon me" (T 44).

Passionately and persistently, Wolf has demanded fair investigation and informed presentation of GDR history, lest it be misconstrued or lost altogether: "We must insist on concrete description and take care that our life, as we really lived it, is not taken from us and substituted by a distorted phantom" (T 28). In this context the threat of closing the Academy of the Arts in Berlin appeared to her especially misguided. Nothing, in her estimation, is more important than an objective analysis of GDR history performed by those having lived under the former regime. Yet, "under fire by the ignorant or ill-intentioned victor, this is incredibly difficult. Our despair, if we dare articulate it, will be stuffed back into our throats as 'nostalgia'" (T 82). Wolf believes that the academy, after carefully instituted changes, has the scholarly and cultural resources to analyze and describe truthfully the past in which it played a major role. A mirror of intellectual life in the GDR, the Academy of the Arts could do much to preserve the accomplishments of East Germany's culture through the "investigation, presentation and publication of its achievements and deficiencies, the conflicts, the courage it mustered to express opposition, the reasons for compliance and compromise, which were not always based on cowardice or convenience" (T 76).

To capture her feelings about the loss of her country, Wolf used the term *phantom pain*. Within a year she observed that many of her fellow citizens felt similarly. They had lost the smile brightening their faces during the *Wende* (turn), as the Germans refer to the immediate period of unification. Instead, she saw sadness, shame, regret, depression, anger, fear, humiliation, hate, self-loathing, disorientation, desires for revenge. "This is not how we had imagined all of this." This quotation from the countless letters Wolf received in response to one of her newspaper articles summarizes the feelings many East Germans have about unification.

Wolf concedes that the West Germans, too, have reason to feel disillusionment. She understands their disappointment about unfulfilled expectations, their indignation for having to make sacrifices and to provide extensive financial and economic aid for the modernization of the East's infrastructure, housing, and industry in order to bring its economy into the fold of the European Union and to make it independent of further support. The pernicious result of many of these often subconscious dynamics is resentment on both sides, increased intolerance, mistrust, and, in some, even the desire to rebuild the Wall because they feel threatened by the other. In "Wo ist Euer Lächeln geblieben?" 1991 (What Happened to Your Smiles?), a description of the two Berlins existing next to each other yet worlds apart after unification, Wolf notes "that we do not know each other, that the mutual feeling of alienation cuts deeper now than before, when the Wall was still standing, keeping us separate so that one can feel pity for the other and the other envy for the one" (T 56). In a speech delivered in Dresden on 2 February 1994 she declared that "a disappointment which we shared separated us, instead of bringing us together in the effort to dismantle our self-delusions" (T 330). The telling title of the speech is "Abschied von Phantomen. Zur Sache: Deutschland" (Good-Bye to Phantoms. Item: Germany). Clearly, Wolf sees little evidence of "unification" and holds little hope for the desired and necessary process to come to a satisfactory conclusion quickly.

The years following unification were extremely difficult for Wolf. They are perhaps the most trying in all her adult life. She published her long story *Was bleibt* in 1990 (*What Remains* [1993]), which powerfully describes the corrosive consequences of Stasi surveillance of the narrator—immediately identified with Wolf herself. In what must be the most painful moment of her career she made the timid and not altogether forthright confession that she herself had been an informant. Preempting the imminent publication of the sensational discovery that she had worked for the Stasi, Wolf admitted that she had been inducted in 1959 and, under the code name "Margarete" (her second given name), supplied the Stasi for two and a half years with inconsequential information about other writers. Inexplicably and unexcusably, Wolf, the author of memory's domain, feigned memory lapses concerning her collusion with the Stasi. Instead of unequivocally admitting the extent and the reasons for her collaboration—which is now public knowledge and documented in embarrassing detail—she issued statements skillfully mingling intentions of honesty with complaints about persecution. The following example illustrates an uncertain and shifting tone as she enumerates her feelings:

> I try to speak as openly as possible about the different phases, about the first shock, the alarm about myself, the despair about the impossibility in this general Stasi hysteria to count on differentiation by the public, on the danger of identifying myself with my new public image, on the therapy through writing and the gradual emergence from depression up to the current phase where I believe that I can include this episode, which will remain a painful, dark blot in my development. (T 291)

Such sidestepping did nothing to satisfy the expectations of either her critics or her sympathetic audience.

The German media gleefully exploited Wolf's revelations to demolish *What Remains* and, not surprisingly, to attack Wolf personally. The list of accusations includes failure to publish the story in 1979, when she completed it and presumably could have made a powerful statement of courage and resistance.

The story's belated publication in 1990 suggested Wolf's opportunistic desire to be cleansed from suspicion of loyalty to the GDR regime and to recast herself as victim. Her critics charged that, instead of concerning herself with the petty surveillance of ordinary citizens, Wolf should have described other and greater horrors perpetrated on innocent people by the regime. Wolf was even accused of having withdrawn her signature from the "Open Letter" of 1976 protesting Biermann's expulsion from the GDR. Ironically, these critics in the West unwittingly fell victim to Stasi machinations themselves: the Stasi had fabricated this lie to discredit Wolf with the other signers and to break up their solidarity. As a result of the hostile media campaign, *What Remains* and, by extension, its author were seen as national embarrassments. There were even attempts to rescind the Geschwister-Scholl-Prize that Wolf had been awarded in 1987 for *Accident*.

Some critics did come to her defense. They argued that this story—any story openly attacking the Stasi—could not possibly have been published when it was written. Furthermore, that there is hardly an East German citizen who did *not* at one time or another function as an informant, including such a prominent writer as Heiner Müller; that Wolf was soon dismissed from the countless ranks of Stasi informants for failure to provide useful information; and that shortly thereafter, as of 1968, she and her husband became themselves objects of constant and intense surveillance, yielding an enormous volume of reports, of which *only* forty-three files, covering the time up to 1980, still exist.

In the midst of such politicized and sensational debate *What Remains* could not have been more misunderstood by Wolf's critics. The narrator-protagonist's failings are not, as critics have charged, weaknesses and inadvertent revelations. By unfolding them quite deliberately in order to expose them, Wolf preempts her critics. The narrator of the story does not merely complain about the spying to which she is subjected, nor does she cast herself in the role of victim. Quite the contrary: while describing the insidious impact of surveillance on her life, she explicitly criticizes her own complacency, her willingness "to dance to the same tune" as the agents who observe her, her cowardly submissiveness, and her passivity. The subject of the story is her painstaking liberation from oppression by the very power to which she has pledged her allegiance, her journey to find the courage and the artistic empowerment to describe this struggle. If read as autobiography, *What Remains* does not present Wolf as victim of Stasi practices or as martyr under the GDR regime. Rather, it exposes her lack of initiative to disengage from the ideological and political practices in the GDR, her insufficient courage to resist its abuses, and her reluctance to speak up. The story contains critical self-analysis and brutal self-revelation, which few other writers would have written, let alone publish.

What Remains describes two distinctly different stages in the protagonist's development: the first one portrays her physical and mental imprisonment while caught in the net of surveillance and intimidation; the second part gradually releases the narrator from her paralysis, ending with a promise to recount her experiences, to describe "what remains." The beginning reveals that the narrator's Berlin apartment is constantly surrounded by "young gentlemen," whom she in turn observes obsessively. Their footprints and a shattered mirror betray the regular search of her residence. The conspicuous presence of these gentlemen exerts an intimidating effect: the narrator, always conscious of strange, relentlessly intrusive eyes and ears, finds her home robbed of its privacy and herself ruled by fear and mistrust. Suddenly subject to exaggerated self-censorship, she feels trapped, immobilized, unable to work. She conducts social interactions with paranoid caution. Simple acts of communication become complex ordeals in which "the true text is always circumvented." Telephone conversations are encoded; voices are lowered and the radio turned up when matters charged with political implications are discussed. She opens and answers her voluminous mail with unusual circumspection. Formerly carefree relationships are poisoned by mistrust, the life-sustaining nature of friendships diminished by suspicions that the friends may be furnishing the authorities with implicating information. All of these results are, of course, desired by the regime.

Governed by anxiety and cowardice, by her "shameful need to be on good terms with all sorts of people" (WB 20), the narrator cannot openly call the agents in front of her house spies or their invasion of her privacy spying. She calls them euphemistically "young gentlemen," "ambassadors of the other," of the "lord ruling this city." The "master" has hired them to practice "barely disguised doing-nothing." Instead of critically analyzing the gentlemen's activities and purpose, she engages in ludicrous reflections about their bald spots, the color of their cars, the content of their lunch boxes, their wives' knowledge of their professions. This is not surprising, because the narrator has revealed herself in many ways as a pawn of the authorities. She admits explicitly to the fact that at least one part of her "multiple being" is obedient to the powers above. It is not the one "which wanted to know itself" nor the one "which wanted to be lenient with itself" but, rather, "that third one that was still tempted to dance to the same tune to which the young gentlemen were dancing out there" in front of her door (WB 57). Yet she expresses hope to expel this "third self" one of these days, once and for all.

The "lord ruling the city" alludes to Bertolt Brecht's story "Measures against the Power of Authority," in which Brecht assigns priority to compliance for the sake of survival over dissidence at the cost of one's life. The literary allusion is perhaps a bit far-fetched: the narrator's life is not in danger. The "lord" is actually an old friend of hers, Jürgen M.—at least in her paranoia she believes so. She encounters him during an aimless outing undertaken to escape the feeling of imprisonment in her own home. Jürgen M. clearly recognizes her but pretends not to know her. Wolf's control of image to portray this moment is remarkable: "How familiar this was: the curtain lowered in front of the other's eyes; the fishy scales covering the white in the friend's eye; the cloudiness obscuring his pupil" (WB 40). He develops the same "glass eye" Wolf has previously associated with other figures representative of an elusive threatening authority; it appears in *Divided Heaven*, "Unter den Linden," and *On the Way to Taboo*. The young gentlemen also assume the "glass eye" whenever the narrator passes them.

Because Jürgen M. apparently occupies a powerful position, the narrator immediately suspects him of masterminding her surveillance. There had to be someone who knew everything about her "except what was really important" (WB 45). He must be the one. But, since he did not know the important facts, he would actually have to admit, if asked, that he knew *nothing* about her; that, in spite of accumulating volumes of files on her, he had accomplished nothing. "But I knew better. He had accomplished a lot, the good man, quite a lot, but he could not know what, because his informants did not hear this, his tapes did not record this, it is of such fine substance that it escaped them" (WB 50). What Jürgen M. did not know was that he had intimidated her into paralysis. The observation that the essence of a person is not captured in the information of confidential personal files is reminiscent of Wolf's statements in regard to files released after the dissolution of the Stasi: they reveal nothing vital about a person and should therefore not be used to pass judgment on anyone's life and conduct. "The fine substance" of the individual can only be recorded by a literary work. *What Remains* makes this attempt.

The very opening lines of the story capture the insidious consequences of the writer's surveillance—her fear and inability to write: "Don't be afraid. In that other language which is in my ear but not yet on my tongue, I will, one day, talk about it, too. I knew, today was too early. But would I sense when it was the right time? Would I ever find my language?" (WB 7). By the dawn of a new day the narrator has found not only the words to describe her ordeal but also the courage for resolute criticism of her failure to take action.

Yet before she is ready to write the narrator must overcome paralysis. The transformation comes about partly as a result of her own rigorous self-examination: "Every day I tell myself, a privileged life like mine can only be justified by exceeding now and then the limits of what can be said, being mindful of the fact that all violations of limitations are punished. . . . How much time was I willing to grant myself?" (WB 22). The other important influences on the narrator's catharsis are two anonymous young women, whom Wolf portrays as the actual heroes of *What Remains:* they represent incarnations of the title's meaning. The personal courage of the two women is ultimately what remains, because they embody the qualities that conquer oppression. Both women remain anonymous. They represent all the East Germans who dared voice their dissidence and question their future under the GDR regime. Thus, Wolf invests the particular individual, not the general will of the masses, with the power to initiate change.

In the afternoon the narrator receives a young woman who was once, as a student at the university, involved in unspecified acts of political resistance "because she did not belong to those who could be bribed" (WB 75). Although she spent time in prison, the young woman intends to continue to express her resistance by publicizing her experiences. The narrator is inspired by the woman's courage. Still dominated by that third self, however, she "forgets" to obtain her address and is unable to return the woman's manuscript or assist her literary debut. Because fear and complacency still rule her, the narrator does not get involved with a dissident whom she greatly admires.

In the evening the narrator is invited to conduct a public reading, a suspect invitation because she has been blacklisted. In the course of the discussion a young nurse boldly asks "how a livable future for our children could possibly grow out of this present" (WB 95). Her question deeply moves the narrator and opens a passionate debate, revealing the public's desperate longing for a better future and true "brotherhood." Of course, the discussion is cut short by the officials, with the narrator's consent.

While the reading is going on inside, several young people who were unable to get tickets are engaged outside in lively debate. They are arrested for provocative behavior. It becomes apparent that the reading had been arranged by the lord, with the primary intent to induce provocations and facilitate the identification of dissidents. The narrator is placidly acquiescing to this plan and intending to heed the organizer's advice to forget such unpleasant occurrences. Yet, on her way home, she does briefly ponder whether young people had actually been arrested. "And what if they . . . ." She does not dare continue her thoughts, but she realizes that she has failed; in a deep sense she has betrayed her profession by going forward with the reading once she suspected its true purpose and by not intervening to protect her innocent young fans. "That was the end. I couldn't do anything anymore. This is what one calls dropped in the deep freeze. With the back to the wall" (WB 104). This realization defines the precise beginning of the narrator's catharsis.

At midnight her daughter telephones to inquire about the reading. Before she hangs up she tells her mother: "What I meant to say: they are quite right to mistrust you" (WB 106). The narrator replies that she is beginning to understand that. The realization that in the eyes of the public she actually serves as an agent of change, and therefore has a responsibility to her readers, unlocks her paralysis. At the dawn of a new day she turns off all the lights in the house which she kept burning as a shield against fear and the feeling of isolation. Symbolically, she is marking the end of the crippling impact of surveillance. Only her desk light is still illuminating paper and pen—a sign that she is ready to give voice to the new language she had in her ears at the beginning of this story. She is finally ready to describe "what remains. What lies at the bottom of my town and what is destroying it. That there is no misfortune other than not to live. And ultimately no despair other than not to have lived" (T 108). At the end she is no longer a victim of oppression but, rather, a victor in the struggle against being silenced.

What Remains records experiences that, although shared by millions of East Germans, were unknown to most people in the West. Neither their collective impact on individual lives and social conduct nor their pervasive evil can be adequately gleaned from the surviving Stasi files. But in this cautionary tale the intimidating and paralyzing effect of surveillance resonates vividly and unforgettably. To dismiss the story as an act of posturing and solicitation of sympathy is a misreading of Wolf's intentions and overlooks its significant contribution to mutual understanding and social reconciliation between East and West Germans.

Conclusion

Wolf's legacy is rich and powerful. Her literary reviews, essays, and fiction chronicle the writer's journey from passionate commitment to democratic socialism, on which the German Democratic Republic was constitutionally founded, to courageous yet judicious resistance to an authoritarian regime that increasingly violated these principles. Her work as a whole reflects her own painful liberation from political doctrine and her struggle toward self-realization under challenging social and personal circumstances, the central pursuit of every protagonist in her novels and stories. Wolf's personal history—early commitment to official ideology followed by disillusionment and emancipation and, ultimately, by discovery of self—is powerfully fictionalized in her greatest novels, *Patterns of Childhood* and *Cassandra.*

A signal property in Wolf's novelistic oeuvre is a profoundly original and varied narrative style. Beginning with strict socialist realism in *Moskauer Novelle,* Wolf continues to experiment with narrative structures, constantly modulating her stylistic approach. Most prominent is how she explores memory and emulates its processes, yielding an idiosyncratic mixture of description and reflection. The striking quality of her narrative voice is already present as early as *Divided Heaven* and becomes fully realized in *The Quest for Christa T.,* notably her first work written in complete defiance of the received principles of socialist realism. In *No Place on Earth* Wolf successfully merges her own voice with the voices of her Romantic precursors to articulate the nature of her similar artistic and personal situation. *Cassandra,* a mythological figure adapted by Wolf to embody contemporary conflicts, speaks partly in the poetic rhythms of antiquity and partly in contemporary jargon, resulting in a voice meaningful to a twentieth-century audience. In her last two novels Wolf turns from the heroic and confines herself to the depiction of ordinary daily life, with its pleasures and pains. In *Sommerstück* this life is seen from the perspective of not just one narrator but many characters who speak their own voices. Wolf's novels, even the last story *What Remains,* describe a circle: the ending invariably feeds back into the beginning, because her resolutions of profound human dilemma are brought about by the very act of writing. This circular narrative structure is but one of many validations of Wolf's powerful dictum: "Books are deeds." Part of the deed consists of her inventing skillful narrative approaches to conceal and veil subject matter not sanctioned by the GDR's cultural bureaucracy. This obstruction scarcely diminishes Wolf's narrative accomplishments; on the contrary, her success in both East and West substantiates the potency of her protean voice and the authority of her style. While her fiction has been published, debated, and criticized throughout the world, much has yet to be accomplished to understand Christa Wolf. Since the portrayal of her novels' protagonists is a species of autobiography, the reader justifiably senses an encounter with the author herself. Very little is known about Wolf's life, however, because the author has always been extremely reticent about her personal circumstances. Not the smallest irony of her extraordinary career is that contemporary Germany's most autobiographical novelist is also the most secretive. A comprehensive biographical study is necessary not only to satisfy the need for a clearer and more detailed picture of Wolf's life and career but also to illuminate the autobiographical components of her work.

It is seldom observed that nearly half of Wolf's oeuvre consists of essays, and certainly most if not all of them are relevant to the history of GDR culture and contemporary intellectual life. Yet very few of these have been examined for their own sake. They are concerned with large and pressing issues ranging from the nature of writing and the role of the artist—the most prominent subject—to international politics, to the position of women in society, to science and medicine. Wolf's prolific observations about other writers and their work are unfailingly original and insightful. Aside from revealing a great deal about her own attitudes toward the function and purpose of literature, they make important contributions to literary scholarship. Thus far her essays have been consulted mainly to substantiate studies of her novels. A thorough examination and evaluation of style, content, and significance of her essayistic writing should be a goal for Wolf scholarship in future years.

In the broad and colorful spectrum of Wolf's recurring themes, one is notably absent: spirituality. Often lurking in the background and tantalizingly indicated in *Accident,* the metaphysical aspects of life have scarcely been addressed by her. Her entire work has been consumed by an ardent interest in the development of self. Although self-realization has an undeniably luminous and spiritual dimension, Wolf usually keeps our perspective focused on consciousness itself, not on what might lie outside of it. In *Sommerstück,* however, she states that, in the course of growing old, her interest in self-realization is disappearing "just like gas is escaping from a balloon that has a leak" (S 207) and that "fear, fear, fear" is taking its place. While it seems unlikely that Wolf will ever abandon the search for self-actualization, she will doubtlessly search for an antidote to the fear that infects old age, and perhaps she will embark on more overtly spiritual quests. Now it is possible that the distance from Marxist ideology, the new and unwanted environment of capitalist materialism, and the experience of aging will combine to impel Wolf to explore this fundamental human drive.

For many years the Democratic Republic of Germany suppressed the Nazi past, on the ruins of which it was founded—essentially because it felt shame about such a horrendous heritage. The title of Wolf's latest work, *On the Way to Taboo* (a collection of essays from 1989 to 1994), expresses her concern that the new and unified Germany of today may once again prefer to ignore its past and thus avoid an informed *Vergangenheitsbewältigung* (coming to terms with the past). Wolf appears to believe that the history of nearly one-third of Germany's population, that of the former East Germany, is in danger of being forgotten because it is, by Western consensus, declared "taboo." The tragic consequences of obstructing or obliterating a country's legacy, whether shameful or otherwise, were powerfully presented in *Cassandra*. *Patterns of Childhood* did much to resurrect, and from a personal point of view interpret, the Nazi years. This pivotal novel described the insidious effects of fascism on *all* postwar Germans, in both East and West, and promoted a better understanding of their common history. Few authors of Wolf's generation have been as fearless or as effective in confronting the Nazi past.

Today the two German societies are politically unified, yet they remain estranged from each other by awe, fear, and a radically different postwar experience. Indeed, they appear merely to coexist. Pervasive ignorance in the West about four decades of GDR life, perpetuated by the shame and guilt that undeniably affects both sides, fuels feelings of confusion and alienation. Yet, to paraphrase William Faulkner's aphorism, the GDR's past is not dead, it is not even past. It still exerts a commanding presence in Germany's life. One of Wolf's most important messages to all German citizens today is that it is imperative to discuss and honestly examine the totality of GDR history, not just selected and politically expedient excerpts of it. Again, Wolf's work can and should contribute significantly to the general comprehension of the GDR legacy. Another irony of her career may well be that her writing will significantly assist the process of a unification she passionately opposed.

The life of East Germany is vividly preserved in Wolf's novels and stories. Her essays answer many perplexing questions about the GDR's political and cultural development. Her recent work describes the varied situations and sentiments of East Germans after the Wall. Because what remains of the GDR and what is worthy of remaining are so powerfully recorded in her writings, Christa Wolf's literary achievement is one of her former country's most stubborn and enduring treasures.

BIBLIOGRAPHY

Works by Christa Wolf

German Editions

If a work appeared in both the GDR and the FRG, both first editions are listed.

Moskauer Novelle. Halle: Mitteldeutscher Verlag, 1961.
Der geteilte Himmel. Erzählung. Halle: Mitteldeutscher Verlag, 1963; Munich: Deutscher Taschenbuch Verlag, 1973.
Nachdenken über Christa T. Halle: Mitteldeutscher Verlag, 1968; Darmstadt and Neuwied: Luchterhand, 1969.
Lesen und Schreiben. Aufsätze und Betrachtungen. Commentary by Hans Stubbe. Berlin: Aufbau Verlag, 1971; republished as *Lesen und Schreiben: Aufsätze und Prosastücke.* Darmstadt and Neuwied: Luchterhand, 1972.
Till Eulenspiegel. Erzählung für den Film. With Gerhard Wolf. Berlin: Aufbau Verlag, 1972; Darmstadt and Neuwied: Luchterhand, 1973.
Unter den Linden. Drei unwahrscheinliche Geschichten. Berlin: Aufbau Verlag, 1974; Darmstadt and Neuwied: Luchterhand, 1977.
Kindheitsmuster. Berlin: Aufbau Verlag, 1976; Darmstadt and Neuwied: Luchterhand, 1977.
Fortgesetzter Versuch. Aufsätze, Gespräche, Essays. Leipzig: Reclam, 1979.
Kein Ort. Nirgends. Erzählung. Berlin: Aufbau Verlag, 1979; Darmstadt and Neuwied: Luchterhand, 1979.
Gesammelte Erzählungen. Darmstadt: Luchterhand, 1980.
Geschlechtertausch. Drei Erzählungen. Mit Sarah Kirsch und Irmtraud Morgner. Darmstadt and Neuwied: Luchterhand, 1980.
Lesen und Schreiben. Neue Sammlung. Mit der Büchner-Preis-Rede 1980. Darmstadt and Neuwied: Luchterhand, 1980.
Kassandra. Vier Vorlesungen. Eine Erzählung. Berlin: Aufbau Verlag, 1983 (abr.); republished in 2 vols.: *Kassandra. Erzählung* and *Voraussetzungen einer Erzählung: Kassandra. Frankfurter Poetik-Vorlesungen.* Darmstadt and Neuwied: Luchterhand, 1983.
"Ins Ungebundene gehet eine Sehnsucht." Gesprächsraum Romantik. Prosa. Essays. With Gerhard Wolf. Berlin: Aufbau Verlag, 1985.
Die Dimension des Autors. Essays und Aufsätze, Reden und Gespräche 1959–1985. 2 vols. Berlin: Aufbau Verlag, 1986; Frankfurt am Main: Luchterhand, 1987.
Störfall. Nachrichten eines Tages. Berlin: Aufbau Verlag, 1987; Darmstadt and Neuwied: Luchterhand, 1987.
Ansprachen. Darmstadt and Neuwied: Luchterhand, 1988.
Sommerstück. Frankfurt am Main: Luchterhand, 1989.
Christa Wolf im Dialog. Aktuelle Texte. Frankfurt am Main: Luchterhand, 1990.

Reden im Herbst. Berlin: Aufbau Verlag, 1990.
Was bleibt. Erzählung. Frankfurt am Main: Luchterhand, 1990.
Reimann, Brigitte. *Sei gegrüßt und lebe. Eine Freundschaft in Briefen, 1964–1973.* Berlin: Aufbau Verlag, 1993.
Auf dem Weg nach Tabou: Texte, 1990–1994. Köln: Kiepenheuer and Witsch, 1994.

English Editions

Divided Heaven. Trans. Joan Becker. Berlin: Seven Seas, 1965; New York: Adler's Foreign Books, 1974. *[Der geteilte Himmel.]* In the Adler's Foreign Books edition Jack Zipes furnished an introduction called "Christa Wolf: Moralist as Marxist."
The Quest for Christa T. Trans. Christopher Middleton. New York: Farrar, Straus, and Giroux, 1971; London: Hutchinson, 1971. *[Nachdenken über Christa T.]*
The Reader and the Writer: Essays, Sketches, Memories. Trans. Joan Becker. Berlin: Seven Seas, 1977; New York: Signet, 1977. *[Lesen und Schreiben: Aufsätze und Betrachtungen.]* Some translations do not accurately render the original.
A Model Childhood. Trans. Ursule Molinaro and Hedwig Rappolt. New York: Farrar, Straus, and Giroux, 1980; London: Virago, 1982. Republished as *Patterns of Childhood. [Kindheitsmuster.]* The English version is incomplete.
No Place on Earth. Trans. Jan Van Heurck. New York: Farrar, Straus, and Giroux, 1982; London: Virago, 1983. *[Kein Ort. Nirgends.]* Includes translator's notes on characters, names, and selected quotations.
Cassandra: A Novel and Four Essays. Trans. Jan Van Heurck. New York: Farrar, Straus, and Giroux, 1984. *[Kassandra: Vier Vorlesungen. Eine Erzählung.]*
The Fourth Dimension: Interviews with Christa Wolf. Trans. Hilary Pilkington: Routledge, Chapan and Hall, 1988. [Interviews from *Die Dimension des Autors.*]
Accident: A Day's News. Trans. Heike Schwarzbauer and Rick Takvorian. New York: Farrar, Straus, and Giroux, 1989. *[Störfall.]*
What Remains and Other Stories. Trans. Heike Schwarzbauer and Rick Takvorian. New York: Farrar, Straus, and Giroux, 1993. *[Gesammelte Erzählungen and Was bleibt.]*
The Author's Dimension: Selected Essays. Trans. Jan Van Heurck. New York: Farrar, Straus, and Giroux, 1990. [Selections from *Die Dimension des Autors, Ansprachen,* and *Im Dialog.*]

Critical Works

Books

Arnold, Heinz Ludwig, ed. *Christa Wolf.* TEXT + KRITIK. No. 46. 1975, 2d ed., 1979; 3d ed., 1985; 4th ed., 1994. Collections of critical essays. The second and third editions are expanded. The fourth edition contains new essays mainly treating Wolf's newest writing.

Behn, Manfred, ed. *Wirkungsgeschichte von Christa Wolfs "Nachdenken über Christa T."* Königstein: Athenäum, 1978. A collection of reviews and essays about *The Quest for Christa T.* from both East and West German critics and scholars. An indispensable source of materials illuminating the history of the novel's controversial reception. With an informative introduction by the editor as well as comments about the authors and notes on the articles.

Drescher, Angela, ed. *Christa Wolf. Ein Arbeitsbuch: Studien, Dokumente, Bibliographie.* Berlin: Aufbau Verlag, 1989; Frankfurt am Main: Luchterhand, 1990. A collection of essays about Christa Wolf and her work, most of which are not easily accessible otherwise—for instance, an essay about the novel *Accident,* originally published in Moscow and translated from the Russian. Articles and letters by contemporary writers from East and West such as Anna Seghers, Heinrich Böll, Ingeborg Drewitz, Günter Kunert, and Günther de Bruyn are included, although some of them already appeared in Sauer's book *Christa Wolf. Materialienbuch.*

Fries, Marilyn Sibley, ed. *Responses to Christa Wolf: Critical Essays.* Detroit: Wayne State University Press, 1989. Includes translations (remarkably well done) of an important interview with Hans Kaufmann and illuminating essays on Wolf's work in general but predominantly on issues of language and female writing. Several articles deal with *The Quest for Christa T.,* the stories of *Unter den Linden, No Place on Earth,* and *Cassandra.*

Hilzinger, Sonja. *Christa Wolf.* Stuttgart: Metzler, 1986. An explication in German of Wolf's work starting with her literary reviews and criticism and ending with *Cassandra.* The author tends to examine a work from a certain perspective rather than explore the various aspects of a text. Contains a comprehensive chapter about the Romantic precursors. Extensive quotations from secondary literature are not always clearly identified.

Hörnigk, Therese. *Christa Wolf.* Göttingen: Steidl Verlag, 1989. An insider's sympathetic view of Wolf's life and work. Circumspect evaluation of her political position and sensitive interpretation of her work in chronological order. More knowledgeable about Wolf's work and thought than most.

Jurgensen, Manfred, ed. *Wolf: Darstellung, Deutung, Diskussion.* Bern: Francke, 1984. A useful collection of scholarly treatments of various aspects of Wolf's work from different philosophical viewpoints.

Kuhn, Anna K. *Christa Wolf's Utopian Vision: From Marxism to Feminism.* Cambridge: Cambridge University Press, 1988. A thorough, thoughtful study of Wolf's novels up to *Accident.* In effect, a demonstration of Wolf's universality and grounding in reality rather than in utopian visions such as Marxism or feminism.

Love, Myra Norma. *Christa Wolf: Literature and the Conscience of History.* New York: Peter Lang, 1991. Intended to ensure Wolf a place in the world's literary canon. Requires intimate knowledge of her entire work.

Mauser, Wolfram, ed. *Erinnerte Zukunft: 11 Studien zum Werk Christa Wolfs.* Würzburg: Königshausen and Neumann, 1985. Studies on pertinent, but not esoteric, issues in Wolf's work.

Reso, Martin, ed. *"Der geteilte Himmel" und seine Kritiker.* Dokumentation. Halle: Mitteldeutscher Verlag, 1965. Indispensable collection of sources reflecting the impact of *Divided Heaven* on the literary scene in the GDR.

Sauer, Klaus, ed. *Christa Wolf Materialienbuch.* Darmstadt: Luchterhand, 1979. New, rev. ed., 1983. Many of the entries can be found elsewhere, especially the essays by Christa Wolf herself. The editor provides an insightful analysis of Wolf's early work. Other contributions are a bit dated, including the extensive bibliography.

Sevin, Dieter. *Christa Wolf, "Der geteilte Himmel," "Nachdenken über Christa T.": Interpretationen.* Munich: R. Oldenbourg, 1982. Clearly developed interpretation of the two novels from various perspectives, including character analysis and discussion of narrative techniques. With useful information about GDR literary history. A fine introduction to the study of *Divided Heaven* and *The Quest for Christa T.*

Stephan, Alexander. *Christa Wolf.* Munich: Beck, 3d expanded ed., 1987. Extensive explication of and often unsympathetic commentary on every work of fiction up to *Cassandra,* with detailed information about its publication history and reception.

Thomassen, Christa. *Der lange Weg zu uns selbst. Christa Wolfs Roman "Nachdenken über Christa T." als Erfahrungs-und Handlungsmuster.* Kronberg: Scriptor, 1977. An in-depth study of *The Quest for Christa T.* from the perspective of finding oneself. The book is fundamental to any scholarly analysis of Wolf's novel but requires the additional reading of more contemporary studies.

Selected Articles in English

Brandes, Ute. "Probing the Blind Spot: Utopia and Dystopia in Christa Wolf's 'Störfall.'" *Studies in GDR* 9 (1992): 101–14.

Cicora, Mary. "Language, Identity, and the Woman in *Nachdenken über Christa T.*: A Post-Structuralist Approach." *Germanic Review* 57 (1982): 16–22.

Clausen, Jeanette. "The Difficulty of Saying 'I' as Theme and Narrative Technique in the Works of Christa Wolf." In *Gestaltet und gestaltend. Frauen in der deutschen Literatur,* ed. Marianne Burckhard, 319–33. Amsterdam: Rodopi, 1980.

Frieden, Sandra. "Christa Wolf's *Kindheitsmuster.*" *Autobiography: Self into Form. German-Language Autobiographical Writings of the 1970s,* 154–77. Frankfurt am Main: Lang, 1983.

Fries, Marilyn Sibley. "Christa Wolf's Use of Image and Vision in the Narrative Structuring of Experience." In *Studies in GDR Culture and Society 2,* ed. Margy Gerber et al., 59–74. Washington, D.C.: University Press of America, 1982.

Jackson, Neil, and Barbara Saunders. "Christa Wolf's *Kindheitsmuster:* An East German Experiment in Political Autobiography." *German Life and Letters* 33–34 (1980): 319–29.

Kane, B. M. "In Search of the Past: Christa Wolf's *Kindheitsmuster.*" *Modern Languages* 59 (1978): 19–23.

Koerner, W. Charlotte. "*Divided Heaven*—by Christa Wolf? A Sacrifice of Message and Meaning in Translation." *German Quarterly* 57 (1984): 213–30.

Konzett, Matthias. "Christa Wolf's 'Was bleibt': The Literary Utopia and Its Remaining Significance." *Monatshefte* 85 (1993): 438–52.

Lennox, Sara. "Christa Wolf and the Women Romantics." In *Studies in GDR Culture and Society 2,* ed. Margy Gerber et al., 31–44. Washington, D.C.: University Press of America, 1982.

McPherson, Karin. "In Search of the New Prose: Christa Wolf's Reflections on Writing and the Writer in the 1960s and 1970s." *New German Studies* 9 (1981): 1–13.

Ryan, Judith. "The Discontinuous Self: Christa Wolf's *A Model Childhood.*" *The Uncompleted Past: Postwar German Novels and the Third Reich,* 141–54. Detroit: Wayne State University Press, 1983.

Sevin, Dieter. "The Plea for Artistic Freedom in Christa Wolf's 'Lesen und Schreiben' and *Nachdenken über Christa T.:* Essay and Fiction as Mutually Supportive Genre Forms." In *Studies in GDR Culture and Society 2,* ed. Margy Gerber et al., 45–58. Washington, D.C.: University Press of America, 1982.

Wiesehan, Gretchen. "Christa Wolf Reconsidered: National Stereotypes in *Kindheitsmuster.*" *Germanic Review* 68 (1993): 79–87.

Voris, Renate. "The Hysteric and the Mimic: Reading Christa Wolf's *The Quest for Christa T.*" In *Writing the Woman Artist: Essays on Poetics, Politics, and Portraiture,* ed. Suzanne W. Jones, 233–58. Philadelphia: University of Pennsylvania Press, 1991.

Winnard, Andrew. "Christa Wolf at the Crossroads: Notes on a Symbol in the Narrative Works." *GDR Monitor* 20 (1988–89): 1–14.

INDEX